PONTIAC'S CONSPIRACY & OTHER INDIAN AFFAIRS
Notices Abstracted from
Colonial Newspapers, 1763–1765

Compiled by *Armand Francis Lucier*

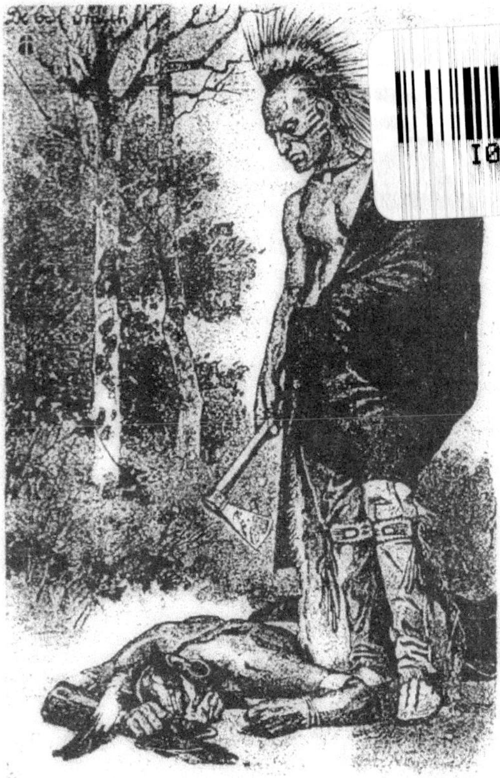

HERITAGE BOOKS
2012

HERITAGE BOOKS
AN IMPRINT OF HERITAGE BOOKS, INC.

Books, CDs, and more—Worldwide

For our listing of thousands of titles see our website
at
www.HeritageBooks.com

Published 2012 by
HERITAGE BOOKS, INC.
Publishing Division
100 Railroad Ave. #104
Westminster, Maryland 21157

Copyright © 2000 Armand Francis Lucier

Index Copyright © 2000 Heritage Books, Inc.

All rights reserved. No part of this book may be reproduced or transmitted in any form or by any means, electronic or mechanical, including photocopying, recording or by any information storage and retrieval system without written permission from the author, except for the inclusion of brief quotations in a review.

International Standard Book Numbers
Paperbound: 978-0-7884-1460-2
Clothbound: 978-0-7884-9303-4

Dedicated
To
My Wife
Dorothy
My Sons
Mark and Joel
My Grandchildren
Sara, Brenna, Carrie and Alexander
My Great-Grandchildren
Madison, Quinton and Aysia

CONTENTS

Foreword vii

List of Contributors viii

Pontiac's Conspiracy & Other Indian Affairs:
Notices Abstracted from Colonial Newspapers, 1763-1765

1763 1

1764 127

1765 271

1766 311

Index 315

FOREWORD

After the French had been conquered by the English and ceded all the forts, settlements, and possessions east of the Mississippi River, (except New-Orleans) the Ottowa sachem Pontiac sent many of his deputies to the other Indian nations to join him in driving the English out of the Indian territories. In two years he was successful in uniting all the Indian nations that were in the French interest during the past war, and also the Senecas, the west-most of the Six Nations.

On the afternoon of the 9th of May 1763 Pontiac established a blockade of Detroit, and began the siege of the fort. The other Indians in the conspiracy fell upon the forts nearest to their nations; and, in a matter of 15 days had captured nine forts and massacred most of the English garrisons.

At this same period of time grants were being issued for lands, to establish settlements in Indian territories and tribal hunting grounds, individuals and groups encroached and established farms, plantations and settlements. At this time young warriors of friendly tribes formed parties and caused havoc with the isolated settlers, burning their houses and murdering and driving the white people east.

All articles are in chronological order of original publication. No attempt is made to correct spelling, punctuation, or composition, except for clarity and understanding.

The reader should keep in mind that these newspapers were published by white publishers for white readers.

By the end of August, 1765, most of the Indian problems had been resolved; and, little thereafter little mentioned in the newspapers on Indian affairs. The publishers devoted most of their newsprint on the acts passed by the British Parliament to enforce the Navigation acts and the new Stamp act.

CONTRIBUTORS

Boston Gazette. Boston Massachusetts.
The Boston Evening post. Boston Massachusetts.
Connecticut Courant. Hartford Connecticut.
Georgia Gazette. Savannah Georgia.
Halifax Gazette. Halifax Nova Scotia.
London Chronicle. London England.
London Gazette. London England.
Maryland Gazette. Annapolis Maryland.
New-Hampshire Gazette. Portsmouth N. H.
New-London Gazette. New-London Connecticut.
New-London Summery. New-London Connecticut.
Newport Mercury. Newport Rhode Island.
New-York Gazette [Weyman's] New-York, New-York.
New-York Mercury. New-York New-York.
North Carolina Gazette. New Bern N. Carolina.
Pennsylvania Chronicle. Philadelphia Pa.
Pennsylvania Gazette. Philadelphia Pa.
Pennsylvania Journal. Philadelphia Pa.
South Carolina Gazette. Charlestown s. Carolina.
Virgina Centinel. Williamsburg Virginia.
Virginia Gazette. Williamsburg Virginia.

MAY 1763

BOSTON May 2. A Proposal is now on Foot for settling a very extensive Colony upon the finest Part of the Ohio, which is to be called New Wales, in honor of his Royal Highness the Prince of Wales, who is to be sole proprietor of the Colony. The Number of Families proposed to form the first Settlement are 4000, who are to rendezvous at Philadelphia, and march from thence in two Divisions, they are to compose two Cities or Towns, for the more convenience of laying out the Land round each.

CHARLESTOWN S. Carolina May 4. Yesterday being the first Tuesday in the month, his Excellency the Governor in council signed warrants of survey for about 160,000 acres of land in this province lying south of the river Alatamaha, which were that day petitioned for. Several plats of land to the southward of the said river surveyed in consequence of warrants issued the first Tuesday of last month, has been returned into the secretarie's office, and grants are preparing for them.

NEWPORT Rhode Island May 16. In the Connecticut papers we find, that letters have been received there from the Secretary of State, signifying his Majesty's disapprobation of the Connecticut people's attempting settlements on the river Susquehanna and Delaware, till the state of the case can be laid before the King: The respective committees have accordingly given notice to all persons concerned, not to proceed to enter upon, or make any settlement on said lands, till his Majesty's pleasure is known.

FORT-PITT May. 31. There is most melancholy News here, the Indians have broke out in divers Places and have murdered Colonel Chapman and his Family; and two of our Men at the Saw-Mill just by the Ford, and the Scalps taken of each Man. An Indian has brought a War belt to Tusquerora, who says Detroit was invested and St. Dusky cut off, and Ensign Pawly taken Prisoner ——— All Levy's Goods are stopped at Tusquerora by the Indians; and last Night 11 Men were attacked at Beaver Creek and 8 or 9 killed ——— We hear of scalping every Hour, Mr. Gray and Allison's Horses, 25, loaded with Skins were all taken.

JUNE 1763

CHARLESTOWN S. Carolina June 1. Their Excellencies Thomas Boone, Esq; our Governor, Arthur Dobbs, Esq; Governor of North-Carolina, James Wright, Esq; Governor of Georgia, His Honour Francis Fauquier, Esq; Lieutenant Governor of Virginia and John Stuart, Esq; his Majesty's agent for Indian affairs in the Southern district, we hear, have received orders from his Majesty to hold a congress or general meeting with the principal headmen of the Choctaw, Cherokee, Creek, Chickesaw and Catawba Indians and their confederates, at Augusta in the Province of Georgia or some other proper place, at which, it is not doubted, his Majesty's gracious intentions, and the abilities of the gentlemen appointed to explain them to the Indians, will conciliate their affections to the British nation and interests and entirely efface any umbrage they may have conceived by the French, being intirely driven from amonst them. —— In March last the goods proper for the presents to the Indians were actually purchased in London by his Majesty's order, to the Amount of about 5000 pounds sterl. and were speedily to be shipped for this port to our Governor, in order to be distributed at the intended congress, which, we hear, his Excellency has proposed shall be held at Augusta the 15th of September next.

The expence of presents for the Indians we are told will henceforth be defrayed by the King.

CHARLESTOWN S. Carolina June 1. From Augusta we are informed, that one Spencer, a trader in the country of the Creek Indians, was killed by an Indian with whom he had quarreled, about the beginning of last month.

Allakullakulla, the Little Carpenter, is gone out with a party against some of the Northern

Indians, who had killed some Cherokees.

It is said the Northern Governors and Sir William Johnson, Bart. his Majesty's agent for Indian affairs in the northern district, are to hold a congress at Albany with the headmen of the several Indian nations in those parts.

NEW-YORK June 7. We hear on Monday last arrived an Express from Pittsburg, by the way of Philadelphia, to his Excellency Sir Jeffry Amherst, advising That a Party of Indians had murdered Colonel Chapman and all his Family; [Residing we suppose near the Place.]

Several other Reports have been spread of mischief done by the Indians, on our back Settlements, but there appear to be no truth of any of them except the above. What Indians have done this mischief is not known. The Companies of Light Infantry of the 17th, 42d anf 77th Regiments are ordered to assemble on Staten Island, to be in readiness to proceed against the Savages, should it appear there is any Thing general intended against the Settlements.

PHILADELPHIA June 7. "We have just received, by way of Redstone-Creek, a conformation of the garrison of Sandusky being cut off, and that the officers and traders were made prisoners."

From Fort Ligonier Jan. 4. "On Thursday last, about seven or eight Indians fired at the garrison and killed some horses, without doing any other damage. They were intimidated by Lieut. Blane and his garrison, who gave them three cheers, and they went off. Some people are come into Logonier from Fort Pitt, in whose company were five men, who set out with them, but had not come in the 4th inst. though the others arrived on the 1st."

SAVANNAH June 9. We hear from New-York that all the independent companies in America will soon be broke, and a number of the regulars stationed in place of them.

We are informed from London, that the Honorable the House of Commons have resolved to provide for 20 battalions of 500 men each, to be kept up in America and the West-Indies for one year, at the expiration of which the colonies are to pay, cloaths, and feed the said troops at their own expence, in such proportion as shall be agreed on and settled by the proper authority.

CHARLESTOWN S. Carolina June 14. The following is what we have been able to learn further about a French prisoner that was taken in the Cherokee nation by Mr. Sumpter in Feb. last. His name is Baron des Joune; he is a Canadian by birth a lieutenant in rank, and has been a partizan this whole war; he was at Fort Pittsburgh at Grant's defeat and Forbe's Triumph; last post he came from was Assumption which he left for killing his man, the duel was an odd one, with guns at fifty paces; he met the great great Warrior in the woods, and returned to the nation with him; and expressed great inclination to return to Canada, notwithstanding his life would be exposed. We are told this and some prevarication, occasioned his being sent as far from the means of breeding disturbances as possible, he being actually on his passage to England in the Nightingale.

Late letters from England affirms it as a fact that the French King has ceded the western part of Louisiana to the crown of Spain; and that the Duke of Nivernois has declared it to Lord Egremont.

In the meantime, we have advice from Augusta, that the Creeks have been informed, the French and Spaniards are to evacuate all they possess on this side the river Missisippi, and do not seem to relish the news; that they declare, they will not suffer them to depart; and insist, that in case the French and Spaniards should be taken from them, we have no rights to possess the lands that were never given to us, and they will oppose all our attempts that way.

CHARLESTOWN S. Carolina June 15. Two gentlemen frome Ninety-six, and the frontiers to the westward, inform us, that the country that way is very settled, people daily coming on the lands thereabout. Some gentlemen in Virginia, who were at Ninety-six, said, the lands there are superior to any they have seen on the continent, and exceeds their most sanquine expectations. The inhabitants have every conveniency that the shortness of the time will allow of, and have a fine prospect of an extraordinary crop of wheat, rye, and barley. They live together in the greatest harmony, and instance of which is, that a number of the inhabitants on Bush river about 200 miles from Charlestown, assembled the 4th inst. and celebrated his Majesty's birth-day in the most joyous manner. The same gentleman inform us, that the Cherokee Indians behave in the most friendly manner to the settlers.

PHILADELPHIA June 16. Extract of a Letter from Fort Pitt. June 2, 1763.

"Thursday last, just opposite the fort, at dusk, arrived a Number of Delaware Indians, with 15 Horse Loads of Skins and Furrs, very early next morning they came over the River, and dealt all off, not seeming to care much what they took for them. Their Indifference, and uncommon dispatch in Trading gave us some Jalousies how they came by them, just before they set off, I was standing with Mr. Alexander M'kee, on the bank of the river, when one of them came up and told him to go away, and that he must not stay more than 4 Days; these, with some other suspicious words, made us imagine they intended some mischief; and immediately after they told Mr. M'gee this, they set off. ——— The next morning we found, that all the Indians that lay on the River, a few miles above us, and planted Corn, left their Towns that very Night, took every Thing with them, which convinced us that they either intended, or knew of some Mischief intended us. ——— Sunday Morning some People, belonging to Col. Chapman, arrived at the Fort, and informed us that the Colonel, and four of his People were killed by the Wolf, and some other Delawares; and since then the Colonel was brought down and buried here, who was tomahawked and scalped; two women were treated in such a Manner, that it would be indecent to mention it. Sunday Night the Enemy killed two of the Soldiers at the Saw-Mill, and on Thursday burnt it ——— Monday, a Man hired with the Alison and Company, came to a Party sent down to bury the Dead, and informed, that he was in Company with

Alexander M'Clure, driving 25 Horse Loads of Skins and Furs, belonging to said Company, Thomas Calhoon and Brothers, and several others, which amounted in all to fourteen, who were fired upon by a Party of Indians, as they were crossing Beaver Creek, and several killed —— Calhoon, and two of his Men having arrived since, but no account of the rest —— The whole Garrison have been very alert in putting every Thing in the Most Order since the first Alarm —— We have destroyed the Upper and Lower Towns, Laying them level with the Ground; and by To Morrow Night we shall be in a good posture of Defence —— Every Morning an Hour before Day, the whole Garrison are at their Alarm Post ——Ten Days ago at Beaver Creek, they killed one Patrick Dunn, and a Man of Major Smallman's; also two other Men —— Captain Callender's People are all killed, and the Goods taken —— There is no Account of Mr. Welsh, or Captain Prentice but it is feared they are likewise killed —— Mr. Crawford is made Prisoner, and his People all murdered —— our small Posts I am afraid, are gone. Detroit was attacked four Days without Intermission —— The French sent the Indians two Belts, and the English three to desist but they determine to continue the Attack, and were fighting when the Indians, who brought this account to the Delawares, came away. We sent two Men with Express to Venango in the Night, but before they got 2 Miles of this Journey were fired upon and returned, one of them wounded."

From Fort Bedford we have the following extract. June 3, 1763.

"As the News current must have reached you with various Circumstances, e'er now, the following is the most authentic that I can as yet depend on, viz. That Col. Chapman, one M'Cormick, two women and a child, were murdered on Saturday the 28th ult. —— That in a few Days after two Royal Americans were killed and then scalped, within a Mile of Fort Pitt. —— And that on Tuesday last one Smith was attacked by an Indian, without Arms at Beaver Creek, who endeavoured to put him under Water; but Smith proving too strong for him, put the Indian under water, brought off a piece of his Ear and left him."

"At this Garrison Capt. Ourry is very alert, in strengthening the Place, and putting in order every last Article that may be necessary. The Fort is tenable, and the Garrison strong, a number of the People having come from the Country. We have a numerous Militia who are under Arms, almost continually. Regular Piquets, Centinals, Town Guards, Post Guards, &c. are observed. Thirteen brave Men, well painted, go out on a scouting to morrow."

Jan. 6. "After sealing the above. I opened it this Morning to inform you, that the thirteen brave fellows above mentioned painted like Indians, have set off from our Parade, in Quest of the Savages to the great Satisfaction of the Commander and the whole Garrison. Just as I am writing, News is brought in of an Indian being seen within two Miles of the Garrison, when immediately the Piquet, consisting of the Militia, sprung after them on a full Gallop."

June 7. We have just now received by the way of Beaver Creek a conformation of the Garrison of St. Dusky being cut off; and that the Officers and Traders were made Prisoners."

BOSTON June 20. Extract of a Letter received from Albany, June 16, 1763.

"We have lately received several Accounts of the Indians murdering our People who went to Trade with them: On the 26th of May 6 Battoes were attacked and fired upon by about 40 Indians, while the People were ashore refreshing themselves, at the Mouth of a River which empties itself into Lake Erie, about 60 Miles from Niagara: two of them were shot dead, and 5 taken Prisoners: the rest made their Escape to Niagara, leaving 5 of the Battoes, valued at 6000 Pounds Currency, in the Possession of the Indians, whose Tribe was called Chepawees, and have a Castle 50 Miles up the River: ——— Eight other Battoes valued at 9000 Pounds are still missing and 'tis feared are also fell into the Hands of the Indians: in those which they had taken, was 100 wt. of Gunpowder, and Lead answerable: ——— In the Affair of Lieut. Cuyler, who was going from Niagara to Detroit with 100 Men, and was attacked in the Night by the Indians, he lost 70 of his People, and 200 Barrels of Provisions which he was escorting, and was obliged to return to Niagara: ——— We hourly expect to hear that Detroit is taken, in which, the other Forts above it, 'tis said there are Goods and Furs belonging to the Merchants of New-York, Albany, &c. to the Value of 500,000 Pounds Currency: ——— 'Tis tho't all the Traders are cut off, some of which went as far as Fort St. Mary's, which is 1000 Miles from this Place."

Extract of a Letter from New-York June 9.

"A Detachment marches on Saturday next for the Ohio, to bring the Indians to an Account for the Murder of Col. Chapman and 18 of his Family; also for that of the Lieutenant of the Americans, who together with his Command was cut off by them."

NEW-YORK June 20. One or two Expresses have arrived here since our last from Albany, with Intelligence, it is said of the Outrages of the Indians on our Out Posts and back Settlements. And a Gentleman who left Albany last Thursday informs, That the Evening before, a Man arrived there who had been wounded by the Indians at a place called Green Bay [we suppose near Fort Detroit] which he said was entirely destroyed; an that Fort Detroit must have been taken by the Time of his arrival. He further added, that the Indians had taken nine Battoes, has kill'd and scalped three Men; and that they were many others missing, particularly Forty of the Queens Independents, supposed to be cut off.

Yesterday a Detachment of the Train of Artillery embarked for Albany, and a few days before Part of the 17th Regiment sailed for the same Place.

CHARLESTOWN S. Carolina June 22. Letters received the beginning of the Week from Augusta dated the 22d ult. say, that the people continued to be very uneasy about the Creeks; that several of the traders amongst them should have been down about a Fortnight, which has increased their apprehensions; and that accounts were bro't there, the 12th, that they had all fled from the nation.

PHILADELPHIA June 23. By Express just now from Fort Pitt, we learn, that the Indians are continually about the place: that out of 120 traders but two or three escaped; that fort Detroit was attacked several days, but the enemy was beat off; that St, Dusky was taken with much goods, and all the people killed, several other small forts are taken; and it is said about 60 men escorting provisions from Niagara to Detroit are also cut off. About 30 inhabitants near Fort Bedford, are all cut off, and several houses burnt, so that now it is out of doubt, it is a general insurrection among all the Indians.

BOSTON June 27. Extract of a Letter received from Albany dated June 21, 1763.

"Letters are just come to Hand from Niagara, dated the 15th inst. by which we learn that Detroit was invested the 7th of May by the Windoits, Cattawaba, and other Tribes; Mr. Fisher and his Wife, were both taken by them and were hanged; Captain Roberson and Sir Robert Davis are killed, Capt. Campbell and Lieut. McDougale, who went out to treat with them, were both carried off: Major Gladwin, who commands the Fort was determined not to deliver it up."

June 22. "This Day the 17th Regiment, and Maj. Rogers with Part of the Rangers, marched to reinforce the upper Posts and every Thing here wears the Appearance of War again, which I fear will end in a general Rupture among the Southern Tribes."

NEW-YORK June 27. On Tuesday Evening an Express arrived from Albany with dispatches for his Excellency Sir Jeffry Amherst, from the commanding officer at the Detroit, and, we hear, brings an account of the most base and trecherous behaviour of the Indians, in those parts; —————— they having, on the 7th of May, to the number of three Hundred, come to the Fort in a friendly manner, to pay as they said a formal visit; but the commanding officer luckily got intelligence of the Evil Designs, the Night before; and was much on his guard, that the Indians, who were armed with Knives, Tomahawks, and a great many with guns cut short and hid under their Blankets, when they saw the disposition of the garrison, and that their design were discovered went off, after receiving a few presents: They however, sent out parties who committed several barbarities on some of our people, who unfortunately happened to be at a distance from the fort; and had afterwards the assurance to come with a Pipe of Peace, desiring to be admitted into the fort no doubt, with an intention to cut off the whole garrison: but the commanding officer having refused to receive any besides their Chiefs, the next day they invested the fort and commenced hostilities; but could make no impression whatever on the garrison, who bravely defended themselves being well supply'd with provisions and ammunition ——— We hear that reinforcements are sent, which, we hope, will get there in good time, not only to save that post, but to pour vengeance on the hands of those barbarians, who have thus perfidiously attacked their benefactors.

NEWPORT Rhode-Island June 27. As the following speech made to the General Assembly of the Colony of Connecticut by the deputies of the Six Indian Nations, is very remarkable, and intimates some causes of the discontent subsisting among them, which has produced such terrible effects, and threatens a general renewal of the war with those savage nations, the publishing of it we doubt not will be agreeable to the publick.

A Conference with the Deputies of the Six Nations of Indians, in the Council-Chamber held at Hartford, in the Colony of Connecticut, on the 28th Day of May last.

Present, the Governor, Council, and Assembly of said Colony.

Deputies from the Six Nations. Toquerole, Mohawk. Saquayanguaraghta, and Toguascanta, Onondagas. Sogheres, and Oghseguarona, Cayugas.

The Deputies, after being taken by the hand and bid welcome into the government, seated themselves; them Saquayanguaraghta arose and delivered a speech, which from the interpreter was taken as followeth, viz.

Brothers, We were sent hither by the chiefs of the Six Nations, and it has pleased God that we arrived safe at this place to see you: Brothers, we are deputies from all the chiefs and we understand that you are not found within, and we give this to clear your eyes that you may see, and open your ears that you may hear, and cleanse your hearts that you may entertain cordially what we shall speak to you. A belt of Wampum from the deputy from Onondagas.

Returned the complement to them that they would open their eyes and cleanse their throats, that they may speak freely.

Brothers, We have no writing of it, but have a tradition that God, the maker of all things, hath given to the Six Nations our large country to dwell and subsist in, and made them a strong people; and our nation have of old established a fire place at Onondaga, by that means united together, and so became a strong and powerful confederacy; afterwards they saw at Albany a white people, and found means to enter into a conference with them, and like them, and made a silver chain, a strong chain of friendship, then from time to time brightened and kept, clean, and at this first interview liked you so well that we gave you room for you to settle upon our land, and you are since become very numerous and prosperous, for which we are very glad and rejoices: And Brothers, we have been very glad we have assisted one another against our enemies, and by the help of God we gained superiority over them: And, Brothers, you will excuse us; we have no records of former proceedings, but hint at such things as were done formerly by our forefathers, and have nothing further to offer on the head.

Now we are come to another head.

Brothers, We have heard grievous news this winter, that you were about to come with 300 families to settle on our lands, which was very astonishing to us, and that you designed to build forts and strong places on our lands, and for what reason our sachems consider upon it, and have sent us down to this place: by that means we are come down here to acquaint you with what news we hear, that you have got a design to settle on the Susquehannah river, and claim the land to the west sea; and have heretofore given away land to the white people, but of this sale of the land the Six Nations nothing, that they have even given or sold it to any; and what little we have left we intend to keep ourselves; we know not of any such sale, and if any such thing hath been, it must have been done in a separate manner, and not in a general meeting or council of the Six Nations, as hath been the usual manner of their giving or selling their lands.

Brothers, Our custom is not to keep any thing secret, we have heard that on Ledias at Albany has endeavoured to purchase some lands at Susquehannah, and it is not the manner of the Six Nations to keep any thing in reserve, he was up among the nation to obtain it; but we have heard that he has since got a deed from the Indians, which he obtained from them singly, or one by one, and that from Stragglers and such as we know nothing of. We have often sold lands to the white people, but then it was done in consent of the whole in some general meeting, and this land we have reserved for ourselves, as we have but little left and we are surprized at such a measure being taken to obtain a deed without our knowledge or consent.

We have been told that Lydias reported that he had paid a great deal of money for this land, which we know nothing of, and this is the hunting ground which we depend upon for our support, and we are not willing by any means to part with it. [Then the speaker presents a broad belt which he held in his hands.] Brothers, we would have you take this matter in consideration; we here present you with the emblem of the six castles belonging to our Nations, and through it the road or path through which we come to strengthen our covenant chain, Brothers, seriously take it into consideration, and think how you would like it to have lands taken from you in an unfair and injurious manner. You are a praying people, better acquainted with books and learning than we, and must needs know better what is right; to have your lands as we may say stolen from you, surly you could not like it to be treated in such a manner, to have your land taken from you that you depend upon for your support. Brothers, take it seriously in your consideration how strong our union used to be formerly, when we were as it was united under one head, and were one body and blood, peaceful and happily united in our affection. Brothers as I have told you before, that we have been sent here by our chiefs to let you know what we have heard about your design of entering on our lands, and we deliver in this belt to shew the minds of the confederate nations, that you do not encroach on our lands which we have reserved and designed to keep for our children to the latest posterity, and will not part with it. They are such as we set by and will not sell, Brothers, if you proceed to encroach on any of our lands we will not be easy, but will return home to your place, and apply ourselves to the king our father to obtain justice, and I myself will go, and on my going out of the house will return home and leave you to consider on it. And now I have said all I have to say.

The Governor directed the interpreter to tell them that he was able to give them a satisfactory answer, and desired they would stay till the beginning of the week, at which time they should have an answer.

To which they answered that their chiefs directed them to make no delay, but as soon as they has made their speech they were to return; but the Governor desired they would stay for an answer; then they withdrew.

The Governor's Answer.

Brethren,
We heartily welcome you to this place, and are glad to see you safe arrived, and that you are sent by your chiefs to brighten the covenant chain made by our forefathers there: You tell us your chiefs think we are not found within, we assure you our eyes are clear, our ears open, and we cordially receive you as friends, and kindly receive your message. Brethren, we rejoice, with you that God has prospered the great

George, our common father, so that your and our enemies are subdued, and now we hope will live in peace and friendship as long as the sun and moon shall endure.

We come now to your message,

Brethren, You tell us the news you have heard that we are about to come with 300 Families to settle on the Susquehannah river, which was vary astonishing to you, and that we design to build forts on your lands.

Brethren, We assure and tell you, this government has not given any orders for any such settlements; we are noways concerned in that matter, only as friends to you have endeavoured to prevent the people from going to settle those lands. We have indeed been told, that a number of particular persons, some living in Connecticut, some in Massachusetts, some in New-York, and some in other governments, were about to settle on those lands, but we advised them not to proceed in their attempts; and lately I received orders from the king our common father, commanding me to use my authority and influence to prevent the people from attempting to settle on those lands, till the matter shall be laid before the king: In obedience to his Majesty's commands, I acquainted the chief men among them with the king's orders, ment for the present; and furthermore, I have now the satisfaction to acquaint you, that I am well informed those people have had a meeting, and have, in testimony as well of his majesty's case as there ready submission to and Acquiescence in his order, unanimously agreed, that no person whatsoever of their company shall enter upon or make any settlement on any of the lands, until his majesty our common father's pleasure be known in that matter.

Brethren, seeing we are your friends, and agreeable to the king's orders have taken so much care to prevent those settlements which are so grievous to you, and have now given you accounts that the attempts are stopt, we think you will be fully satisfied, and inform our brothers your chiefs and your nation of this, and rest easy and quiet. We assure you of our cordial friendship, and wish you a safe journey home, and desire you to present our king complements to the sachems of the Six Nations, Farewell.

To which the deputies of the Six Nations replied;

Brethren,

We have heard with attention what you have said, and we are well pleased with the same, and we hope you will endeavour to prevent any more people from making purchases of us; and as to those lands we talked about, we do not at present design to part with them, but if ever we do, it shall be to those purchasers of your people before any others, if they desire it. We are to receive no persons on these occasions, but as to your offer to discharge our expences while in town, we gratefully accept and acknowledge the same, and heartily bid you farewell.

NEW-YORK June 29. Letters from Albany on the 15th inst, say, that the French Indians have cut off all the posts & battoes between Niagara and Detroit, and is generally believed, that Detroit is cut off also. We have an account of one Evert Wendell being killed, and John Wendell mortally wounded; they were attacked about 40 miles above Niagara having battoes and 35 men, 11 Of which escaped.

Lieut. Cuyler with 100 men, was attacked the 28th ult. within 50 miles of Detroit, and has only brought to Niagara 30 of the number.

PHILADELPHIA June 30. Tuskerowas, May 27, 1763 11 o,Clock at Night.

King Beaver, Shingas, Wyendougjeta, Wingeenum and Daniel and William Anderson, all chiefs of the Delawares, came to my House, and by the string of Wampum, delivered the following message,

Brother,

Out of the love we have for you, & the friendship that has always subsided between our Grandfathers and the English (which has been lately renewed by us) we came now to inform you what news we have heard, which you may depend upon.

Brothers, At Detroit we hear there is not one Englishman left alive. At St. Dusky all were put to death five days ago, except the officer, who is taken prisoner. And at Cedar-Point six man were killed, and two persons taken prisoner, being Hugh Crawford, and a boy that speaks Shawnese.

Brother, We have learned to-day from the Salt Lick, that five white men were killed there. We have likewise heard that a number of tracks, have been seen an the road from St. Dusky here, not far off, and we have sent out a man to watch their motions. We have likewise seen some tracks passing the road, between here and Gaiahouga.

Brother, We love you, and would be sorry to see you killed in our town: So we desire you not to think of any thing you have here, but, with all speed, make the best of your way to some place of safety, carefully avoiding the road, and all places where Indians resort.

Brother, We desire you to tell George Grogham, and all your great men, that they must not ask us any thing about it; for we don't know any thing. When they went to speak first to those people, they did not tell us, but went another road: Now if they want to know the reason of this, they must go the very same road to enquire of it. And if they want any thing of us, they must only send one or two men, and we will hear them.

Brothers the English, We thought that your King had made a peace with us, and all the western Indians: For our part we joined it heartily and hold it always good, and will not be cheated any more, as we sit in the middle; but we will move a little to one side of the road, so that you may pass to one another, and do what ye please, and we will take no notice of it.

Brother, There is one white man at Gaiahouga; don't be concerned about him; we will take care to send him safe home.

Brother, As to what goods you have here, we promise they shall be kept safe for six months; perhaps by that time we may see you, or send you word what you may expect us to do further.

Thomas Calhoon.

Extract of a Letter from Carlisle, June 20.
"We are yet in suspense whether the Indians

will carry the war into our inhabited part, but that they certainly intended it, is to me beyond any doubt. ⸺ About the 14th instant a man who went out to catch a horse at Ligonier, was killed or carried off, almost in view of the garrison. ⸺ An Indian who has a white woman to his wife, is now on his way, with some white people, flying from the Potowmack, and says the Indians has acquainted him with their intentions, viz. That they design to carry the war to us great and extent as they can, in which many tribes are joined. That they are to attack the inhabitants in the season of harvest: That they are to burn and destroy all sorts of provisions: And that they are determined to make no prisoners, but kill all that fall in their hands. ⸺ The country is in great distress, occasioned by the people leaving their plantations."

By several letters from Fort Bedford, of the 18th inst. we have the following particulars, viz. That the poor farmers who had left their places and come into the fort, had returned to their plantations, at the risk of their lives, for the preservation of their crops, in order to prevent starving in the winter: That the enemy ever watchful for such opportunity, had struck a severe blow on Denning's creek, where three or four families were murdered and scalped on the 17th. That it was not known what course the Indians would take next, but that it was absolutely necessary for every one to be on his guard: Some who left the garrison were returned, lamenting, from their fatal experience, that they did not, as they had been advised go to each others plantations in bodies: A dog (belonging to James Clark, who had gone with another man to plough corn, about 12 miles from the fort) came in wounded, on which a scouting party went out, and returned with a spear they found sticking in the body of the said Clark, who was scalped, an inhamanly mangled; but were afraid the hunt for the other man, as they perceived a number of Indian tracks in the woods: A man and his wife, who lived about 8 miles from fort Bedford, had just come in, and informed, that being in a corn-field, they heard a gun go off when a cry insued, and soon after six guns more were fired, which obliged them to set off for the fort; and that about an hour after they got in, their house was seen in flames, and it was feared that all that were in it were destroyed.

Extract of a Letter from Pittsburgh, June 16.
"We are informed by a prisoner who had been amongst the Shawanese Indians, that in making his escape he overtook Mr. Calhoon, and 9 of his men driving their loaded horses from the Shawanese town, who told him that the Delaware Indians informed them, that St. Dusky was surprized and taken by the Indians, the garrison and the traders murdered, except Lieut. Pauley: That Detroit had been besieged ten days before this happened: ——— That the Indians had killed 6 men who were in company with Mr. Crawford, coming down the Meami River; That the Delaware Indians desired Mr. Calhoon to leave the place, lest he should be killed; they seized his goods, disarmed him and his men, and sent two Indians to conduct them to this place, but about 30 miles from hence they led them into an ambushcade of Six Nation Indians, who he believed killed all the other men, and he saw none escape but himself; however, in three days after, Mr. Calhoon and two of his men arrived; the rest, 8 in number, were all killed. ——— The 7th inst. an express arrived, who informed that a large quantities of provisions and powder, from Niagara to Detroit, with 100 men; was attacked in the night by the Indians who destroyed the provisions, and killed 67 of the party. Detroit is the only garrison we have beyond this that can make any defence. The rest of the garrisons to the westward, I think before this time are all massacred. Not a man goes without gun-shot of the fort, but he is fired at by the Indians, whose numbers we are yet entirely ignorant of. ——— Yesterday we had one man killed who ventured out a little farther then he had orders; and last night the Indians had the impudence to fire pretty briskly upon our centries in the fort. The garrison are in good spirit under no apprehension of the Indians being able to take

the place."

Extract of a Letter from the same date.

"We have alarms from, and skirmishes with the Indians every day; but have done us little harm as yet. —— Yesterday I was out with a party of men, and were fired upon, and one of the Serjeants was killed, but we beat off the Indians, and brought the man in with his scalp on. —— Last night the Bullock guard was fired upon, and one cow killed. —— The Indians have cut off 100 of our traders in the woods, besides all our little posts. —— We have plenty of provisions, and the fort and in such good state that we are able to defend it against 1000 Indians."

Extract of a letter from Winchester June 22.

"I have been at fort Cumberland several days, but the Indians having killed 9 people, and burnt several houses near fort Bedford, I tho't it prudent to remove from those parts, from which I suppose, near 50 families have run away. —— It was a most melancholy sight to see such numbers of poor people, who had abandoned their settlements in such consternation and hurry, than they had hardly any thing with them but their children. And what is still worse, I dare say there is not money enough amongst the whole families to maintain a fifth part of them till the Fall; and none of the poor creatures can get a hovel to shelter them from the weather, but lie about scattered in the woods."

A Letter from fort Bedford of june 20, mentions a scouting party being just come in, and brought a confirmation of three houses being burnt, and 7 people being killed, but none were scalped.

SAVANNAH Georgia June 30. By His Excellency James Wright, Esquire, Captain General and Governor in Chief of His Majesty's said Province, chancellor and Vice Admiral of the same;

A PROCLAMATION.

Whereas the General Assembly of this province stands prorogued to Tuesday the fifth day of July next ensuing; and whereas no business of great importance requires the immediate attendance of the said General Assembly, but the same may be postponed till a more convenient season, I have therefore thought fit to issue a proclamation, further to prorogue the said General Assembly, and it is hereby prorogued accordingly, to Wednesday the twelfth day of October next ensuing then to meet for the dispatch of business.

   Given under my hand and the great seal of his Majesty's said province, in the Council Chamber, at Savannah, the twenty-fourth day of June, in the year of our Lord One thousand seven hundred and sixty-three, and in the third year of his Majesty'd reign.

By his Excellency's Command
 John Talley, Dep. Secr.   James Wright.
   God Save the King.
    Georgia.

By His Excellency James Wright, Esquire, Captain General and Governor in Chief of his Majesty's said Province, Chancellor and Vice Admiral of the same,

   A PROCLAMATION.

Whereas his most sacred Majesty has been graciously pleased to signify to me, that he is determined, upon all occasions to support and protect the Indians in amity and alliance with him, in their just rights and possessions, and to keep inviolable treaties and compacts which have been made and entered into with them by his royal predecessors; and whereas I have received his Majesty's command to declare his royal will and pleasure, that all persons whatsoever, who may, either willfully or inadvertently, without any lawful authority for so doing, have seated themselves upon any lands reserved to, or are claimed by the Indians, under any of the treaties or compacts aforesaid, do forthwith remove therefrom, I do therefore, by his Majesty's ex-command, issue this my proclamation, in his Majesty's name, strictly enjoining and requiring all persons whatsoever, who may, either willfully or inadvertently, have seated themselves upon any lands so reserved to, or claimed by the said Indians, forthwith to remove therefrom, as they will answer the contrary at their peril.

Given under my hand and the great seal of his Majesty's said province, in the Council Chamber, at Savannah, the twenty-fourth day of June, in the year of our Lord One thousand seven hundred and sixty-three, and in the third year of his Majesty's reign.

By his Excellency's Command
John Talley, Dep. Secr.   James Wright.
God Save the King.

JULY 1763

PHILADELPHIA July 7. Extract of a Letter from Fort Pitt, June 26.

"Since my last the Shawanese, Delaware and the Mingoes have frequently appeared in small parties, and have taken one scalp, shot and stole some horses, and some cows, and came and fired on the fort. After this the sent-in-to-hold a treaty, and Mr. M'gee was hardy enough to go out to them, but within musket shot of the fort. —— They endeavoured to persuade us to leave the place and said, it was impossible to count the number of Indians that are coming against us, and that we should be destroyed in two days &c. But the commanding officer let them know that a large army was sent round the lakes to their towns, in order to cut all off; upon which they desired to stand neuter, and brighten the chain of friendship. —— Ensign Price, commander of Le Beuf, came in here to-day, with half his garrison, six in number; he kept possession of his wretched post, till the savages set it on fire with their arrows, when he found means to slip out, and travelled here in six days, without provisions, having left the rest for his poor people behind, who were so far exhausted, that it was impossible for them to come on. —— Venango was destroyed before he came there, and every soul perished. —— Just now came in a soldier from Presque Isle, who affirms that the place was attacked, and had been defended for two days, when the Indians undermined the blockhouse, on which the garrison capitulated, with liberty to come here; but the Indians fell upon them, and, as he supposed, massacred them all. —— We credit this account, as we have had former examples of their inhumanity. —— The last account of Detroit are, that the garrison makes a noble defence. —— The Indians put in practice the following piece of treachery there, they proposed a treaty, and sent two chiefs —— Our people sent out two officers to them; on which they came in great numbers, desiring admittance, but were refused. —— they then fired on the guards, and our people returned the complement, and killed forty of them on the spot."

Extract of a Letter from Fort Bedford June 29.
"Last night a young man who went out in pursuit of a horse, but a few paces from him, was taken in view of the garrison.

30th. This morning a party of the enemy attacked 15 persons, who were working in Mr. Groghan's field, within a mile of the garrison, and news is bro't in of two men being killed. 8 o'clock Two men are brought in alive, tomahawk'd and scalp'd more than half their head over. —— Our parade just now presents a bloody and savage cruelty: 3 men, two of which are in the bloom of life, the other an old man, lying scalped (two of the still alive) thereon: Any thing feigned is most fabulous romance, cannot parallel the horrid sight now before me; the gashes the poor people bear are most terrifying. —— 10 o'clock. They are just expired —— One of them, after being tomahawked and scalped, ran and got on a loft in Mr. Croghan's house, where he lay till found by a party from the garrison."

Extract of a letter from Fort Pitt, June 26.
"Every day see more or less of the Indians. — We have had two men killed by their own folly, in leaving the party contrary to orders; one killed by accident, taking down his gun on an alarm; and one wounded in the fort, by a shot from the opposite side of the Ohio. —— A party of Delaware are appeared in sight of the fort, three of which came down and desired to speak with Mr. M'Gee who went out to them; when they let him know, that there was a great body of Indians, of different nations, ready to attack us, but the had prevailed with them not to do it till they had spoke to us, and desired we would go off. —— The commanding officer let them know that he had men ammunition and also

provisions enough to defend the place against all the Indians in the woods; and that troops were marching to attack them in their towns; upon which they altered their tune, and said their nation would hold fast the chain of friendship."

"They told us our small posts were cut off, that Vennango was taken, and Mr. Gordon, the officer that commanded taken prisoner, but put to the torture every night till he died.

"This morning Ensign Price of the Royal Americans, with part of his garrison, arrived here, being separated from the rest in the night. The enemy attacked his post, and set it on fire, and while they watched the door of the house, he got out the other side, and the Indians continued firing long time afterwards: imagining that the garrison was in it, and that the were consumed with the house: He touched at Venango, found the fort burnt to the ground, and saw one of our expresses lying killed on the road: Mr. Price received an account from Mr. Christie, who commanded Presque Isle, that the Brig Detroit, had passed by there, on her way to Niagara for provisions: that the French did not fight for us, that the sloop lay opposite one side of town, to cover it; That Capt. Campbell & M'Dougall were sent out to the Indians, on their approching the garrison, to know what they wanted, but that the Indians had first given two of their chiefs as hostages for their safe return: That the Indians then attempting to force the gate; upon which Major Gladwin ordered the troops to fire & killed 40 of them: That the enemy had been about the fort for 3 weeks, when the Brig left it: That they were 1500 strong; that they had attactk the Brig coming down Detroit river, wounded the master, and lodged a great number of the shot in the vessel and that Sir Robert Davers and Capt. Robeson, with two others, were killed, while they were sounding the Lake. Mr, Price is afraid that Presque Isle is taken as the Indians that attacked his post came from there, or that way. By the last accounts the Indians will be here in a day or two, to make an attack upon this place; if they are not afraid, and will come on boldly they will be well drubbed.

"Ligonier was attacked the 22d by the Indians, for a day and a night, but were beat off; was killed one scoundrel from the fort, who had trusted himself a little too near.

"Four o'Clock in the Afternoon. Just now come in one of the soldiers from Presque Isle, who says Mr. Christie fought two Days; that the enemy fifty times set fire to the Block-house but that they as often put it out; that they then undermined the house, and was ready to blow it up, when they offered Mr. Christie terms, who accepted them, viz. that he and the garrison was to be conducted to this place. ——— The soldier also said, he supposed they intended to put them all to death: and that on hearing a woman scream out, he supposed they were murdering her, upon which he & another soldier came immediately off, but knows noting of the rest; that the vessel from Niagara was in sight, but believed she had no provisions, as the Indians told them they had cut off little Niagara, and destroyed 800 barrels; and that he thinks, by what he saw, Venango had capitulated."

From Cumberland County our accounts in general are most melancholy; the poor inhabitants coming continually into Carlisle from their places having hardly any thing with them but their children.

SAVANNAH July 7. Extract of a letter from a gentleman in Philadelphia, to his correspondent here, dated June 6, 1763.

"Two expresses from Fort Pitt since last night brings the disagreeable accounts of the Indians breaking out and have already killed several people, taken many horses and goods, one of our small posts, and it's feared many more before this; and expected to be surrounded at Fort Pitt in a few hours. They have burnt several settlements near the forts; fear every hour to hear more disagreeable difficulties."

Several copies of his Majesty's royal instructions to his Excellency the Governor, relating to the treaties entered into with the Indians, and the hunting grounds and land reserved and claimed by them, have been printed, and are, by order of his Excellency, sent throughout the settlements in this province, and also into the Indian country, to be explained and published amongst the several tribes of Indians, agreeable to his Majesty's royal commands for that purpose.

By late accounts from Fort Barrington we learn that Capt. Elsick was returned from the nation, and says, there are bad talks among the Upper Creeks, in which they want the Lower Towns to join them, but they have refused.

NEW-YORK July 11. The General Assembly of the Province of Pennsylvania, have resolved to take into pay 700 men (exclusive of those already in the service of the Government) to be employed in protecting the frontier inhabitants, during the time of harvest.

New-York July 14. By a Letter received yesterday from Philadelphia, we are informed that 100 Indians are come in to Lancaster, and declared that they had no Hand in any of the late hostilities.

Williamsburg July 15. "An Express arrived last night from Winchester, with a letter to his honnour the Governor, dated July 11th, giving an account that all the inhabitants of Hampshire, intimidated by some stalking parties of Indians, who have murdered several families thereabout, had left their houses and plantations, and taken refuge in the different little forts to the South Branch of the country; and that many of the inhabitants of Frederick have followed their example, amounting in all to 648 men, 538 women and 1191 children. His Honour, we hear, has sent up orders to the commanding officers of the counties adjoining to draw out their militia; so that, it is hoped, they will be able to drive off those merciless savages, and let the inhabitants return to their fine plantations, which otherwise must be inevitably destroyed."

WILLIAMSBURG July 15. We hear that two Indians have been taken within four miles of Winchester, who said there had been 400 Indians for a fortnight past about the south branch of the Patowmack, and waited there in expectation of being joined by four times that number; they are apprehensive of a visit from the Indians; Capt. Robert Rutherford is gone out with a party of eight man, to learn, if possible, their disposition and numbers. Indians have been seen on the Blue Ridge and Col. Cresap's being cut off is told with fresh circumstances. Those Indians who have appeared on the Ridge have done no mischief, they are suppose to be a party from the main body to reconnoitre the country before the fall on the back inhabitants, which it's imagined they have put off for a few days that they might perpetrate their intentions upon the people in the time of harvest.

From the face of the circumstances, the beginning of last war was not so alarming or effecting. What a shocking consideration it is to see the harvest fields abandoned, plantations deserted and the poor wretched inhabitants, obliged to fly, or be scalped in surprize!

CHARLESTOWN S. Carolina July 16. On the Evening of the 8th instant three Catwaba Indians came to town, with a complaint, that some time ago two of their women had been killed in the nation, and about the 1st instant three more taken and carried off, by enemies, one of the women that escaped said, that these acts of violence were committed by Cherokees, and that a fellow that she knew called Red-Horse was of the gang; which was confirmed by the track being followed into their country. Upon this we hear, his excellency the Governor has wrote to the Cherokees desiring restitutions of the woman agreeable to the treaty.

NEW-YORK July 18. By a latter from Albany we are informed that 4 men belonging to the garrison at Niagara, who had ventured to some distance from the fort, were cut off by the Indians.

BOSTON July 19. By His Excellency Francis Bernard, Esq; Captain General and Governor in Chief in and over His Majesty's Province of the Massachusetts Bay in New England, and Vice Admiral of the same.

A PROCLAMATION

Whereas on the breaking out of the late War with France the Indians of the Norriggewalk,

Arasingutacook, Wewenock, St. John's and Penebscot Tribes, and the Indians of the other Tribes inhabiting the Eastern and Northern Parts of New-England, having committed Hostilities against the Inhabitants of this Province were declared and proclaimed Enemies, Traitors, and Rebels; And Wheras, for some time past the said Indians forebore any hostile Acts against the Province, and have shown Disposition to live for the future in Peace and Friendship with all his Majesty's Subjects; and the Chiefs of some of the said Tribes have lately made Application to me to permit them to come to Boston to open a Treaty for a formal Submission and through Reconciliation of themselves and this Government.

I have thought fit, by and with the advice of his Majesty's Council, to issue this Proclamation, hereby commanding and requiring all his Majesty's Subjects within this Province not to commit any Act of Violence or Hostilities against the said Indians or give them any Trouble or Molestation whatsoever; but on the contrary, to afford them all the necessary relief and Assistance as Occasion shall require.

And His Majesty's Justices of the Peace, Sheriffs, and all Officers civil and military, are hereby commanded and enjoined to take care that the said Indians be protected in their Persons and Properties, and all Persons who shall do them any Wrong or Injury to be brought to Justice.

> Given at the Council Chamber in Boston, the Nineteenth Day of July, 1763, in the Third Year of the Reign of our Sovereign Lord George the Third, by the Grace of God, of Great-Britain, France & Ireland, King, Defender of the Faith, &c.

By his Excellency's Command   Fra. Bernard.
A. Oliver, Sec'ry.

God Save the King.

PHILADELPHIA July 21. Extract of a Letter from Carlisle July 12, 1763.

"Our present state of affairs is indeed very distressing; every day almost affording some fresh object to waken the compassion, alarm the fears, or kindle into resentment and vengeance, every sensible breast, while flying families, obliged to abandon house and possession, to save their lives by a hasty escape; mourning widows bewail their husbands surprised and massacred by savage rage; tender parents, lamenting the fruit of their own bodies, cropt at the very bloom of life by a barbarous hand, with relations and acquaintances pouring our sorrow for murdered neighbours and friends, present a varied scene of mingled distress.

"On Sunday morning the 16th inst. at the house of William White, on Joniata between 30 and 40 miles from hence, there being 4 men and a lad, the Indians came rushing upon them, and shot White at the door, just stepping out to see what the noise meant. Our people then pulled in White and shut the door; but observing thro' a window, the Indians setting fire to the house, they attempted to force their way out the door; but the first that step'd out being shot down, they drew him in, and again shut the door; after which, one attempting to escape out of a window, was shot thro' the head, and the lad wounded in the arm. The only one now remaining, broke a hole thro' the roof, and an Indian who saw him looking out, alleging that he was about to fire on him, withdrew, which afforded him an opportunity of escaping. ——— The house with the other four in it was burnt down.

"The same day, about a mile and a half from said White's, at the house of Robert Campbell, six men being at dinner, three Indians rushed in at the door, and after firing among them, and wounding some, tomahawked in an instant one of the men; whereupon George Dobbs sprung back into a room, and taking down a gun, shot an Indian thro' the body, who was presenting his piece to shot him: the Indians being mortally wounded was carried off by the others. Dobbs, with one more broke the roof, in order to escape, and looking out, saw one of the company (Stephen Jeffries) running, but very slow, by reason of a wound in his breast, and an Indian pursuing; and it is tho't he could not escape. The first that attempted to get out of the loft was fired at and drew back; another was shot down; and of the six Dobbs only one made his escape. ——— The same day about dusk, about 5 or 6 miles up Tuscorara, they murdered one Anderson, together with a boy and a girl, all in one house.

"Six men belonging to one of the parties which went out are returned, and inform, that they passed through several places in Toscorara, and saw the houses in flames, or entirely burnt down: that the grain that had been reaped the Indians burnt in the shocks: that the Hogs had fallen upon and mangled several of the dead bodies; that the said party suspected danger dusrst not stay to bury the dead; and that about 18 miles from hence they were fired at by about 30 Indians, and John Graham and William Robinson, were certainly killed, and 4 others missing. We expect every hour more messages of Melancholy news. On hearing of the above defeat another party of 30 went out under the command of our High Sheriff: There are also a number gone out from the place below us, so that we have now over the hills 80 or 90 volunteers out scouting the woods. The inhabitants of Shearman's Valley, Toscorara &c. are almost all come in, so that in a few days there will be scarcely an house inhabited North of Carlisle."

Extract of a Letter from Carlisle, July 13.

"From what appears, the Indians are travelling from one place to another, along the Valley, burning the farms and destroying all the people they meet with. This day we have an account of 6 more being killed in the Valley, so that since last Sunday to this day, we have an authentic account of 25 persons being killed and 4 or 5 wounded."

Advice since the above says that the Sheriff's party had returned; that about 18 miles from Carlisle, they fell in with a number of Indians at a house, & shot down one of them; upon which the others took to the fields, when our people pursued, and knocked down 2 or 3 more of the enemy, but tho' they followed for some time they could not come up with them, nor find one of those that were wounded. Two of the Sheriff's men were wounded one of which is since dead.

Extract of a Letter from Paxton, July 8.

"Three Indians have come in and brought some intellegence of the Senecas and Cayougas tribes having declared war against the English, and joining the Indians Westward; and that the accounts they have from the Ohio are, that they have destroyed all the forts there, except fort Pitt; that they expect to do that in a little time; and afterwards to march in a body to the west branch of the Susquehannah, and from thence to come in a body of 900 men, to attack fort Augusta, which they likewise expect to reduce, and then to march with their body down the country."

ANNAPOLIS Maryland July 21. A Gentleman in Virginia writes, in his Letter of the 18th,

"I have been at Lord Fairfax's since I saw you, and only returned this day; while I was there, we were alarmed every day with accounts of the Indians being in the neighbourhood, which occassioned many of the inhabitants to leave their plantations, and retire with what effects they could carry into the most convenient forts. The militia of the five frontier counties have been draughted and sent up to Frederick and Hampshire, and many gentlemen are gone volunteers."

SAVANNAH July 21. By runners from Lower Creek towns in nine days we learn from Augusta, that the French and Northward Indians have killed and scalped several of the Cherokees.

NEW-YORK July 25. The Highland Regiment that lately marched from hence for the Southward, was at Carlisle the 12th instant; and it was thought, that the two Companies that marched before them, were got as far forward as Bedford (which is 100 Miles from Pittsburg.)

We hear that the Frontiers of Virginia and Maryland are now, or will be soon in most deplorable situation. Several parties of Indians have appeared in different parts of Winchester and Hampshire counties, but their numberes are uncertain. A Letter from Winchester dated the 11th says, "A great number of people have been scalp'd and taken prisoners in both counties within these two days. Many have already deserted their plantations in this county, and Hampshire is entirely abandoned, except by some who have betaken them selves to forts, were they must fall a sacrifice, unless speedily relieved."

PHILADELPHIA July 26. As what follows seems to be wrote with a truly charitable and benevolent Intention, we chearfully, insert it, not doubting but it will answer the expectation of its worthy Author.

"It appears, by many accounts, that the distresses of our Frontier Inhabitants, who are driven from their Dwellings, thro' fear of the Savage Indians are exceedingly great. Many from Juniata, and other places near the Susquehannah, fled from Danger, and brought their Families, and little else, down the River in Canoes. Some escaped by Land in almost as great Distress having nothing to support them but a few Cattle, for which they can hardly find range in the inner Parts of the Country, where they fled for Shelter. Their Neighbours, among whom they reside, must suffer greatly, and be oppressed, while they strive to accommodate such numbers as crowd in among them. They cannot see any perish from want while they are able to relieve them. Above a Thousand Families are driven from their Houses and Habitations, and all the Comforts and Conveniences of Life. Of these a great Number are so poor, as to have neither Money nor Credit to purchase the Necessities of Life. Many Families on our Frontiers, and in other places, live comfortably, who, for many Months in the Year can command Money, and as soon as such Persons are driven from their Plantations, they are poor and distressed beyond Expectation. Many of these very Families that now suffer, were a few Years ago exposed to the same Losses and distresses. They lost all their worldly Substances and some of their dearest Friends and relatives. They were obliged to seek shelter among us, and endured Poverty and Hardship for some Years. They gladly returned to their forsaken Habitations as soon as there was any Prospect of Safety; and many of them, with the Help of Friends, or even burdened with debts, were scarce able to begin the World anew; how hard then and discouraging is their Condition, to be again reduced to extreme Poverty, and all the Dangers of an Indian War: There are Men & we should, for this Reason pity their Distresses; they are our Christian Brethren; they are our Fellow Subjects; their Distresses are our Distresses; for they are Part of this flourishing Province; all these tender Connections call forth our Sympathy and Bowels our Compassion. It is our Interest as well as our Duty to encourage them to stay in Cumberland County; or even to return to their foresaken Dwellings, if it can be done in safety. For if that County be deserted, where shall we make a Stand? Shall Lancaster or this City be the Frontiers of this Province? Our Governor and Assembly have granted Men for their Protection, and it is to be hoped the Charity of good Christians will not be wanting to enable the most needy and distressed to find the necessaries of Life, until we see how these Calamities will end. Our Excellent King, and the English Government, will never oppress nor do what is unjust, even to the most barbarous and savage Nations, and if reasonable terms will not satisfy them, we are able to correct their Insolence, and bring them to Reason; so that we have cause to trust in God that this Storm will soon blow over."

   PHILADELPHIA July 27. "I returned here last Night being as far Westward as Fort Loudoun with Colonel Bouquet, who set out for Fort Pitt with his Command of more than 450 Men of the 42th and 77th Regiments. He took under his Convoy thirty six Waggons, and near five hundred Pack Horses, loaded with Provisions and Stores; they went off with good spirits, as two small Detachments sent forward had the good fortune to escape the Enemy, and got into their Stations without being attacked (which I hope will be his good fortune) Should he be beat, these Provinces would have Work enough on their Hands for two or three Years. There has been a great deal said in the Papers but not more than is like true. Shippensburgh and Carlisle is now become the Frontiers, none living on their Plantations but such as have their Houses stockaded. Upward of 200 Women and Children are now living in Fort Loudoun, a Spot no more than 100 Feet square. I saw a

Letter from Col. Stevens, late of the Virginia regiment, to Colonel John Armstrong, wherein mentioned that Green Brier and Jackson's River are depopulated, upward of 300 Persons killed or taken Prisoners; that for one hundred Miles in breath, and 300 Miles in Length, not one Family is to be found on these Plantations, by which means there is near 20,000 People left Destitute of their Habitations. The 700 Men voted by the Assembly recruit very slowly; the People that have Grain, are more intent on saving it than accepting the Bounty offered: By the lowest calculation made there cannot be less than 400,000 Bushels of Wheat fall to the Ground, which cannot be saved."

PHILADELPHIA July 28. Extract of a Letter from Fredericks County Maryland, July 16. one in the morning.

"Just now I received a melancholy account from Col. Cresap's in which is as follows. viz. That on the 12th inst. the Indians fired upon six men shocking wheat, and killed one man, but were prevented scalping him, by another firing upon them as they came up. On the 14th five Indians fired upon 16 men as they were sitting, standing, and lying under a tree at the end of Col. Cresap's lane, about 100 yards from his house and wounded one man, but being fired at by the white men, who wounded one or more of them, as appeared by the great quantity of blood found on the tracks, they ran off, and were persued, but could not be overtaken. On the 15th, Mr. Welder, was going to a house of his about 300 yards from Cresap's, with three men and several women, the Indians to the amount of 20, rushed on them, but on being perceived by the people in the house, they immediately went to their assistance, on which the Indians fired, and killed Mr. Welder; the white men returned their fire, killed one, and wounded several more, as appeared by the blood left in the field and on the tracks. ——— The Col. expects daily to be more distressed, as is in much want of assistance. ——— The Indians were very bold and daring for some time, and one in particular, who cut Mr. Welder in the back, and divided his ribbs from the back bone, after he was shot down, but we prevented his being scalped. Mr. Cresap's youngest son scalped the Indian. A party that went up the river are just returned and inform, that they found a hog killed and laid upon a shelf of a house, bleeding fresh, by which conjecture the Indians had not been gone above a half an hour from which they track'd them along the old warrior road, that leads up to Will's creek, and soon after perceived a great smoke coming thro' the gap of said creek, which made them think the enemy had burnt all the houses there."

Our advice from Carlisle, are as follow, viz. "That the party under Sheriff, Mr. Dunning, mentioned in our last, fell in with the enemy at the house of Alexander Logan, supposed to be about 15, who had murdered said Logan, his son, and another man, and mortally wounded a fourth, who is since dead; at the time of their being discovered, they were rifling the house and shooting the cattle. Our men on seeing them, spread themselves from right to left, with a design to surround them, and engage the savages with great courage, but from their eagerness, rather too soon, as some of the party had not got up; that the enemy returned our fire very briskly; but our people regardless at that rushed on them, when they fled, and were pursued a considerable way, till tickets secur'd their escape, 4 or 5 of them, it was tho't, being mortally wounded: Our people brought in what cattle they could collect, but great numbers were killed by the Indians, and many horses carried off. On the 22d, one Pummeroy and his wife, and the wife of Johnson, were surprized in a house, and left for dead; but one of the women, when found, she gave some sign of life, was brought to shippensburgh, where she lived some hours in a most miserable condition, being scalp'd, one of her arms broke, and her skull cracked with a tomahawk; and that since the 10th instant, there was an account of 54 persons being killed by the enemy.

There are many letters in town, in which the distresses of the frontier inhabitants are set forth in a most moving and striking manner; but as these letters are pretty much the same, it would be endless to insert the whole, the following therefore is the substance of them. ——— "That the Indians had set fire the the houses, barns, corn, hay, and in short, to every thing that was combustible; so that the whole country seemed to be in one general blaze. ——— That the miseries and distresses of the poor people were really shocking to humanity, and beyond the power of language to describe; that Carlisle was now become the barrier, not a single inhabitant being beyond it; that every stable and hovel in the town was crowded with miserable refugees, who were reduced to the state of beggary and despair; their houses, cattle and harvest destroyed; and from a plentiful, independent people, they were become real objects of charity and commiseration: that it was most dismal to see the streets filled with people. in whose countenances might be discovered a mixture of grief, madness and despair; and to hear now and then, the sighs and groans of men; the disconsolate lamentation of the women and the screams of children, who had lost their nearest and dearest relations; and that on both sides of the Susquehannah, for some miles, the woods were filled with poor families, and their cattle, who make fires, and live like the savages."

A Gentleman from Carlisle informs us, that in a letter from Augusta county in Virginia, dated the 16th inst. it is said, that the settlements of Great Briar and Jackson's river, in that colony, were cut off by the Indians, a few of the inhabitants only escaping; and that a prodigious extent of country was entirely evacuated by the people.

CHARLESTOWN S. Carolina July 30. By letters, from Beaufort, and Port Royal, we are informed that Joiner, in the scout boat, was returned from St. John's river. The lat. at the mouth of said river he found to be 30 deg. 12 min. north. After he got up the river about 15 miles, he found its course to be S. and about 60 miles farther up, s. S. E. half E. The Indians affirm there is a passage into the bay of Apalachee.

About 50 miles up the said river and 18 miles from St. Augustine, the Spaniards have a small fort called Picolata.

AUGUST 1763

BOSTON Aug. 1. The Philadelphia Papers give us further Accounts of Mischief being done by the Indians at the Southward. ──── On the 10th of July 4 Men and a Lad being in a House at Juniatta, about 30 Miles from Carlisle, a number of Indians rush'd in upon them; they set fire to the house, kill'd 3 of the Men, wounded the Lad whom they made Prisoner, the other Man made his Escape. ──── The same Day six Men being at another House about a Mile Distant, were attacked by the Indians; in this skirmish one Indian was mortally wounded, five of the Men lost their Lives, and only one got off. ──── On the same Day a Man and two Children were also murdered in another House. ──── The next Day several Parties were sent out in quest of the Savages, one of which Parties were fired upon by a large Number of them, and oblig'd to fly. Another of the Parties fell in with a Number of Indians and shot one of them; the rest took to the Fields: our People pursued them but could not come up with them: ──── The 13th of July Accounts were received of 6 being killed; so that from the 9th to the 13th of July, there has been 25 Englishmen killed, and 4 or 5 wounded. ──── The inhabitants of Shearman's Valley are in the greatest Consternation; their Houses are burnt, and their Grain destroy'd; it was thought that a few Days there would not be left a single Inhabitant North of Carlisle. ──── It is further mentioned in the Papers, That the Senecas and Cayugas had declared War against the English: That all the Forts on the Ohio, except Fort Pitt are destroyed, and that the Indians expected to do in a little Time; after which they intend to attack Fort Augusta with a Body of 900 Men, which they likewise expect to reduce; and then to meet with the Body down the Country.

NEW-YORK Aug. 1. From Albany we learn that Sir William Johnson has held a congress with five of the six nations, at German Flats. ——— The Senecas refused to send any of their nation to the congress. ——— The five nations that met Sir William brightened the Chain of Friendship, declared their firm attachment to the English, their concern at the foreign nations having taken up the hatchet; that it was owing to some French emissaries amongst them; that each of the nations met at this congress would send one of their sachems to endeavour to persuade the Indians now at war with us, to lay down their hatchets, and would endeavour to make peace between them and us: That they would give us the earliest notice of the enemy's march or design: That in consequence of this promise, they had since congress broke up, sent Sir William intelligence, that a number of enemy Indians were on their march towards the German Flats, whereupon Sir William ordered all the Militia on the Mohawk river to march to the support of that settlement and the frontier; and had sent orders to Vanderheyden at Albany, to march 5 companies of their militia to Scenectady, for the defence of that part of the country, as occasion might require; and the same time ordering the 5 companies to be replaced by 5 others, from the lower part of the County.

CHARLESTOWM S. Carolina Aug. 3. Last Week Expresses were sent off to all the Indians in the Southern District, on account of the War began to the Northward.

The Accounts from the Creeks are, that all things are quiet among the Indians there.

SAVANNAH Aug. 4. It is said that part of the British troops in garrison at Martinique, and Guadelupe will be ordered to Florida, and that part of Louisiana ceded to the English; and that the Spanish troops that remove from Florida will be sent to La vera Cruz.

Capt. George Johnston of the Navy, we hear, is appointed Governor of Florida.

PHILADELPHIA Aug. 4. The following Advices from Detroit, of the 8th of July, may be depended on as authentic.

The conduct of Major Gladwin who commanded at Detroit, seconded by the spirited Behaviour of his whole Garrison, having bested all the schemes of the Indians, even before any Reinforcements arrived, the Savages seem'd to sicken of their attempts, and some threatened to leave the others and go home, when the Letters came away; but these Letters discovered such a continued Scheme of Barbarities committed by the inhuman Villains as stagger Credibility, and are shocking to human Nature.

It appears that the Savages massacred all the Men of Lieut. Gyler's Party, who fell in their Hands, on their Way to the Detroit; excepting three Men, who had resolution enough, when they came within Sight of Detroit, to attack the Indians who were guarding them in the Boat; threw the Brutes overboard, and got safe into the Fort.

The Posts at Sandusky, Miamis, Michillimackinac, Ouiatanon and St. Joseph, are all cut off by Treachery, chiefly owing to the Savages having taken the Oppertunity of securing the Commanding Officers, when treating with them as Friends. The whole Garrison af Sandusky (except Ensign Pauli, the Commanding Officer who made his Escape, and got safe into Detroit) with all the Traders who were there, fell by the Hands of the Savages: the same fate attended Ensign Holmes, at the Miamis, who was betrayed by a Squaw, that begged him to go 200 Yards, to bleed one that was dying, when he was shot by the Indian, who way lay'd him. The Commanding Officer of Michillimanckinac is Prisoner; but too many of his Garrison have suffered: All the Goods at those places have fallen into the hands of the Indians. Several of the Traders massacred, Ensign Schloffer, who commanded at St. Joseph's got safe into the Detroit but the Villains, who came Friends, butchered every Man of the Garrison excepting 3, and plundered the Fort. Lieut. Jenkins, who commanded at Auatanon, is carried to the Illinois; and 'tis feared his Garrison have met with no better Treatment than the others. ——— Ensign Christie, who cammanded at Presque Isle, and who was said to be killed, was carried by the Savages, with Part of the Garrison to Detroit.

On the 30th of June, the Schooner arrived from Niagara, with a Reinforcement of Men, and a Fresh Supply of Ammunition and Provisions, and on the 14th of July, Major Gladwin sent out a Party, who attacked some Indians, killed three (one of whom was a Chief) and pursued them for some Distance: But soon after he had Mortification to learn that the Villains had butchered Capt. Capt. Campbell, in the most shocking manner: This Officer had been determined ever since he went out to treat with them; and there cannot be stronger Proof of the Ingratitude of that brutal Race than in this Instance; for while Capt. Campbell commanded at Detroit, he was remarkably hospitable to the several Tribes of Indians who came to that Post; and made it his constant study to befriend them. The other Officer who accompanied Capt. Campbell, had the good Fortune to make his Escape, and was safe in the Fort, when the letter came away.

PHILADELPHIA Aug. 4. Our Accounts from the Westward are as follows, viz.

Lancaster July 28. They are certain Accounts that the Indians passed the South Mountain, and gone into York County; and some of them have assuredly been seen near Carlisle. ——— The want of the distressed Refugees have been greatly relieved, by scads of money collected in the different Congragations in the County. ——— The Quakers and Menonists have been very liberal on this Occasion, having raised a considerable Sum, and hired Men to assist the poor People in gathering in as much of their Harvest as possible. ——— And we are told, that several large Parties have again attempted to go over the Mountains, for this necessary and laudable Purpose; but the Risk they run is so great that we cannot think of them without dread.

Carlisle July 25. Two Indians were seen at Connadogwynoch-Creek about four miles from Shippensburgh, on Thursday or Friday last, who attempted taking a Man that saw them, but he escaped. ——— They write from Virginia that great Numbers of People are reduced to the utmost

Distress by the Savages: but that several Parties of them had been repulsed by our Men, who had taken to the Forts.

July 30. On the 25th a considerable Number of the Inhabitants of Shearman's Valley went over (with a Party of Soldiers to guard them) to attempt saving as much of the Grain as might be standing, and it is hoped a considerable Quantity will yet be preserved. —— A Party of Volunteers between Twenty and Thirty went to the farther Side of the Valley South of Tuscarora Mountain to see what appearance there might be of the Indians, as it was thought they would most probably be there, if any where in the Settlement, to search for, and bury the Dead at Buffaloe Creek; and to assist the Inhabitants that live along, or near the Foot of the Mountain, in bringing off what they could; which Service they accordingly performed, burying the remains of three Persons; but saw no Marks of Indians having lately been there, excepting one Track, supposed about two or three Days old, near the Narrows of the Buffaloe Creek Hills, and heard some Hallowing, and firing of a Gun at another Place. —— A Number of the Inhabitants of Tuscarora Valley go over to morrow, with a Party of Reapers, to endeavour to save part of the Crops. —— Five Indians were seen last Sunday, about 16 or 17 Miles from this Place up the Valley, towards the North Mountain; and two the Day before Yesterday, about five or six Miles from Shippensburgh, who fired on a young Man, but missed him. The eight Companies allowed for the Defence of this Frontier, are now very near, if not quite compleat.

On the 15th of July they were in Shippensburgh 1384 of our distressed Back Inhabitants, viz. Men 301; Women 345: Children 758, many of whom we are obliged to lie in Barns, Stables, Cellars and under old leaky Sheds, the Dwelling houses being crowded.

From Fort Bedford we learn, that Col. Buquet, with the Army under his Command, were well at that Place the 27th ult. having met with no Interruption from the Enemy; and that he was to proceed on his March the next Day. —— That no mischief had been done in that Neighbourhood for three Weeks; and that the Number in all killed thereabout is fifteen: But they had received Advice there from Fort Cumberland, that on Sunday, the 24th of last Month, as a Number of People were assembled at a Place of Worship, at a Calf Pasture, in Augusta County, Virginia, they were attacked by a Party of Indians, who killed 26, or upward of them.

SAVANNAH Aug. 4. Extract of a letter received from Philadelphia dated, 5th inst.

"Our Indian affairs at present have a most melancholy aspect indeed; every day brings a conformation of the farmer's bad news, with an addition of losses. Last night we had account of Presque Isle, Vanango, and another post being cut off; that D'Etroit was closely besieged, and 1000 Indians were going against Pittsburg, for the safety of which I will not answer, if attacked by so great a body. We suspect Frenchmen, Painted, dressed, and every way disguised like Indians, to be amongst them, and to have fomented of this dreadful defection. As to our Traders, they are all either murdered or ruined, and many considerable men here will suffer very largely; some will not lose less than 2 to 10,000 Pounds currency. God grant the defection may not be general, and extend to the southern provinces; for if it should you will be in a woeful situation. ——— Three or four companies of Highlanders have already passed through this city to strengthen the frontiers, and Gen. Amherst it is said, orders every man (who he thinks fit for duty to march to Albany, &c."

BOSTON Aug. 8. We hear that a Detachment of the 17th Regiment, which marched from Albany the 22d of June, to assist at D'Etroit, were safe arrived at Niagara; but that they had met with a skirmish, of which 'tis said they had the Advantage considerably, [This Party was reported to be commanded by Major Rogers; but it appears since to be under the Command of a Captain belonging to the Regulars.]

We hear that several Regiments just arrived, and a great Number of other Men from different Corps are forthwith ordered Up to endeavour to check the further Progress of the Savages.

By a Maryland Paper we have the following Account from Frederick County, viz. That the 13th of July the Indians fired upon 6 Men, and killed one of them: On the 14th five Indians fired upon 16 Men, one of whom they wounded; upon the English returning the Fire, they fled, and were pursued, but could not be overtaken: On the 15th about 20 Indians fell upon 4 Men and several Women, who were soon assisted by some of their Friends in a neighbouring House: At this Time one Englishman was killed, and barbarously Mangled, but was prevented being scalped by his Son: An Indian was also killed, and several wounded: A Party of English who had been on the Road that leads up to Wille's Creek, towards Bedford, perceived a great Smoak from whence they were fearful the Enemy had burnt the Houses there, but could not be certain of it, as Night came on.

By a Philadelphia Paper we have the following Account, viz. That one of the Parties sent in quest of the Indians, as mentioned in our last fell in with about 15 of them, in Shearman's Valley, that they had murdered 3 Men and a Lad, and were then shooting the cattle, being as it was tho't about to return home with Booty: Our Men surrounded the Savages, and engaged them with Resolution, and having finally put them in flight, pursued them 'till the Tickets forced their retreat, 4 or 5 of the however it is supposed were mortally wounded. ——— On the 21st ult. 3 Indians were discovered near Shippenburg who next day murdered a Man and two Women, one of whom they scalped and mangled in a cruel Manner: Not less than 54 Persons have been killed in about 15 Days.

By the New-York Papers we learn that at a Congress lately held by Sir William Johnson, At German-Flats, all the Chiefs of the Six Nations were present, except the Senecas, and brightened the Chain; promising to give the earliest Intelligence of the Enemy; and also to endeavour to bring them to a Friendship with us: Soon after which they bro't Intelligence of a Number of them marching towards German Flats; upon which Sir William immediately took the necessary Steps to the Protection of that Part of the Country.

We hear by the Hartford Rider of the Indians continuing their Ravage to the Westward, that the German Flats was beset by them: That Major Rogers, who was in pursuit of the Indians having a Party of 500 Men with him, were cut off; with some additional Accounts; which, if true, will doubtless soon be received. These reports were by two Persons, one of them left Albany last Wednesday and arrived at Springfield on Saturday, the other left Albany on Thursday and was at Hartford on Monday. They both agree that such advices were received.

NEW-YORK Aug. 8. The last Accounts from Albany are, That Captain Dalyell was met at Presque Isle, by our Vessel that brought Letters from D'Detroit, and which was attacked in the River within six Miles of that Place, by a large Number of Indians, covered by a Breast Work, on a Pass that interrupted our Communication very much, and where the River is very narrow. This Information, it is said, has determined Captain Dalyell to entrench before he got there with his Detachment, consisting of 300 Men, and wait the return of the Vessel from Niagara, which is well armed, and play'd Havock with the Indians in that affair, in which he had five Men wounded.

―――― By what the Indian Traders report, it looks probable some of the Indian Nations are inclined to make Peace having delivered up their Prisoners gratis, and restored some of the Goods they had plundered from the Traders.

We have the Pleasure to inform the Public, That the Alarm upon the Mohawks River (as mentioned in our last) has turned out not to be so bad as represented, although our information at that time came well authenticated. It appears to have been occasioned by a couple of Idle Fellows belonging to the Oneidas, the Sachems of which Nation were very much surprized when Sir William Johnson's Messengers arrived among them anxiously enquiring what Grounds there were for the Intelligence: And desired that Sir William might be acquainted, That the Reports were groundless, and according to their promises to him their last council, would from Time to Time acquaint him every Thing that might tend to the disturbance of our Settlements; requesting withal, that if we could with the Fellows that reported the Falsehood, to secure and punish them. This has greatly satisfied the People of the Frontiers, who have settled again in Peace; and the Detachment of the Militia that were ordered Up in consequence thereof, are returned to their respective Homes.

NEW-YORK Aog. 8. Extract of a Letter From Fort Ontario, dated July 24, 1763.

"By Vessel arrived from Niagara Yesterday, and by some Traders from Detroit, who came Passengers in her, we are informed, that Maj. Gladwin, and his Garrison were well the 12th Instant, and that he had only 1 Man killed, and 4 Wounded, and that the Indians about Detroit, when the Traders came away, some of the Nations are very desirous to make Peace; all the out-posts are cut off; the Garrison of Presque Isle, were delivered up to Major Gladwin; at St. Joseph's, all the Men murdered except Ensign Schlosser and 7 Men, who are also given up to Major Gladwin; Lieutenant Jenkins, with his Garrison, are sent to Illinois, Ensign Holmes, killed; the Garrison of Michillimakinac were surprized; they sent in a Number of Squaws with short Guns under their Blankets, which they had cut off for that Purpose, and a Number of Indians playing at Ball round the Garrison, when at last the Ball was struck into the Fort, and the whole push'd and seized the Garrison. Captain Ethrington, and Lieutenant Leslyare Prisoners, the other Officers that were there Lieutenant Jennett, was killed, Captain Campbell was butcher'd in revenge of one of the Sachem's Son that was killed in a Skirmish at Detroit, they boiled his Heart and ate it, made a pouch of the skin of his Arms; Lieutenant McDougal who was prisoner with Captain Campbell made his Escape with an Indian Trader ten Days before.

They attack'd the Vessel the last Time she went to Detroit, but were beat off; they also attempted to burn her with Arrows. The Vessel that came from Detroit saw Capt. Dalyell 10 Miles beyong Presque Isle; they gave him information that a Number of Indians being on a Point in the River, 6 Miles from Detroit, which it is thought will stop him; the Detachment is about 300 Men. We found only the Major and Hill, with a few Men. Capt. Hope of the 17th, with his Company, which consisted of about 15 Men goes Tomorrow; it is thought the French are at the bottom of this Affair, very few gave Major Gladwin Assistance till the first small Reinforcement arrived from Niagara. —— Our Traders are all Prisoners none killed but them you heard of before."

Extract of a Letter from Fort Detroit, July 6.
"We have been besieged these two Months, by 600 Indians; we have been upon Watch Night and Day, from the commanding Officer to the lowest soldier, from the 8th Of May, and we have not had our cloathes off, nor slept one Night since it began, and shall continue so till we have a Reinforcement up, than hope soon to give a good Account of the Savages; their Camp lays about a Mile and a half from the Fort; and that's the nearest they choose to come now; for the first 3 or 4 Days, we were attacked by 3 or 400, but we gave them so warm a Reception that they don't care coming to see us, tho' they now and then get behind a House or Garden, and fire at us at about 3 or 4 Hundred Yards distance, the Day before Yesterday, we killed a Chief and 3 others and wounded some more, and Yesterday we went up with our Sloop, and batter'd their Cabbins in such a Manner that they are glad to keep farther off."

Extract of a Letter from Detroit July 9, 1763.
"You have heard long ago of our pleasant situation, but the storm is blown over. Was it not very agreeable, to hear every Day, of cutting, carving, boiling eating our Companions; To see every Day dead Bodies floating down the River, mangled dirk-gored, and Frenchmen daily coming into the Fort, with long wry Faces, tellin us of the most shocking Designs to Destroy us. But Britain, you know, never shirks; we also appear Gay, to spite the Rascals, and our little handful

of Men were always in good Spirits, and very Healthy; and thrashed Nytchees when ever they appear: They boiled and ate Sir Robert Davers; and we are informed by Mr. Pauly, who escaped the other Day, that he had seen an Indian have the Skin of Capt. Robertson's Arm for a Tobacco pouch. These are their Trophies."

Three Days ago a Party of us went out to demolish a Breast-Work they had made. We finish'd our Work and were returning Home; but the Fort espying a Party of Indians coming up, as if they intended to Fight, we were ordered back, made our Dispositions, and advanced briefly; our Front was fired upon warmly, and returned the Fire for about five Minutes, In the mean Time Capt. Hopkins, with about 20 Men, filed off to the Left, and about 20 French Volunteers filed to the Right, and got them between their Fire; the Villains fled immediately, we pursued as far as it was prudent, for a centry who I had placed informed me he saw a Body of them coming down from the Woods, and our Party, being about 80, was not able to cope with their united Bands; in short, we beat them handsomely, yet did not do much hurt to them, for they ran extremely well. We only killed the Leader, and wounded three others as we are told. We had only one Man slightly wounded, which is surprizing from their Situation and their first Fire. One of these fired at me at a Distance of 15 or 20 Paces, but I suppose my terrible Visage made him Troubled; I think I shot him. The killing of their Chief was cause for another tragical Affair; they brought Capt. Campbell out, and cut him to Pieces, McDougal had the good Fortune to escape two Nights before; and Pauley, who commanded at Sandusky, being told of Captain Campbell's Fate, jump'd out of a Window and arrived safe at the Fort.

SAVANNAH Aug. 10. We hear from New-York of the 12th of July, that the Indians about the Ohio and the Lakes continue their depredations, and have almost depopulated the western frontiers of Pennsylvania, they are determined and resolute and take no prisoners. All our Forts beyond fort Pitt and Niagara, in number eight or nine, are cut off. Detroit only excepted, which has been blocked up for some weeks. The General has ordered up 1200 man to recover these Forts and chastise the Indians. Pittsburgh has been entirely surrounded by the savages. The Six Nations continue quiet as yet. Among those that are murdered by the savages are Mr. Gordon of Venango, Sir Robert Davers, and English Gentleman, who had been some time in America taking surveys of the country, and Lieut. Grant and Robertson of Montgomery's Highlanders. &c. &c.

SAVANNAH Aug. 11. Last Sunday put in here, the Adventure transport, from Havana bound for Pensacola, having on board his Majesty's 35th regiment, amounting to 200 men, under the command of Major Forbes, and about 80 women and children. The Adventure being thought unfit to proceed on the voyage, two other ships are taken up, which are preparing to carry the troops, &c. to their destination.

SAVANNAH Aug. 17. The presents provided by the King for the several nations of Indians who are to meet the southern Governors in October next, are arrived here.

In Philadelphia Papers to the 4th inst. Just received, we have dismal accounts of the very distressed conditions of the inhabitants of the western frontiers of Virginia, Maryland, and Pennsylvania, against whom the Indians continue their horrid barbarities with unrelenting cruelty. ——— The regiment sent by Gen. Keppel for New-York are arrived there, and they, with other forces, we are told, are ordered against the savages. Col. Bouquet was marching with a body of men towards Pittsburgh, and had got to Fort Bedford the 25th past without being molested by the Indians.

BOSTON Aug. 15. The Reports we had last Week of Major Rogers and a Party of 500 Men being cut off by the Indians it is said, are not true, as the New-York Papers mentioned that the 17th Regiment was got up the Niagara, with which Detachment went Major Rogers.

NEW-YORK Aug. 15. We have no news of any consequence from the Frontiers, since our last. That the Hurons and Pottawattamies, who were partly forced into the War by the menaces of the Ottawas, begin to withdraw, they have already delivered up at Detroit, Ensign Christie and 8 prisoners, taken at Presque Isle, being afraid of the arrival of the army, also that the Indians who lately consisted of 800 men before Detroit, cannot at present muster 500. They were in confident of succeeding, that they began to divide the Land with the French, and have planted large fields of Corn, which we hope the English will reap. They have plenty of provisions and ammunition at Detroit, and the men are in high spirits, and are also happy in having one of the best commanding Officers the army can afford, under whose direction we doubt not a good account will be given of all the Indians that come against them.

CHARLESTOWN S. Carolina Aug. 17. All the accounts from the countries of the Southern and Western Indians continue favorable, Not a week passes in which the Cherokees do not lose some of their people by the Nottowagas or other northern Indians; and they seem to be a settled animosity between the Cherokees and all those Savages. One hundred Creeks, with two Cherokees as Guides, are gone against the Yactanoes, who killed a Creek Indian of note in May last.

His Excellency Governor Dobbs has signified his intention of being at the congress with the Indians in October next.

NEW-YORK Aug. 18. By particular accounts come to Hand of the Indian Attempts upon Detroit and other remote Posts, it evidently appears that some of the Canadians, and other French residing in those Parts, were the secret instigators of the Savages, in their villainous and bloody Attempts; and had persuaded them that all their former Possessions might be retaken from us; and that, finding themselves mistaken, the Indians are daily deserting, the Cause returning to their own Homes, not a fourth part of them now remaining in their Camps.

Coilita, (about 70 or 80 Miles from New-York,) August 5. Last Week the following Accident happened in this Place. Several Men having been out upon the Hills hunting for Deer, in their return met with a flock of Partridge, at which 4 Guns were discharged, three of them pretty quick after each other; this being an uncommon accident in the Place was mistaken by some of the Inhabitants of the Wall Kill, for the firing of Indians. ——— Immediately alarm Guns were fired, and spread over the whole Place, which produced an amazing Panick & Confusion among the People, near 500 Families: Some for Haste cut the Harness of their Horses from the Plows and Carts, and rode off with what they were most concern'd to preserve. ——— Some who had no Vessels to cross the River plunged thro', carrying their Wives and Children on their Backs, some we have already heard, proceeded as far as New-England, spreading the Alarm as they went, and how far they may go is uncertain.

The Men who were the innocent Cause of the Alarm inform'd as many as they could meet with of the Truth of the Case; but they were far from being able to quit the Disturbance they had raised. ——— Hence it is hoped People will be warn'd not to be frighten'd before they are certain of Danger.

PHILADELPHIA Aug. 18. Yesterday an Express arrived from Ligonier, by whom we have the following.

Extract of a Letter from Fort Ligonier, dated August 10, 1763.

When I wrote you last, the 2d inst. we had no Account of our little Army since the March from here on the 28th ult. As a great deal depends on that Convoy getting to Fort Pitt, so, doubtless, every One must be anxious for its safety. ——— The whole got safe to Ligonier the second Inst. without a single shot being fired at them. ——— On the fourth Colonel Bouquet resumed his March, leaving the Waggons with Capt. ____, and some other Officers, at Ligonier. On the Fifth, about One in the Afternoon a full Mile on this Side of Bushy Run, he was attacked (I don't hear of the Number) the fire continued till six; when the Col. took Post on a Hill for the Night. Next Morning the Indians, having been reinforced renewed the Attack, which was very warm, about Ten o'clock, when the colonel having drawn up a Line formed by his Flags, rushed upon the Savages, and pursued the upwards of a Mile and a Half, and then, ordered a retreat. ——— In these different Attacks we have lost some Men and Officers; but as this Intelligence is founded upon the Report of six Rangers who returned to Fort Ligonier, because, as that say, the Enemy got between them and our People, I am cautious of relating Particulars, till a more authentic Account comes to hand. ——— In the mean time, it appears from the whole, that the Enemy has been repulsed; and in all probability, the Convoy may have got to Fort Pitt, unless the Troops were attacked again, the 7th the furthest. ——— I have reason to believe, that the whole Force the Enemy had on this Communication was collect- for that Stroke, for from the Time the Troops arrived here to this Day, we have not seen nor felt the Effects of the Indians, And the reapers under cover, by the Assistance of a Captain and his Company have cut almost all their Grain, without the least Interruption; but now I shall expect they will visit us again."

  The Following are the Names of the Officers killed or wounded in the above Affair.
  Killed. Captain John Graham.
        Captain John Campbell.
        Lieutenant Menzier, either killed or Prisoner.
        All of the 42d Regiment.
  Killed. Captain Robert Grant.
        Lieutenant Donald Campbell of the 77th wounded.
        Lieutenant Dow, of Royal Americans shot in the Breast, and since dead.

  CHARLESTOWN Aug. 20. On Monday last arrived here, in the Ship Friendship Capt. Ball from London, the long expected Indian presents which are to be distributed at the ensuing congress, to be held the 15th of October; the place of meeting will be Augusta, unless the expiration of the Small-Pox should admit of another being fixed, more commodious for the northern Governors; boats we hear are hiring, provisions are engaged or engaging, and Fort Moore is repairing or repaired for the reception of the Governor and a detachment of independents. The Cherokees have received their invitation and accepted them, some will come from all the Towns, but not many, as they are sadly harassed and alarmed by the Northern Indians; the more distant nations can send no answer; and the Creeks have not yet, that we can learn, however, there is no sort of doubt but many of them will be at the meeting, and perhaps a little more humble than usual, for the hostilities of the Northern Indians are directed against them also. There are abundance of Virginia Traders in the Upper-Cherokee nation, of which the Indians heavily complain.

CHARLESTOWN May 24. Attakullakulla or the Little Carpenter, and all the other headmen and warriors of the Cherokee, have sent down assurance of their resolution to be at the intended congress, and expresses great thankfulness to his Majesty for the care he has taken of the lands belonging to his children the Indians.

The Northern Indians continue to cut off numbers of both Creek and Cherokees, several gangs of them from 70 to 100, have been met by some Virginian readers going to the Cherokee country, whom they did not hurt further than by staving all their kegs of rum, and searching for ammunition of which however found none.

The Settlement made by the Mortar headman of the Creeks, on the Ceosaw river, is broken up by these inroads of the Northern Indians.

BOSTON Aug. 22. Thursday last three Chiefs of Penobscot Tribe of Indians arrived in Town from the Eastward, in order to have a Conference with his Excellency our Governor, which we hear is to be held at the Council-Chamber this Day.

PHILADELPHIA Aug. 25. Extract of a Letter from Lancaster August 21, 1763.

"Just as I had closed my letter to you John Hart, the Indian Trader arrived here from Pittsburgh, and brings the following Account, which you may depend upon: That on the 5th and 6th Colonel Bouquet was attacked by the Indians and lost and had wounded 110 Men: On the 8th he arrived at Pittsburgh. The Officers killed are Captain Graham, and Lieutenant Campbell; Lieut. Dow wounded. Mr. Hart declares, the Indians never had so severe a drubbing since they knew the use of powder, &c. 20 of their Great Warriors were found dead besides a great Number wounded, and dragging away by their Fellows."

Another Letter from the same Place, mentions, Colonel Bouquet's getting to Pittsburgh, with all his provisions; and that he had been able to carry all the wounded with him to the Fort.

And a third. " That the Hearing of the Colonel's arrival at Pittsburgh, was as agreeable News to them, as any they had heard the last War."

Extract of a Letter from Niagara, July 25.

"Since my last, a Man of the New-Jersey Provincials, belonging to the Garrison, was scalp'd within a Mile and a Half of the Fort, as he was going Express to Fort Schloffer, a Place about 18 Miles from hence, and where they embark after having crossed the Portage. Two Sailors, belonging to Commodore Loring have also shared the same fate at the Mouth of Lake Erie, where they had gone to embark for Detroit."

In another Letter from the same Place, of August 17. Mention is made, that one John Martin, in the Great Cove, seeing an Indian coming up to a House where he was, fired at him; upon which the Indian raised a Yell, and took to a Tree: That Martin imagining they might be more Indians near him, ran to a Company at Work, and told what had happened, when they went to the Place, and found some blood and excrements; from which they concluded he was shot through the Bowels. They followed his Track down to a Bottom, where they saw the Tracks of six or seven more; but being a small Party pursued no further. In the same letter it is also said, that a young Man, at a Plantation about 9 Miles from Carlisle near the Foot of the Mountains, saw an Indian and fired at him, at about 50 Yards Distance, but was not sure that he hit him; the Indian took on a Tree and the Lad went back a little Way, in order to load again, but on his return could not find the Indian. He then alarmed the Neighbourhood; and the Soldiers being all out in Parties covering the People gathering in their Grain, upwards of 20 young Men turned out immediately from Carlisle, to scout the Woods.

From Berks County we have advice, that on the 16th Instant they had Intelligence of Captain Kern's Post, on the North Branch of the Shuylkill, above the Blue Mountain, of some Indians being seen about 8 Miles from thence; to which a Party was sent out, who found the Tracks, but could not come up with them: That the same Day they received further Intelligence, that the Enemy was about a Mile off, when a Party pursued, came up with, fired on them, and wounded one Indian, who was seen to fall three times but there happening to be severe Gust, they escaped. That soon after the Indians came within 80 Perches of the Guard, and carried off some Horses; And that a reconnoitring Party was sent on by them from a swamp, when our Men immediately rushed into it, but the Place and Larrels were so thick, that they could not find them.

Extract of a Letter from Fort Cumberland, August 9, 1763.

"I have just received Advice by Express, that this Day the Savages killed one Capt. Staunton, and another Man, of the Virginia Militia and wounded three others dangerously of a Fort above Pearfall's on the South Branch, but scalped none.
There were eleven Men in the Fort; the Party of Indians was between Thirty and forty, three of whom were thought to be killed. Colonel Stephens will be here to morrow with 140 or 150 Men. As he commands the Militia of several Counties, he has promised to assist all in his Power, by protecting Bedford and this Garrison."

By a Person from Fort Augusta, we learn that our people were all well there, about 14 Days ago; but that the Indians, who used to live on the Big Island, on the West Branch of the Susquehannah were all gone off, excepting one old man and his two Sons, and are suppose to have joined the other Indians in the War against us.

Extract of a Letter from Halifax, august 4.

"Last Night an Express arrived from Annapolis Royal in this Province, with an Account of a Number of St. John's Indians having fired on the Fort, and killed several People thereabout;

upon which News a Regiment is ordered up there from this Place and is thought will break up all the New Settlements in this Province."

NEW-PORT Aug. 22. By a Vessel from Halifax we are informed, that a considerable Number of Indians had assembled, together in Nova-Scotia, but with what Design we have not yet learnt. We have not heard of any Hostilities being committed by them.

BOSTON Aug. 29. Last Thursday se'nnight the Province sloop Massachusetts, Captain Saunders, arrived here from the Eastward, in which came Meserwanderoment, Eclambuit, Saure Woraromegasa. Indians of the Penobscot.

An on Monday and Tuesday last his Excellency the Governor in Council, aad a Conference with them at the Council Chamber.

The Conference related chiefly to the proper method of Trade to be carried on between the English and the Indians.

The above Indians informed his Excellency that they were empowered by the Penebscot, Passamaquods and Machis Tribes to declare their willingness to submit to King George and the Government, and be governed by English Laws: and that they were desirous of renewing the ancient Treaties, to live in Peace, and never be at War again with the English.

The Governor in answer to this Declaration, told them that as his Majesty King George had subdued all the Country which the French used to hold, He was now become Sovereign of the Whole: That the French who remain here were now become Subjects to King George; and both French and Indians would be treated as Children as long as they behave dutifully to him.

His Excellency ordered some small Presents should be delivered them before they went away; and informed them that if they should be desired to make submissions to the Government, and renew the Treaties heretofore made with it, in a formal Manner, they might signify their Desire to him.

The Indians on the whole expressed themselves well satisfied.

They say, that the norridgewalk Tribe consisted

of about Ten who were with the Wawemacks, and live amomg them at Becacour.

BOSTON Aug. 29. By a Gentleman who came to Town Yesterday from Quebec and Montreal, we learn, that there is not the least Disturbance among the Indians in those Parts, but that they daily bring in Furrs, &c. and track with the Inhabitants in the most amicable Manner; we also learn that they had brought in most of the English Prisoners who had been so unfortunate as to be taken Captive by them in the late War.

Extract of a Letter from Quebec, Aug. 11.

"There are Thirty Canoes of the Indians arrived at Montreal, with three of the Traders from Michilimackinac also Sixteen Battoes loaded with Furrs. ——— These Indians are suppos'd to be Ottowaaous, and want to make Peace. ——— The cutting of the Michilimackinac is suppos'd to be a loss to the Merchants of Quebec and Montreal od Fitty Thousand Pounds Sterling ———."

NEW-YORK Aug. 29. Friday last at 2 o'clock in the Afternoon, Captain Basset, and Engineer, arrived here from Pittsburgh, Express to his Excellency Sir Jefrry Amherst, which Place he left the 13th Instant. The Account brought by him, we hear are as follows, viz. That on the 5th Instant, in the Evening the Troops under the Command of Col. Bouquet amounting to about 450 were attacked by 400 Indians, with about a mile and a half of the Place called Bushy Run (26 miles from Pittsburgh,) the most convenient for an attack on all that Road; but after a smart Fire for some Time, Night obliged both Parties to withdraw: that on the Morning of the 6th, by break of Day, the engagement was renewed again by the Indians: that they advanced on our People with the greatest Undauntedness, but met with a Reception contrary to their Expectations and were soon convinced they had People to come with that understood Bushfighting as well as themselves: Notwithstanding which, the Engagement continued till Ten o,Clock, very Smart, and very bloody, many being killed and wounded on both Sides, The Indians still continuing to behave with uncommon Bravery; but two Companies of Light Infantry having found means to surround them, they soon found themselves between two Forces, when they immediately gave Way, and fled with the greatest Precipitation imaginable, leaving killed on the Field of Battle at least Sixty of the Savages, among which Numbers was a Sachem called Kikahusica, that had been often well treated at Pittsburgh. Our Men pursued the Savages two Miles, but could take only one Prisoner, and after a little Examination he received his Quietus. Our Army did not scalp and of the Indians, nor thinking it prudent to delay Time, but proceeded on to the Relief of the Garrison, where they arrived, with all their wounded Men, and Supplies, the 10th following.

In the Engagements above mentioned, we had Captain Lieutenant Graham, and Lieutenant M'Intosh of the Hignlanders, with a Lieutenant of the Rangers killed; and Lieutenant Dow wounded, besides 40 Privates killed, and 60 wounded; The Waggoners and several other People that followed the Army, scalped most of the Enemy that were left on the Field; and the Indians the Night following the Action returned and scalped as many of our People as they could find. The 10th the Indians crossed the Ohio, in sight of Pittsburgh, when they gave 30 Scalp Yells, to denote the Number of Scalps taken.

We are told Lieutenant Dow shot two Indians before he received his wound, and broke the thigh of a third afterward.

We are also told, the Indian Army was composed of 8 different Nations, and as Braddock and Grant were conquered on the Road, they expected to have served Col. Bouquet in the same Manner: but thank God they have been disappointed. And we hope the Province of Pennsylvania will reap the sweets thereof, and many be convinced that the Indians are no more invulnerable than other Men, when attacked on equal Terms, and especially by British Troops.

We hope to give the Public a better Account of this Affair: as also agreeable Advices from from the Dutchmen; That is gone to the relief of Detroit, commanded by Capt. Dalzel.

By an Express that arrived in this City on Saturday last, we learn that Fort Detroit still held out strongly against the Savages; and that they were no ways likely for the Savages to succeed in their attempts.

SEPTEMBER 1763

NEW-YORK Sept. 5. A Letter from Detroit, August 8, 1763.

"The 25th of July we landed at Sandusky (where the Fort formerly stood) about break of Day; and instantly marched, 8 Serjeants, and 160 Men, with 5 Subalterns, for the Indian Town that lay about 6 Miles off from the Lake; Capt. Dalyell and myself, was on the Detachment; I commanded an advanced Guard of Light Infantry, leaving Capt. Grant, of the 30th, to secure our Boats and Retreat. We came to the Town about 8 o'Clock in the Morning, and directly surrounded it, but could find none of the Enemy there, all that we could do was Fire their Huts, which were made of Bark, and bring off some Peltry that the Enemy had hid there; we likewise cut up some Corn, but it is of so small value, that it's hardly worth mentioning. We returned to our Boats about two o'Clock the same Day and that Night rowed about 5 Miles to an Island and there encamped. The 27th in the Morning, the Wind blew fair at South to carry us across by the Islands, to the North of the river Detroit; and, with a fair Wind did good sails, we came to it at 3 o'Clock in the Afternoon, having Distance from Sandusky about 50 Miles. When we came there, I got in to Leeward of a small Island, and waited for the rear; the whole arrived very soon. Capt. Dalyell ordered us to proceed; we got undiscovered to the center of Villages, where the Savages fired on both sides of us, just at the Dawn of Day; but we kept the Center of the River, which is about 600 Yards across. The Indians wounded 20 Men slightly, but killed none; we arrived at the Fort about Sun-rise the Morning of the 28th.

In the Morning of the 30th, a Detachment was ordered to march under the Command of Captain

Dalyell of 140 Men, with Gray of the 55th, Maj. Rogers, Capt. Grant of the 8th, Lieut Brown, Lake, and Narthlow of the 55th, with Lieut. Bain and Cuyler of the Queen's Rangers, Lieut. M'Dougal and Ensign Paury and Anderson of the Royal Americans, Ensign Anderson and Fisher, with Lieut. Catchel of the 55th, with a proper proportion of Serjeants, Corporals and Drummers and 8 Volunteers from the Traders, with Mons. Babee and Martine, on whose intelligence depended. We marched up the River Side along the Road that led to the Indian Encampment, having on the Left Fields of Wheat, and Orchards, and on the Right a Sandy Beach to the Water Side, with no other Cover to the Detachment than two Battoes, with Swivels in their Bows. In this Manner we marched about a Mile two deep, with an advanced Guard of 25 Men, under the command of Lieut. Brown, about 20 Yards a head. We continued our March with fixed Bayonets; the advanced Guard got about the Center of the Bridge we had to cross, and the Main Body just entering of it, we received a Fire from the Houses, (of which there was many there) and Hedges in Front, which killed and wounded the greatest part of the advanced Guard; the Fire we returned in Platoons, and soon after, received a Fire on the left Flank; but we marched over the Bridge, and beat the Enemy from the Houses, &c. by the Assistance of the Boats aforementioned, where we halted the Detachment for some Time to get the dead and wounded on board the Boats. The Indians in the mean Time got between us and the Fort, in this Situation the Detachment was ordered to Face to the Right about, and fall into two deep, and retreat slowly, Capt. Dalyell in the rear with the Light Infantry; in this Manner we returned, followed by a heavy Fire from the Hedges, Orchards, Houses, keeping close to the Fences that divided the Inhabitants Fields from the Road, and once in a while sent out a Party to beat them back a little; when we had marched half a Mile, the Enemy came close upon our Right, and attacked us with heavy Fire; upon which, Capt. Gray was ordered out with his Company to beat them back, and myself ordered with another

Detachment to take Possession of a House the Enemy had got into opposite the Centre of the Detachment. I took Possession of the House with some Loss, and Capt. Gray drove the Enemy back from the Fence, but with Loss, himself being wounded.

  About this Time, Capt. Dalyell was killed, and Lieut. Brown wounded; Capt. Gray was brought to the House, and the Rear came up; the Boats fired with their Round of Grape Shot, which by the Help of our Musquetry from the House broke the Enemy to some distance, and gave me an Opportunity to put Capt. Gray, Lieut. Brown, and several other wounded Men on board the Boats; which delay caused the Front and Back to be divided by Reason of the Front's marching forward to which I sent a Messenger to Capt. Grant, to desire him to Halt in the progress, (as I was then the Commanding Officer of the Party) and marched up with the Rear, followed closely by the Savages which continued coming closer, in so much that I was obliged to take Possession of another House which I did with Lieut. Narthlow, and Ensign Anderson, and about 30 Men, which was the only way I could think of to secure the Retreat. I went forward to acquaint Capt. Grant, that he might secure the Retreat in the same Manner, for as he tho't best, which he did, by taking Possessions of the Houses; Also as the House the whole Enemy fell on me, thinking to force the House, the Boats having gone down to the Fort with the wounded, and to return directly with a fresh Supply of Men and Ammunition. Here I stood then about two Hours, with only the lose of two Men; They were in Number 200 at least, and they kept up a very brisk Fire through the Windows of the House; which were very large but I fortified them with Beaver Skins, as there were many in the House, and also the Chamber, beating the Boards off the Roof and making a Breast-Work with them and Skins. About 8 o'Clock the the two Row-Boats came up, one with a 3 Pounder in her Bow; she immediately threw in a shower of Rounds and Grape to the Right and Left of the House, to a leanto and a cover which was there, and drove the Enemy back, with the Help of our

small Arms. This gave us the Opportunity of making our Retreat to the Fort, where we arrived a half past Eight. Capt. Dalyell, one of the Serjeants, one Corporal and 19 Men of this Detachment were killed Capt. Gray shot thro' the Body and the right Arm; Lieut. Brown thro' the Thigh, Lieut Luke in the Leg, and 48 wounded. ———
Since the above we have had several Skirmishes, but none of any Consequence, having no Men killed or wounded.

Pondiac who is the Indian chief, calls himself King from the Rising of the Sun to the Setting; is encamped 4 Miles above the Fort where he is well entrenched; and declare he never will leave that Ground 'till he has Possession of the Fort."

The Savages since this affair, have been reinforced, continued in this encampment, but make no impression on the Fort, as the Garrison has ample supplies of all Kinds.

Great part of the reinforcements that are ordered to Detroit must be well advanced by this time, and, we trust, we shall soon have the pleasure of giving the publick an account not only of their arrival, but of their success in clearing the country of the barbarians, as well as punishing them severely; that they shall never dare to attack any of our settlements hereafter.

NEW-YORK Sept. 5. Last Friday his Excellency General Amherst received the following account of the unsuccessful attack made by Capt. Dalyell to surprize Pontiac's Camp near Detroit, on the 31st of July, viz. ———

On the 29th of July at day-break, the garrison of Detroit were most agreeably surlrized by the appearance of Capt. Dalyell, with a detachment under his command, who, altho' attacked on both sides the river, by the Savages, made his way, without loss of a man, only a few wounded. ———

On the way thither Capt. Dalyell landed at Sandusky, in hopes of surprizing the Indian village at that place, but found it abandoned; whereupon he burnt the village and destroyed every thing he found therein, and proceeded to Detroit without molestation, until he reach'd the river, where he was attacked as the above mentioned.

The garrison being now reinforced, and the Indians still continuing in their Camp, Captain Dalyell, formed a design of surprizing Pontiac, under cover of the night. The corps intended for this service being got ready; about half after two in the morning of the 31st, they marched out, under the command of Capt. Dalyell; two armed boats sailed along shore, to cover their retreat, and take off the killed and wounded: The distance of the enemy's camp from the fort, was only about two miles, so that our troops were soon close to the Indians breat works: but found the Savages had got intelligence of the design, and prepared themselves accordingly, by taking possession of all the houses on the road, from whence they kept an incessant fire, which galled our troops excessively: ——— Many efforts were made to dislodge the Savages, Capt. Dalyell exerting himself, with the most undaunted Bravery and resolution, and the other officers and troops seconding his endeavours: but as it was now evident that the Savages had been thoroughly apprized of the desigh, it was judged advisable not to pursue in the attack, but to think of a retreat. ——— Capt. Dalyell, who, before this, had received two wounds, was trying to bring off some of the wounded, when he unfortunately received a third, which put a period to the life of a brave officer, animated with a noble thirst for glory, Zealous for the honor of his King and country, most assiduous in executing the orders of his General. ——— Our greatest loss in his death, for Capt. Grant. who commanded the retreat, made so proper a disposition, that the detachment returned to the fort, in good order, about 8 o'clock in the morning, in sight of the enemy, who had all joined, and were much stronger that at the beginning of the affair. ——— Capt. Gray, and Lieut. Brown and Luke of the 55th Regt. were wounded; but all like to do well: in the whole, we had nineteen men killed and thirty-nine were wounded.

Major Rogers went out with the above party, but received no hurt.

PHILADELPHIA Sept. 8. In a Letter from Fort Bedford it is said that the Indians were much quieter than they had been for some time; and it was thought they began to dread the consequences of their late horrid cruelties.

Extract of a letter from a Gentleman who went out with a party on volunteers from Lancaster County, dated Sept. 1, 1763.

"Last Friday at 5 in the afternoon, we had the happiness of meeting a large party of the great island warriors on their way to the frontier of this Province. They had the first Fire on our advanced party, which was forced back on out front, and pursuing, engaged us briskly for some time; but, after an hour's hot firing they were obliged to run, with considerable loss. I killed two myself, and saw several others fall, by the good behaviour of our men. We had four of our men killed, and four wounded, who we brought in with us. ——— We hid the killed, so that the Indians did not get one scalp, ——— We bro't in four scalps, and killed at least six more. ——— but did not think it prudent to follow and scalp them, for fear of some of the Indians falling in with our wounded men. ——— We lost several Horses."

Other letters say, that the Indians were seen dragging off several of their dead and wounded: That next day the party was attacked twice by the Indians but beat off without loss: ——— It is said the Indians fought all naked, and were painted black.

BOSTON Sept. 12. The extract of a Letter from Nova-Scotia of Aug. 4, published in our last under a Philadelphia Head, relating to the St. John's Indians firing on the Garrison and killing several People, must be a mistake, as Mr. Hancock has received Letters from a Gentleman of distinction at Annapolis Royal, dated the 8th and 13th of August, and from Halifax on the 5th, 10th, 13th, 23d, and 25th of August, therein there is no Mention of any assault made on the Fort at Annapolis, or any Mischief done by the Indians there.

SAVANNAH Sept. 14. On Thursday a Catawba Indian arrived here with a letter from Samuel

Wylly, Esq; at Wateree, by which we learn, that some Indians, thought to be Shawanese, had killed a man and his two children on Alison's-creek, a branch of Fishing-creek, they likewise tomahawked his wife, who it was hoped would recover. They also killed the wife, and child of Thomas Robinson.

The Lower Creeks have sent down assurances of their intentions to be at the ensuing congress; the Upper Creeks have received the letters of inviting them to the same congress, and their answer is daily expected. Capt. Colbert who went with the invitations to the Chicesaws and Choctaws, is arrived in the Chicesaw country.

By Letters from Fort Prince George, Keeowee, dated the 3d inst. we are informed, that on the 1st three Cherokee women were killed by the Northern Indians in the corn field at Estatoe; and scalped them. The Cherokees have lost between 50 or 60 of their people. Two Northward Indians were seen the 2d about four miles from Fort Prince George, and were pursued, but to no purpose.

PHILADELPHIA Sept. 15. On Monday last Express arrived from Reading in Berks County, with the following Intelligence, viz.

"That on Thursday last, about two o'Clock in the afternoon, 8 Indians came armed in the House of John Fincher (one of the people called Quakers) about three quarters of a mile distant from a party of Capt. Kern's consisting of 6 men commanded by Ensign Sheffer, and about 24 miles from Reading over the Blue Mountains. That said Fincher, his wife, two sons and a daughter, Immediately went to the door, and asked them if they would eat any thing hoped they were come as friends, and entreated them to spare their lives; That however after some deliberation, they then killed Fincher, his wife and two sons, the daughter said also to be missing: but as she being heard screaming by some of the neighbours, and crying murder, we fear she is likewise killed: That a little boy made his escape from the Savages, and came to the Ensign, who immediately went to the place with his party, but the Indians were gone, and finding but their marks which way the went, pursued them to the house of one Nicholas Miller, where he found four children massecred. The enemy having carried off two others of them; but that said Miller and his wife being at work in a field, saved their lives, by flight, the man being pursued near a mile by one of the Indians, who fired at him twice: That our party still pursued and soon come up with the enemy, and fired on them, which they returned, but the soldiers rushed on them so furiously that they quickly ran off, and left behind them two prisoners, two tomahawks, and hanger, and a saddle, three of their number being badly wounded. That the two prisoners recovered were the two above mentioned Miller's children, which they had tied together, and drove them before them; That the persons murdered were scalped, except the child about two weeks old, which they in a cruel manner dash'd to pieces against the Wall: That the number killed near the mountain was eight, and two missing; and all the Inhabitants were all come off to this Side, and were in the utmost distress.

That as the Express was setting out from Reading, certain Information was brought there, that the House of Frantz Hobler in Berns Township, about 18 miles from Reading, was attacked, on Friday Evening last by the Indians, Frantz himself was wounded; his Wife and Children carried off; and three other of his Children scalped alive, two of whom are since dead."

Since our last arrived here an Express from Fort Bedford, which he left the 7th. By him there is advice, that all was well at Pittsburgh; That Capt. Hay with the convoy from Ligonier had got safe there. That there had been no disturbance from the Indians in that Quarter since Colonel Bouquet's Victory over them: And that every thing was likewise very quiet in Cumberland County, where there seem to be a noble spirit, many brave Men being ready to go out in service of the King and Country, if properly encouraged.

Extract of a Letter from Fort Cumberland, of September 8, 1763.

"One Henry Adams informs us, that yesterday he

was at John Forman's Fort, about 30 Miles from this Place, on the South Branch, when an Express arrived there from Fort Pleasant, who informed, that Capt. Luke Cullins, with some Men, had followed a Party of Indians to Chief River, one of the main Branches of the Monongahela, where he attacked them, and killed six of their number; took 11 Guns, 14 Pouches, several Horses and a large Quantity of other Plunder, to the amount of One Hundred Pounds, or more, exclusive of the Horses. He also released a son of Capt. John Walton's from the Enemy. It is remarkable that not one of the Guns taken from the Indians was loaded, and when attacked, they were butchering a Buffuloe, not thinking of Danger. It appears that their Party did not consist of above eleven; some of the Shot pouches being taken from the Inhabitants."

SAVANNAH Sept. 15. Extract of a letter from Philadelphia August 8, 1763.

"In my last I Acquainted you of the rupture with the Indians; they have since that time made great devastation on our frontiers, as well as on the frontiers of Virginia, where it is said whole settlements have been deserted. Carlisle is now our frontier, where thousands have fled for shelter, and lie under old sheds and trees, who are supported by the charity of the people round about the place, several of our merchants and officers (the latter since gone to Fort Pitt) gave very liberally to the distressed; and in this City subscriptions are handed about by several congragations, who have already got near 1000 Pounds subscribed; toward the fall it is imagined large sums will be added to their relief. ——— Col. Bouquet marched from Carlisle some weeks since for the support of Pittsburgh, and, by the last accounts, his corps, amounting to between 4 and 500 men, had reached Fort Bedford without molestation from the enemy. Since the Army left Carlisle we have no account of any mischief done. The noble Defence made by the brave garrison of Detroit has rendered the Attempts of the Indians on that fortress unsuccessful. We have accounts lately of a reinforcement getting in, since which the Indians have been quiet there, tho' they have cut off by surprise a great many of the small forts on the lakes; the garrisons they have inhumanly butchered, excepting some few that made their escape. ———— A number of the troops have safely arrived at New-York from the Havana, and others are expected from the Missisippi; those, with what are already there, and on their march, &c. and many hereafter raised, it is hoped will reduce the savages to their reason again, by destroying them with as little remorse as they have shewn our unhappy countrymen that have fallen under their savage cruelty."

WILLIAMSBURG Sept. 16. An Express arrived in Town yesterday, with letters for his Honour the Governor from Col. Stephen, of which we have the following advices, viz. That a party of Indians attacked 6 men in Welton meadow at Louring's creek, the 20th of August about XI at night; when the killed Michael Harness and Jonathan Welton, wounded John Welton, and took one Deles prisoner. The Indians that wounded Jacob Welton and was on the point of repeating the stroke with a tomahawk, and killing him, when the savage was shot by Deles, brother to the prisoner of that name; This discharging of his piece he was attacked by several Indians at once, the first that made up to him he knocked down with his gun, but the savages wresting it out of his hand he knocked down another with a tomahawk, which he carried under his belt, by this time the Indians had jostled him to the place where his brother lay tied; upon seeing him taken prisoner he immediately dropt all thoughts of further resistance and gave himself up, expecting likewise to be taken prisoner; but they hurried him away to the Indian that was shot, tomahawked him, and scalped him, then wounded him with a knife, leaving him for dead; but some time latter he crawled to some hay, undiscovered hid himself up till the next morning, perfectly in his senses, told the whole affair circumstantialy, and lived two days afterward. On receiving this intelligence, Col. Stephen ordered Maj. Wilson and Capt. Collins of the Hampshire militia to raise two companies of volunteers, and pursue the enemy as soon as they could possibly provide themselves with provisions. ——— Major Wilson took the way of Loiry's creek; and Capt. Collins being ordered to reconnoitre the head-waters of Patterson's creek, he fell in with the Major's party at the foot of the Alligahany mountains. After communicating this intelligence they thought it advisable to pursue the Indians over the mountains; accordingly on the 30th of august, after a pursuit of 120 miles over as rugged a mountains as can be found, they came up with them on a branch of the Monongahela. Being in on fresh tracks in the evening. Major Wilson was certain that their encampment was of no great distance; he therefore detached parties different ways in the night, to listen for horse-bells, or see if they could discover fire: the noise of the bells directed them to the encampment, and before day they had crept within 30 paces of the enemy and surrounded them. The order not to fire until it was light enough to see all the births, where the Indians lay: but a big fellow rising to make the fire, one of the party fired at him a little to soon, which brought on the engagement. This is to be attributed to the young man's eagerness to revenge the death of his father, who had been killed and scalped by the savages. Major Wilson, however, routed the party, took three Indian scalps, wounded many more, and took 11 rifles and 2 smooth barrel guns, from them, with all war equipage, and retook a number of horses. They likewise released Deles the prisoner, and got back the 3 scalps taken at Walton's meadow.

NEW-YORK Sept. 19. We hear from Albany, That about the beginning of this Month Sir William Johnson was greatly encouraged by a Congress with the Five Friendly Tribes; who signified their Hearty inclination to the English, assuring him of their Endeavours to reconcile the distant Tribes to the same Interest.

We hear from South Carolina, that the difference between the Governor and Assembly has never yet been accommodated, and that the means while the public business lies neglected.

ANNAPOLIS Maryland Sept. 21. Extract from a

Letter sent by Col. Stephen, dated the 30th of last Month, to Henry Lee, Esq; County Lieutenant of Prince William, in Virginia.

"I am sorry to acquaint you, that we are constantly harassed with Parties of Indians amongst us, either in Hampshire or Frederick in which we have taken two scalps, recovered three Prisoners carried off by the Savages, and according to their information, and our opinion, kill'd five more Indians that we could not scalp. I am obliged to apply to you, Sir, for a Detachment of your Militia, consisting at least of one Captain, one Lieutenant, an Ensign, and five Serjeants, and sixty Rank and File; and I must request you to have them well appointed with Arms and Ammunition, and dispatch them all to Winchester with the greatest Expedition, where I shall wait to give them further orders."

PHILADELPHIA Sept. 22. Extract of a Letter from Michilimackinac.

"On the Second of June, about twelve o'Clock, the Nation of Chipaway Indians came to the Fort, and played at Ball, as is usual for Indians to do, as they had done for three or four Days before, 'till they got the officers, out of the Fort to look at them. Immediately they seiz'd them Prisoners and fell on the Soldiers with their Tomahawks and Knives, killed fourteen Soldiers, Lieutenant Jamett, and Mr. Tracey, a Merchant from D'Troit, the rest of the Soldiers and English hid themselves. They first pludered the commanding Officer's House, then fell on our's and soon the rest of the English, all but Mr. Oakes who lost nothing, neither was there a French House in the Fort touched. Bostwick hid in the Garret under some Bags of Corn, till they carry'd all the Goods off, then they took the Corn that hid him, so he fell into their Hands. He took hold of one of the Men, and begged for his Life; in the mean Time another lifted his Tomahawk and made a stroke at him which he fended off with his Arm, till the other saved him: He was carried to their Cabbin, about half a Mile, they stripped him immediately, and dressed him to their own liking with Paint and Feathers and carried him to another Cabbin to see the Captain and Lieutenant. After Councelling a while, they agreed to let him come to the Fort, on condition they deliver all the Soldiers that were hid. On their Way to the Fort they were separated, and the Captain taken back 'till the Soldiers were sent to relieve him. All being done, they were put into a French House, and threatened every Minute of their Lives by those who were drunk. In the mean Time was sent for, the Nation of Ottaways, who are our Friends and live about twenty Leagues from the Fort. They arrived three Days after the Fort was taken, and marched into the Fort with their Callumets of Peace, all armed; and they took Possession of the Fort, and relieved those that were Prisoners from the other Nations. They begun a Council between the two Nations, to reconcile matters, which held ten Days, and the result was, that the Ottaways should take them to their Village, and not Permit them to stay at the Fort, Mr. Bezzo the Grecian, arrived the same Day, and was taken with them to the Ottaways. The Cruelties, the Day of the unhappy Massacre, are hardly credible, tho' they were not many murthered, yet those it was terrible to see. Lieut Jamett was knocked down, had upwards of twenty Stabs in his Body by Tomahawks and knives, then his Head cut off, and his Body quartered. Mr. Tracey likewise was stabbed in many Places, all the Soldiers were barbarously murthered, and one of them cut in quarters and eat. Mr. Solomon and Mr. Henry were taken in a Canoe by some of the Savages that Murthered Mr. Jamett with an intention to be murthered and they expected that every moment would be their last; and to aggravate the Thing, and make death appear to them more horrid, the Villains shewed them the bloody Knives and Hands that had murthered Mr. Jamett, and cut his Head with the knife and gave it to them, and obliged them to eat thereof; and because they thought there was not a sufficient Quantity of Blood to make it appear horrid to them, they spit upon the Handles and every other Part where it was dryed on, and put it upon their Bread. Henry and Solomon were rescued from the Villains who intended to Murther them, by several Ottaways, who bro't them back to the Fort. On our approaching the Shore at Michilimackinac, we were immediately pulled out of the Canoes, and were made Prisoners. Mr. Oakes was taken to the Fort, Mr. Levy to one of the Cabbins, and myself to another: in their drawing me to their Cabbin, they attempted to murther me, and struck me with a knife five times, which I watch'd and averted every Blow with my Arm: Once the top of the knife touched my Head; and scratch'd it to draw a little Blood, and it wanted a little Time to have given me my Quietum, and rescued me from a Life which seems to promise me nothing but Discontent and Misery. Our Loss is very considerable, I am seperated from Oakes and Levy, the two and Mr. Henry are together with the Chinoway Indians, and I continued in the Fort, their Lives are safe, but mine depends on the News we shall receive from D'Troit. The Savages, have given us a Report that there are many Officers who were taken at Niagara, arrived at the Illinois and have with them at that Place, an Army of two Thousand Regulars, and they are in the Missisippi, Ten Thousand Regulars more, who are making all the Haste they can, to come forward for this Place; that they have great plenty of Brandy at Des Illinois. We have likewise bad News by the Savages that the Garrison La Baye and St. Joseph, are cut off, and the greatest part of the People who were there are murthered: we don't much rely upon it, as we hope that it is all false: A few Days more will determine if it is so. We have but little Prospect of escaping, for they have stopped up the Way bout for Montreal and for D'Troit; as for that in Regard to Des Illinois, and the French Army, we are not concerned about, knowing that it must be false, but the other two Garrisons being cut off, we have but to much reason to fear. The Savages are sorry that they have done this, but as they have begun, they shall be obliged to go thro' with it, and therefore have blocked up the Way, to continue their plunder. I have this Moment heard from Oakes, Levy and Henry, and they are all well which is as much as can be expected. I shall not fail to write by every Opportunity;

it is out of the Power of Pen to point out to you our Distress. I shall keep a Journal as long as I have Permission.

SAVANNAH Sept. 22. By letters received this week from Augusta, we have a confirmation of two of our traders being killed, their horses and goods taken, and the store at the Fish pond plundered, by the Mortar and some of his party. Both Upper and Lower Creeks are greatly exasperated at his proceedings, and some of the former have promised to carry the Chickesaw horrors through the nation. Every thing we are assured is at present quiet among them; The Lower Creeks have promised to be at the congress to be held at Augusta next month, and many of the Upper Creeks ar also expected. The people who went over to the Carolina side were only a few stragglers, who, having no fixed place of residence, are ready on every occasion of this kind to alarm and disturb the country.

Savannah Sept. 22. On Monday last his Excellency received an Express, a letter from Col. Richard Richardson one of the members of assembly for the parish of St. Mark, informing of several depredations being committed by the Northward Indians, and referring him a letter inclosed, written to the Colonel by the Rev. Mr. William Richardson at the Waxsaw settlement near the Catawbas. By this express we learn, that those Indians have killed one woman on the south fork of Catawba, and lower down the country they killed one Man and two children, and miserably cut another woman. These murderers filled the inhabitants at Broad-river with such apprehensions that most of them fled to Waxsaw. The people about Fishing-creek are crowded into houses, and about building forts again.

Aug. 27. The Northward Indians killed the brave old King Heigler, of the Catawbas, almost in the middle of the Waxsaw settlement, which caused such terror as nothing was seen but flying on every side, when the minister, Mr. Richardson, wrote a representation of the miserable state of these parts, In the name of a number of the inhabitants, and sent it to Col. Richardson, to be forwarded to our Governor, and requesting assistance, otherwise the poor people would lose their crops, and be reduced to the utmost distress.

NEW-YORK Sept. 25. We hear that one of our vessels from lake Erie was lately cast away on her voyage from Niagara to Detroit loaded with provisions.

BOSTON Sept. 26. Extract of a Letter from a Merchant in Halifax dated Sept. 8, 1763.

"I am sorry to inform you of the late uneasiness in this Place, occasioned by an Order from Sir Jeffry Amherst, which deprive the Soldiers of their Provisions under the pay 4 Pence Stering per Day: allowing them only Two Pence per Day for subsistence, fresh Provisions, Necessaries, Surgeon and Spruce Beer. The consequence of this order was, all the Troops (except the Company of Artillery) mutinied and threw down their Arms, and refused to serve without their usual Allowance: They said. That they had behaved like Soldiers on all Occasions, and had drubb'd the Enemy of Great Britain in almost every Quarter of the World: asked if this was the Recompence, is this the Parliament's care in their address to the best Sovereign, is this the Reward of all our Services? We are the Remains of a once great and victorious Army: and we must not starve. ——— In consequence of this Col. Foster called a council of the Field Officers and Captains of the Garrison, who came to a Resolution to continue their Allowance without making them pay for it, till the General's pleasure is further known."

BOSTON Sept. In an Account lately published of Col. Bouquet's engagement, Capt. Robert Grant and Capt. John Campbell were said to have been killed; but we are now informed that they both escaped unhurt, and that Lieut. Dow is not dead of his wounds.

PHILADELPHIA Sept. 29. Extract of a letter from Carlesle Sept. 20, 1763.

"Of late we have had no Disturbance on the Frontier from our savage Neighbours; which is by no means, I apprehend to be accounted for from any change in their Disposition, but from their Time being taken up by removing their

Families, and putting themselves into a better situation to accomplish their bloody Designs, ——— I was last Week through the upper End of this Country, where People are, at present, following their Labour as usual, and will, unless prevented by such Trouble, have a large Fall Crop. ——— A considerable Number of the Inhabitants of both Coves were then gone home, and designed to put in same Grain, for the further Support of their Families. Many of the Inhabitants had likewise returned to the Canalloways, but, on fresh Alarms along the Virginia Frontier, were, as it was informed, come back to Fort Frederick. ——— Through all the late schene of Troubles one man and his Wife, kept their Place in the Little Cove, though entirely by themselves.

"On Tuesday, the 13th Instant, a small Party of Indians were chaced, in the Little Cove, by a Party of Maryland Scouts. ——— The Inhabitants of Path Valley, and a Number of Reapers will I expect have the Crops sufficient for the next Year's Support, if no new Troubles come upon us, and a Guard be continued; but ranging Parties, and a Reward for Scalps, are the means which under God, would most likely answer the End."

PHILADELPHIA Sept. 29. We hear from Virginia that about three weeks ago, a large party of Indians came down on the Frontier of Augusta county, designing, as was supposed, to strike a town there; but being discovered by some men, who were out hunting horses, the inhabitants, were alarmed of their approach and turned out, in a large body, to meet them. which they accordingly did, and an obstinate engagement ensued, wherein, though the white people lost a considerable number, yet they kept the field, and brought off with them 15 Indian scalps, and a considerable quantity of plunder.

We are also informed, that a party of Virginia Rangers, having, the same week, come on some Tracks of Indians going out from the inhabitants, followed them till evening; when, sending some of their party to the top of a hill, they discovered the Indian fire, and made towards it;

and as they went along, they heard the enemy fire 15 guns, which they supposed was the party emptying their pieces, as the day had been wet, in order to clean them; upon which they hasted up, and immediately fired on the savages, as they sat round the fire, and killed three of them; the rest fled, leaving behind 13 guns, and a number of Moccasons.

PHILADELPHIA Sept. 29. Extract of a letter from Carlisle Sept. 20, 1763.

"A number of the back settlers have returned home, and, unless prevented by fresh troubles, will get in a large fall crop."

OCTOBER 1763

BOSTON Oct. 3. The following is inserted by desire of the Governor of Nova-Scotia.
Council-Chamber, Halifax, September 15, 1763.
Whereas a Paragraph has appeared in the Boston News Papers, relating an Account from Annapolis Royal in this Province as follows.
Extract of a Letter from Halifax Nova-Scotia, Aug. 4th.
"Last night an Express arrived from Annapolis-Royal in this Province, with an Account of a number of St. John's Indians having fired on that Fort and killed several People thereabout; upon which News a Regiment is ordered up there from this Place, and 'tis thought will break up all the new Settlements in this Province."
All which Accounts being without Foundation, no hostilities whatsoever having been committed, nor any such Disposition having appeared among the Indians, the Commander and Chief, with the Advice of his Majesty's Council, has thought fit to contradict this groundless Report, that the Publick may be undeceived, and the ill tendency and design of all such Rumours render ineffectual.   Richard Bulkley, Secr.
NEW-YORK Oct. 3. On Friday the Albany Post came to Town in the Manner of an Express, bringing the mail, and tiding extraordinary, on the following doleful Occasion, Viz.
Copy of a Letter from a Gentleman at Niagara, dated September 16, 1763.
"Sir,
I have just Time to tell you we arrived safe at Niagara the 13th Instant, delay'd much on Lake Ontario, by hard Gales, and Storms of Rain: Next Day had an Express from Little Niagara (a Post above the Falls) that our Convoy, with it's Teams employed in carrying Provisions to Lake

Erie, was attacked; we sent off from the Fort an reinforcement of a Major, and about 70 Men, which was followed by a Captain and 50 more an Hour after to support them: The whole of the Indians by best Accounts, amounted to about 300, divided into two Bodies, one of which (i. e:) the most inconsiderable was that attacked the Convoy, the other lay in ambush about two or three Miles Higher our Post, near the Carrying Place, and possess'd themselves of a most advantageous Piece of rising Ground near the Road to intercept our Escorts: On the first hearing of the Firing by the Convoy, Capt. Johnston and three Subalterns march'd with about 30 Men, mostly of Gage's Light Infantry, who were in a little Camp adjacent; they had scarce Time to form when the Indians appeared in the above Pass: Our People fired Briskly on them, but was instantly surrounded, and the Captain who commanded mortally wounded the first Fire; the three Subalterns also were soon after killed, on which a general confusion ensued; The Indians rushed in on all Sides, and cut about 60 or 70 Men in Pieces, including the Convoy: Ten of our Men is all we can yet learn has made their Escape; they came here through the Woods Yesterday. From many Circumstances, it's believed the Senecas have a chief Hand in this affair. I wish our Affair at Detroit may not suffer by this, all the oxen and Teams on the Carrying Place is destroyed, and the Horses missing, which 'tis believed are drove off by the Indians: Our Reinforcement came up to late to save them, so the People return'd that night, and next Day marched and buried all they could; most of them who came in are wounded. We shall be in an ugly situation having a weak sickly Garrison, if Detroit should fall (which God Forbid) to stand the Fury of those rascally Indians; but dare say our wise General will provide against the worst, and will in Time send such a Force as will be able to chastise these Savages so effectually that they will dread the Name of the Englishman latest Posterity.

Our People too had a Brush at the Wreck, in Lake Erie with a small body of Indians, who we beat them off, but lost about four or Five Men, they promised when Reinforcements should join them they would pay us another Visit there; but we have little to fear from that Quarter, as we have 170 Men there, strongly intrenched, to guard the Provisions saved from the wreck.

Extract of another from Niagara, Sept. 17.

"Wednesday the 14th Instant a large body of Indians some say 300 others 400 or 500 came down upon the Carrying Place, attacked the Waggon escort, which consisted of a Serjeant and 24 Men, ––––––– this small Body immediately became sacrifice, only two Waggoners escaped. Two Companies of Light Infantry (the General's and La Hunt's) that were encamp'd on the Lower Landings, and on hearing the Fire instantly rushed out to their Relief, headed by Lieutenant George Campbell, and Frazier, Lieutenant Rosco of the Artillery and Lieutenant Deaton of the Provincials; this Party had not march'd above a Mile & half when they were attacked surrounded, and almost every Man cut to Pieces; the Officers were all kill'd 'tis reported, on the Enemy's first Fire: the Savages rush's down upon them in three Columns. The officers being kill'd the Men fell into Confusion: of both our Parties only 24 are come in, Waggoners included, eight of which are wounded. Lieut. Campbell, Frazier, Rosco and Deaton killed, and about 75 Rank and File killed: Capt. Johnson of the Jersey Blues, who was coming down on some business with a Waggon escort, killed. The Savages killed 16 Oxen on the spot, destroyed most of the Carriages: The Horses, in Number 20, they have carried off loaded with Plunder. As soon as the Alarm reached this Post, Major Wilkins marched out with the most Part of this Garrison to the Lower Landing, but Night coming on, were obliged to return back; the next Day he march'd out again to the Place of the Action, buried the Dead, which were every one scalped and strip'd naked, brought of four or five waggons and three Firelocks, the Enemy having carried off all the rest of the Arms, Catouch boxes &c. The Bodies were so mangled, they could not discover either Rosco or Deaton: we don't imagine here they carried off any Prisoners: The consequence of this Blow is better imagined than described; 'tis we have been long been apprehensive of: That together with the Loss of the Sloop on Lake Erie, will render it very difficult to support Detroit this Winter unless a large Reinforcement is soon sent up."

NEW-YORK Oct. 3. A Letter from Niagara, Dated September 16, 1763.

Most of the provisions that was on our sloop, when cast away on her voyage to Detroit, was saved, and the people under the direction of Capt. Montrefor, intrenched themselves. Capt. Cockran with 90 men, was sent from hence to succour them, and take command. The Indians attacked Capt. Montrefor in his unfinished encampment, and after killing him and three men, they were repulsed.

The 12th instant Capt. McCloud, of the 80th, with 10 officers, 200 men, 2 scows, and 20 Battoes, set off in order to Join Capt. Cockran, whose entrenchment was at Catfish creek, 12 miles from the mouth of the river. The 13th in the morning, a party with a serjeant, 20 oxen, 16 horses were sent off, and withe them went Capt. Thomas Johnston of Amboy, and Mr. Stedman our sutler. ——— At 10 o'clock, Mr. Stedman returned on horseback, and said, that about 3 miles from the landing, between two bridges, in a ticket, sixty Indians all naked, attacked the party to which he belonged, and killed all but himself; and indeed, on burying the dead, we found he had not deviated much from the truth. Lieutenant Campbell, who commanded at the landing, hearing the firing, took part of two companies, with Lieutenant Frasier of the 80th, Lieutenant Rosco, of the Artillery, and Lieut. Dayton, of the Yorkers, in order to succour our people; but he was soon attacked, in a situation so disadvantagious to him, that his men could not do their duty, and in short none of the whole party save two, who came in the 14th in the morning, were either killed or taken; we imagined Mr. Campbell made a noble resistance with few of his people, as his body, with several others, were found lying together. On making a computation of the loss it was found, that Lieutenant Campbell, Lieutenant Frasier and 78 men of the light infantry, with Lieut. Rosco, of the artillery, Capt. Johnston of New-Jersey, Lieut. Dayton, and 8 Drivers are missing, and also suppose to be killed, as we have reason to think the Indians made no prisoners. ⎯⎯⎯ All the oxen were killed, but no horses, that we know, the enemy having carried them all away.

NEW-YORK Oct. 10. We hear from Quebec, that there has been a Mutiny among the Soldiers there on the same Occasion as at Halifax, but it was quickly surppresed, and the matter accommodated by the Care of General Murray.

By the Philadelphia Post we have the Pleasure to learn that all is quiet on the Communication between the Place and Fort Pitt.

Detroit, Sept. 9, 1763.

"Since my last to you we have had several Skirmishes with small Parties of the Enemy, in taking Possession of three Houses about 500 Yards up the River, which prevents the Indians coming so near the Fort to discover our Motions. The 9th Inst. about half after 8 o'Clock in the Evening 3 or 400 Indians in Canoes went off to attack our Schooner that way coming up the River from Niagara with Provisions. They met her becalmed about 6 Miles from the Fort, with only 12 Hands on board, who defended themselves so bravely that the Indians, after attacking with great Resolution on all sides, were obliged to retire with the Loss of many killed and wounded, 7 of which are since dead of the Wounds. The Indians attempted to enter the Schooner by a Cabin Window, but were obliged to fall astern, and several were killed by endeavouring to board by the Bowsprit. The Number of Indians killed on the Spot is uncertain; some say 10; but they have been very busy for several Days fishing and searching for Dead Bodies. Mr. Horsey, Master of the Schooner, and one Man was killed, three wounded, and another burnt by the bursting of a Cannon Cartridge.

"The Indians were so roughly handled, that they have declared, they never will attempt to attack the English by Water any more; and they have having heard the Captain of the Schooner say to his Men, in the Action, Stand by my brave

Fellows, to the last, and then blow up the Vessel: which was answered by the Crew with three Cheers, the Indians imagine they would neither give up or take Quarters, left the Schooner in the greatest Confusion, and two Canoes were overset by our Shot. By the blood on the Spears and Lances on board the Schooner, and the Spirit of the Indians being much staged since, they must certainly have met with a considerable Loss; but as we are surrounded with a Parcel of Rascals who never bring us any News to the disadvantage of the Enemy, its impossible to know what mischief we have done them.

"Immediately after the Action which was short and smart, 4 armed Battoes, with a four Pounder in each, and 2 officers and 24 Men, were ordered on board the Schooner, who brought her safe here the 6th Instant.

"The Indians confess they had 10 killed at the Attack with Capt. Dalyell, Five Indians belonging to the Six Nations come up on the Schooner, and went on shore in the Morning, when the Vessel was attacked in the Evening; it is therefore not impossible but that they either intended to betray the Vessel, or else were compelled by the Ottowawas to discover our Strength on board the Schooner, on which they attacked her, as was afterward told us."

PHILADELPHIA Oct. 13. Extract of a Letter from Bethlehem, Oct. 9, 1763.

"Early this Morning came Nicholas Marks, of Whitehall Township, and brought the following Account, viz. That Yesterday just after Dinner, as he opened his Door, he saw an Indian standing about two Poles from the House who endeavoured to shoot at him; but Marks shuting the Door instantly, the Fellow slipt into the Cellar, close by the House. After this said Marks went out of the House, with his Wife, and apprentice Boy, in order to make their Escape, and saw another Indian standing behind a tree, who also tried to shoot at them, but his gun missed Fired. ——— Then then saw a third Indian running through the Orchard; upon which they made the best of their Way, about two Miles off, to one Adam Tashler's, where about 26 Men in

Arms were assembled, who went first to the House of Jacob Mekly, where they found a Boy and a Girl lying dead, and the Girl scalped. From there they went to Macks Plantations and found both the Houses on Fire, and a Horse tied to the bushes. They also found said Sneider, his wife and three children dead in the Field, the Man and Woman scalped but not the Children. ——— On going further, they found three Girls, one dead, the other two wounded one which scalped, After this they returned, with the wounded Girls, to Adam Tashler's and saw a Woman, Jacob Allmong's Wife with a Child, lying dead in the Road, and scalped. The Number of the Indians, they think was between Fifteen and Twenty.

"I cannot describe the deplorable Conditions this poor Country is in: most of the Inhabitants of Allen's Town, and other Places, are fled from their Habitations. Many are in Bethlehem, and other Places of the Brethren and others further down the Country. I cannot ascertain the Number killed, but that it exceeds 20. The People at Nazareth, and the other Places belonging to the Brethren, have put themselves in the best Posture of Defence they can; they keep a strong Watch every Night, and hope, by the Blessing of God, if they are attacked, to make a good stand."

In a Letter from the same County, of the tenth Instant, the Number of killed is said to be 23 besides a great many dangerously wounded; that the Inhabitants are in the utmost Distress and Confusion, flying from their Place some of them with hardly sufficient to cover them: And that it was to be fearful there were many Houses, &c. burnt, and Lives lost, that were not then known. ——— And by a Gentleman from the same Quarter, we are informed, that it was reported, when he came away, that Yost's Mill about 13 Miles from Bethlehem, was destroyed and all the People that belonged to it, excepting one young Man, cut Off.

Extract of another Letter from Carlisle dated Oct. 6.

"I greatly fear the Communication between Fort Pitt and Ligonier is cut off again, as the Indians have been seen about Ligonier, and have killed one Man, and done some other Damage. It is now upward of five weeks since any accounts from thence."

WILLIAMSBURG Oct. 14. The following is an extract of a letter from Col. Andrew Lewis to his Honour the President, dated Oct. 3, 1763.

"Our men on duty have of late been constantly harassed by the enemy, especially those on Jackson's river. The lookouts in that quarter, about the end of August, discovered the tracks of a party of Indians on Green Brier. As soon as they made their report, I ordered Capt. Bawyer and Moffat, with 100 men, to go in quest of them, who found the Indians, about 20 in number, forted in. As soon as our people fired on them, they took to their heels, though not without returning the fire; two of their men were however killed on the spot, and many of those who made their escape wounded.

"About the 12th of last month, Capt. Ingles, with 30 of his men, fell in with a party of Indians, 20 in number, on New River, as they were returning from the frontier of Halifax with 4 prisoners, 30 horses, and a considerable quantity of baggage: The Indians being unwilling to part with so valuable a booty, disputed the ground for near half an hour, when Capt. Ingles remained master of the field, scalped two Indians, wounded many, released the prisoners, and brought in the horses and baggage.

"On the 26th a more unlucky affair happened on Jackson's river between Fort Dinwiddie and Fort Young. As Capt. Moffat and Philips (the latter from Louisa) were on their march with 60 men, to join Capt. Cunningham, they were attacked by a far superior number of the enemy. The engagement lasted a considerable time, but at last our men, overpressed with numbers, were obliged to give way, leaving 12 of their number dead on the spot, one of them Capt. Philips's lieutenant. By all accounts the Indians must have lost a good many men."

PHILADELPHIA Oct 20. Extract of a letter from Virginia, Oct. 12.

"The Capts. Moffat and Philips, passed on Jackson's River, in Augusta County Virginia, were surprised, with sixty Men, by a Number of Indians, and totally routed on the thirteenth of last Month; tho', notwithstanding this stroke, the Savages in general, have met with great loss on the Frontiers of Virginia. Capt. Field, with about 100 Volunteers, from my Department joins Major Campbell in escorting the Convoy to Fort Pitt."

Extract of a Letter from Fort Bedford, Oct. 8.

"This Day the remains of a brave Officer, Lieut. Richards of the Provincials, was buried here; he was killed and scalped about five miles from the Garrison. The Indians are seen every Day. ——— This Moment a Boy was taken in View of the Garrison; and, at the same Time, a sister of his wounded, but not mortally. 'Tis remarkable this Boy was taken this Year before on the same spot by the Enemy, but made his Escape from them."

Yesterday a Gentleman arrived here Express from Northampton County, who brought Advice, that on Saturday last, about Noon, the New-England Settlement at Wyoming, was attacked by a Body of Indians (supposed to be the Wyalusings) when, we hear, Thirty two People were killed or carried off by the Enemy. This Account was bro't to Fort Penn, in Northampton County, by seven of the People that belonged to the Settlement, and made their Escape.

PHILADELPHIA Oct. 20. Extract of a Letter from Lancaster, Oct. 13, 1763.

"The Paxton Volunteers are returned ——— They went as far as the headland, but met with no Indians. They destroyed all the Houses, and above 3000 Acres of fine Corn, &c. Col. Armstromg, and his Party, proceeded twenty Miles farther, and are not yet returned."

SAVANNAY Oct. 20. Monday last arrived from Charlestown by water, the Hon. Peter Randolph, Esq; one of his Majesty's Council in Virginia, who came with his Honour Lieut. Gov. Fauguier, in order to attend at the congress; and next Day he set out again in the South-Carolina scout boat, Capt. Joiner, for Charlestown.

On Tuesday morning an express arrived from John Stewart, Esq; at Augusta, to his Excellency our Governor, by which we learn, that part of the Upper and Lower Creeks, Chickesaws, Choctaws, and Catawbas, were come there to the congress, but absolutely refused to go to Dorchester; 200 Cherokees were daily expected. In consequence of this express, a party of 50 rangers commanded by Lieuts. Moses Nunez and Mungo Graham, were yesterday ordered to march to Augusta; and his Excellency, attended by gentlemen and Captain Gilliveay's troop of horses, set out this day, under a discharge of the great guns at Fort Halifax.

CHARLESTOWN S. Carolina Oct. 22. Monday last an express arriv'd from Augusta, with letters of the 15th instant which contained the following intelligence, viz. That a number of the Lower Creek Indians, a very few of the Upper, headed by Mistificah (a fellow of no great note, but who led the party that lately killed the two Cherokee women near Estatowih and is generally known by the name of Struther's Friend) one Choctah leader called the Red-Horse, about 20 Chicasah's and Catawba's of different ages and sexes, were then there, in consequence of the invitation sent them to a congress: That the Cherokee's were hourly expected: That many more Choctahs had been on their route, but turned back, upon hearing of two of their people being killed by the Creeks: That the Creeks had never been known to be so audacious as lately; that they had treated Capt. Colbert, who carried the invitations, with utmost contempt and insolence, and more than once shook a Tomahawk over his head; that the young people seemed all for war, and were almost too powerful for the headmen: That some of them had already been to Pensacola, were received kindly, and well treated there, yet had the insolence to shake their hatchets over some of the soldiers heads, as they were drawn up on their esplanade; but the commanding officer did not then take the least notice of their insult, lest the consequence of his shewing resentment, should be, the immediate massacre of the traders in the nation: That our friend the Wolf King, seeing the ill disposition of his countrymen, and apprehending they would begin hostilities against us at Pensacola, had fallen upon an expedient in order to gain time, which was by calling an assembly of all the headmen on the Tallapoosih river, the beginning of last month; proposing to go to Pensacola himself, to know what was intended to be done in regard to their hunting-ground (which the French had incessantly insinuated was intended to wrest from them, as well as deprive them of their liberty) and exhorting them to be quiet till he should return with an answer: That several traders intended to take the opportunity of the Wolf's going to Pensacola, to withdraw themselves; amongst them one that had been in the nation, above 30 years, who writes of the 15th and 20th of September, from Muecolassah, "That he had never seen so dangerous a time; that for three weeks before, he had been obliged to have a guard of Muecolassah Indians constantly about him, day and night; that no white man dare stir half a mile from his house without such a guard; and that the Wold King had found it very difficult to persuade the Indians to be peaceful till he should return from Pensacola, for which place he was then about to set out." That the Mortar had publickly declared, he would have the goods going to the Choctah's, if they were to be found upon the face of the earth. That Captain Stuart had had a very long talk with the Creek Indians at Augusta, to persuade them to come to Dorchester, but it has so little influence with them, that they positively refused to move a step further, or stay for the governors at Augusta, more then ten days, and that upon these express conditions, viz. "That the Indians should have doubled the usual allowance of provisions; that they should be lodged in good houses in Augusta; that good pasturage should be provided for their horses, and that any loss they might sustain, in horses, should be made good to them." in consequence hereof, the congress is at last to be held at Augusta, notwithstanding the many inconveniences attending it; and, we hear, their Excellencies Arthur Dobbs, and Thoman Boone, Esquires, His Honour Francis Fauquier, Esquire and all the gentlemen That propose to attend they will accordingly set out on Tuesday morning next.

The Young Warrior of Estatiwih had declared to Capt. Taylor at Fort Prince George, "That the Creeks have sent him repeated invitations to take up the hatchet against the English; that he proposes being at the congress, and there will be ready to prove it; and that two large bodies of Creeks were encamped on Broad-River for the purpose not known.

The Creeks it seems were apprized of the pace of the meeting for the congress being changed to Dorchester, before Capt. Stuart delivering his talk to them.

BOSTON Oct. 24. We hear on the 9th Instant, a Woman with three Children, one about 3 Months old, the others between 1 and 3 Years of age, going from her Dwelling to Half-Moon near Albany, she missed the Road in the Woods, being tired she set the Children down while she sought a Path, but she wandered about till she could not find the Children; for some Hours after she got to a House and the next Day a Number of People went in search for the Children, who had not found them when our informant came away.

It has been reported at Halifax, that three large French Storeships were gone up the River St. Lawrence in Order to supply the Indians, &c. with Necessaries for the carrying on another War, which it was fear'd would soon break out, the French making great difficulty, and using many subtle Arts to avoid complying with the Terms of the late Treaty of Peace.

NEW-YORK Oct. 24. On Monday last his Excellency Sir Jeffry Amherst with some other officers embark'd for Albany.

From Sir William Johnson's Intelligence, we have reason to expect great trouble too near this city in a very little time, by means of the Indians; and what seems to confirm this opinion is, that orders are actually sent for the Militia within 80 and 100 Miles from this Place, to hold themselves in readiness to march, &c.

Philadelphia Oct. 27. Letters from Carlisle of the 18th mentions that a small army under Col. Armstrong, was returned from the expedition to Grand Island, which they found abandoned by the Indians; that the Colonel then proceeded up the river to a small town called Myonaghaquea, which he also found deserted; but four Indians being discovered a few miles further up, the Colonel imagined the Enemy's encampment was not far off, set out with 150 Men, and after a very difficult march, through excessive bad road, and on the same Day about 5 in the evening they observed several Indians running among the houses, upon which our people immediately rush'd in, but here the Indians also made their escape, leaving their victuals warm on pieces of bark, used by them for a table. Here our people found large quantities of corn, a number of swine, some black cattle and 7 horses, with a variety of implements which had been taken from our frontier: ——— To pursue these Indians farther was judged in vain, from thence therefore they returned to the Island, and the whole of the plunder, amounting to 70 pounds was divided among the private men. ——— The damage done the enemy in this expedition, is the having destroyed 7 or 8 towns, and upwards of 3000 bushels of corn, and 'tis hoped that such an additional terror is thrown into the minds of these Savages, that more quiet may be expected on the exposed Frontier.

Accounts from other parts are not so favorable; From Winchester, that 60 of the Virginia rangers were drawn into an ambuscade, and fired on from both sides by the Indians, and only 21 escaped.

From Northampton county, that on the 16th inst. the Laghowexin settlement, on the branch of the Delaware, was cut off by the Indians, and 9 People killed and wounded: ——— That on Thursday last a party of Indians rushed into a house in Allemingle township, and tomahawked a man, his wife and four children.

PHILADELPHIA Oct. 27. "From Winchester we have intelligence which may, I think, be depended on. That a Party of Virginia Rangers, amounting to Sixty being out on Jackson's River, discovered a small Party of Indians, who they pursued, till being drawn into an Ambush, they were fired on from both Sides by a large Body of Indians, and obliged to fly; and of the whole Party Twenty one had only come in when the Person that bro't the account came away; the rest, it is thought being killed, or made prisoners."

On Tuesday last we received the following melancholy Advices from Northampton County, viz. That on Sunday the 16th Inst. the Laghowexin Settlement, on a Branch of the Delaware, betwixt Wyoming and the Minisink, was cut off by the Indians, when nine People were killed, and four wounded one of which, and two Boys had got in to Upper Smithfield:

And that on Saturday the following Persons were killed in a flat going over to the Jerseys viz. Stephen Brink, Garret Brink, Esther Brink, Peter Vangada, Benjamin Hacer, and a Negro Woman, and Jacob Shoemaker, and Samuel Guin missing. These People had removed their Families into the Jerseys, but had to be over to milk their Cows, and were on their Return back again. when the Enemy fired on them.

The Number of Indians said to be about twenty, who swam into the River, brought the flat ashore, and scalped all the People, excepting the Negro Woman.

And in Sussex County, in the Jerseys, we learn that the Indians have been seen in different Parts thereof; and that the Militia of that Province are out after them.

Extract of a Letter from Paxton in Lancaster County dated October 23, 1763.

"Our party, under Capt. Clayton is returned from Wyoming, where they met with no Indians, but found the New-Englanders, who had been killed and scalped a day or two before they got there; they buried the dead, 9 men and a woman who had been most cruelly butchered; the woman was roasted, and had two singes in her hands, supposed to be put in red hot; and several of the men had awls thrust into their eyes, and spears, arrows, fitchforks, &c. sticking out of their bodies. They burnt what houses the Indians left and destroyed a quantity of Indian corn, the Enemy's tracts were by the river, up towards Wighalousing."

SAVANNAH Oct. 27. His Excellency the Governor,

who set out on Tuesday last for Augusta to meet the different nations of Indians who had been invited to the congress there, above five miles from town was met by Capt. Ewen at the head of his company of militia, mounted, who, escorted him to the Hon. Clement Martin's at whose house his Excellency lodged that night; the next morning Capt. Kiesser's company of militia escorted him beyond Ebenezer, where Capt. Rahn with his company of militia attended, and escorted him to Barton's Branch, the rendezvous of the detachment from the two companies under the command of Lieut. Newnez, who, with Capt. MacGillvray's troop of horse militia, are to escort his Excellency, and the several gentlemen his attenddants, to Augusta, where it is expected they arrived Monday last.

We hear from Charlestown, that they have been obliged to press horses and carriages there for the conveniency of his Excellency Governor Boone and the Governor of North Carolina and Virginia, going to attend at the congress at Augusta. occasioned, it is said, by they not having had sufficient notice to provide properly for the journey, the time and place for holding the congress being fixed only in June last.

QUEBEC Oct. 28. "We had a visit from an Indian Chief, the Sachem of the Christian Hurons, and Squaw; they were neatly dressed and spoke good French: The Sachem is a man of sense and probity and you would scarce believe possible, well-bred: he is by no means a bigot; and, if proper means were used, might easily be made entirely English. I made shift to muster a little bad French, to make him sensible, that the English were free, tho' under a King; that he was Father of his people, and loved by us as much; that we were governed by just Laws of our own making, to which the King himself was subject, as well as his people. Speaking of the French King, he thought I called him one of his subjects; on which his eyes sparkled, and he said, with some indignation, 'That the Indians were not governed by the French, but were free all over the world.'

"We are soon to pay them a visit, when you may expect a further account of our good Ally

Atanas. He told us, he would gladly cross the Great Lake, to visit the Great King, if the General would give him leave.

"We are apt to despise the Indians too much, General Amherst, by neglecting them, has brought on an Indian war to the Southward, which is feared will have terrible consequences."

NOVEMBER 1763

CHARLESTOWN S. Carolina Nov. 1. We are told, that two more women have been murdered in or near the Waxaw settlement; and that the fears of the people there increase; Apprehending a general Indian war, and that the Cherokees are the perpetrators of the late murders, notwithstanding the severe chastisement they have been constantly represented in, in consequence of it.

SAVANNAH Nov. 3. By express which arrived yesterday from Augusta, which place he left on Saturday last, we learn, that his Excellency our Governor, with his attendants, arrived there on Tuesday morning the 25th ult. the other Governors were expected the day the express came away, and it was thought they would proceed to business as on Monday. About 200 Cherokees, together with the Chickesaws, Catawbas, two Choctaws, and 60 Upper and Lower Creeks, had been there some days, and near 100 more of the latter were daily looked for. A good understanding subsists between the Cherokees and Chikesaws, but the Creeks and Cherokees seem not to be upon the best terms.

Philadelphia Nov. 4. On Thursday, the 20th ult. The Barn and Stables of William Thomas, on Lizard Creek in Northampton County were burnt by the Indians; when he lost about 400 bushels of Grain, and many Tons of Hay; also had eight of his horses carried of, and eight of his cow kind: and what were left were so badly wounded with arrows, &c. that some of them are since dead and others rendered useless.

Since our last there is advice from Ligonier, that a Convoy of Provisions was safe arrived there from Bedford in their way to Pittsburgh where we hear, they were all well, having met without disturbance from the Indians, ———

near Bedford five Indians have been lately seen but we do not learn that they had done any misschief.

NEWPORT Rhode Island Nov. 7. By a Letter from London, we are informed, that it was currently reported there, that the Government will require Ten Thousand Troops to be kept in Pay by the Northern Colonies, and at their sole expence, in order to prevent for the future, any such encroachments as gave Birth to the last War.

PHILADELPHIA Nov. 10. The following in an authentic account of the damage done by the Indians in Northampton County, on the 8th of Last Momth, viz. That at day-break they attacked the house of John Stenton, where 3 persons were killed and wounded, 7 of which were shot, some dead, others died of their wounds; they afterwards went to the house of Andrew Hezlet where they shot one man dead, upon which Hezlet got his gun and attempted to fire at the enemy, but it missing fire, he was shot himself by them; they then tomahawked his wife and two children, and afterwards plundered that and several other houses.

We have advice from Pittsburgh, of the 26th ult. when all was well there, and the convoy mentioned to be at Ligonier, was safe arrived.

Extract of a letter from Stanton Virginia of Oct. 18, 1763.

"The following are the particulars of an engagement with the Indians the 3d Instant. It was with a party of the enemy that passed the frontier in June last as friends, who had a pass and English colours; but on their return homeward they met with some of our militia on Jackson's river, and killed 15 of them, 13 of which were scalped. ——— On receiving this news 100 of us immediately started after them, and pursued till we came to Fort Dinwiddie, where we were joined by 50 more, and got intelligence of the enemy. We marched three days after them, thro' very bad roads, till we came to the head of Patowmack and discover'd their camp unperceiv'd, when we killed and scalped six of them on the spot, and wounded about 20 more, or upwards, as could be seen by the blood on so many different tracks; ——— but it raining very hard, we could not pursue them far; however we took 14 firelocks, 64 budgets, with all the ammunition, 26 shot bags, 38 brass kettles full of meat boiling, and 5 horses, with all their plunder, which sold for 250 Pounds besides the value of the horses, and the poor devils went off stark naked. The Number of the Indians imagined to be about 80. Of our party we lost none, but had six wounded. We also recovered the 13 Scalps."

By the person that brought the above letter we are informed, that about the end of Sept. a number of Indians came into Halifax county, where they killed a man, and took his wife and children prisoners; but on their return, were observed by two of Capt. Inglis's men, who acquainted him therewith, and he directly pursued with 29 men, came up with and engaged the enemy, retook the prisoners, killed three of the Indians, and wounded several others, 6 or 7 badly, recovered 30 horses, and a great deal of plunder, 5 guns and 13 shot pouches. Capt. Inglis generously restored the woman some of the horses, and plunder which belonged to her; and did the same to others of the country people, who had been plundered by the enemy; and, after all, his men shared of the booty nine pounds each. The Capt. had one man killed, and one wounded.

PHILADELPHIA Nov. 10. A letter from York of the 12th instant says, "That they had three persons killed and scalped by the Indians, and one taken prisoner, a few days before: That the same morning a man came in to Carlisle, and informed, of a man being found in the path way, killed and scalp'd, and several parties of Indians have lately been discovered near the place."

Philadelphia Nov. 10. We hear that the General Assembly of Maryland have passed a bill, for allowing 50 pounds for every enemy Indian's scalp or prisoner taken in or by the inhabitants of this Province.

SAVANNAH Nov. 10. Our account from Augusta are, That Wednesday the 2d the three Governors from Charlestown, with their attendants, arrived there; on Saturday the congress was opened at Fort Augusta, with the Indians, in number between 7 and 800, received a talk, to which they were to return an answer on the Monday following. It is thought that the whole business will be finished, and that the four Governors will set out on their return in the Georgia and Carolina scout-boats the end of this week, or the beginning of next. A bad understanding still subsists between the Creeks and Cherokees.

We hear that the boundaries of this Province are extended to St. John's River.

PHILADELPHIA Nov. 11. By a Letter from Carlisle, the 31st ult. we hear that all was then quiet on the Frontiers, bit that they were apprehensive of another visit from the Indians before winter sets in.

We have advices from Pittsburgh, of the 26th of October, when all was well there, and the convoy mentioned in our last to be at Ligonier for that place was safely arrived.

BOSTON Nov. 14. By the South-Carolina Paper in October last, we learn, that their Excellencies Arthur Dobbs, and Thomas Boone, Esquires, and the Honor Francis Fauquier, with all the Gentlemen that propose to attend them, set out to the Congress to be had with the several tribes of Indians at the Southward. The intended Place was Dorchester in that Province, but the Upper Creeks would not come further than Augusta. ——— At which place there were on the 15th about 20 Chicasaws & 60 Catawbas, of different ages and Sexes; the Cherokees were hourly expected, a number of the Lower Creeks and very few of the Upper, one Chactah leader: ——— many more of the Chactahs had returned back upon hearing that two of their People had been killed by the Creeks: ——— The Creeks had never been known to be so audacious as lately; they treated the Person who carried the invitation to the Congress, with the most contempt and insolence; that the young People were all for war: that some of them had been at Pensacola and had been treated well, yet had the insolence to shake their hatchets over the Soldiers heads as they were under Arms, but the Commanding officer did not then take the least Notice of the insult, lest the consequence of his showing resentment, should be the immediate massecres of the Traders in the nation. The French immediately insinuated we intended to wrest all their hunting grounds from them, as well as deprive them of Liberty. A number of their Emissaries were still in Alabahams, and give out; ——— "That the French are once more alive, and were coming out with a powerful Fleet to Quebec, and an Army to the Illinois."

NEW-YORK Nov. 14. An Extract of a Letter from Capt. Rogers, of Hanover, dated the 6th Day of November, at the Head-Quarters, 12 Miles above Colonel Vav Camp's on the River Delaware, on the Frontier of the Province of New-Jersey.

Sir,

"I arrived here with my detachment of 90 Men, by Order of his Excellency William Franklin, Esq; &c. where I found 150 Persons, Men, Women and Children, who were driven to this station by the cruel Savages of the Wilderness; of these, fifty at least, lodge every Night in a small Room, in a very uncomfortable and confus'd manner; in the Morning they throw what Beds and coverings they have out the Door in one heap, which in a sort, resembles the Chaos before the Elements were separated from one another. These poor People it seems (if ever they can be such) are the most proper Objects of our Commiseration, for they have been compelled to quit their little all; their Provisions, their Corn, and in short, the whole Dependence to be devoured and consumed without any Hope of Security: What can ever animate a Christian to unsheathe the Sword, and bathe the same in Blood, if the inhuman Cruelty of Savages will not? And what will not the Noble & Generous deny himself of, that he may rescue such miserable innocents as are daily presenting to our View? Every Time I see those piteous Objects and hear the Lamentation methink, I feel something within that makes me uneasy without Revenge. Two Indians were seen on this side the River Yesterday, by Capt. De Poe, in which he was qualified: ——— and what will be the final Issue of this troublesome Indian Affair, is yet in the womb of Providence. ——— O may God grant repentance to his People, that this anger may be turned away, that we Perish not.

I am Sir, Yours, &c.   Lemuel Bowers.

CHARLESTOWN S. Carolina Nov. 16. An Officer belonging to the three companies of the Royal Americans, which are to replace the three independent companies now in this province, is arrived from New-York.

PHILADELPHIA Nov. 17. We are desired to publish what follows, as being a more authentic Account of the damage done by the Indians in Northampton County, on the eight of last Month, than what was inserted in the Gazette of the 10th. viz.

"That on the 8th October, betwext Day break, and sunrise, The Indians attacked the House of John Stenton, when eight Persons (instead of three mentioned) some dead, and others died soon after of their wounds, in the greatest agony; the eight likely to do well: That after they went from Stanton's they plundered the House of James Allen, a little Way from thence; they then attacked the House of Andrew Hezlet, but half a Mile from said Allen's, where they shot one man dead, and scalped him; upon which Hezlet got his gun and attempted a fire on the Enemy, but in missing Fire, he was shot himself by them: whereupon his Wife, being at some distance, and seeing what had happened, run off with two of her Children, but was instantly pursued by the Indians, who overtook and tomahawked her and them in then in most barbarous Manner; notwithstanding which, she and one of the Children lived four Days in the most exquisite pains and the other Child it is thought will recover; After which they plundered Hazlet's House; and that about a quarter of a Miles distance from thence they, or was supposed, plunder'd the House of Crocher, and burnt it down."

The following Account we have from Reading in Berk's County viz. That on the 8th Inst. in the morning, the House of Frantz Balley of Albany Township, was wrecked by a Party of Indians who fired several Times thro' his Windows; upon which he got up, and fired at the Enemy, when he received a wound in his Wrist and one of the Children, a Boy, was killed. That one Hagenbush and two of his Sons, hearing the Firing, went to his assistance which made the Indians go off, without destroying the House or Barn. That they next went to the House of Stapleton, but one of his sons seeing them fired off a Gun which occasioned their passing by the House, and going to George Schifler's, where they tomahawked and scalped his Wife, mangled her in a bad cruel Manner and left her in a condition which a regard to Decency forbids to mention; they likewise killed one of Schifler's Sons who they scalped and half roasted; and burnt his Dwelling House and Barn and all other Buildings; That from Schifler's they went to Jacob Tree's killed one Shober and destroyed the House and Barn: That then they Plundered Daniel Smith's House and burnt it, with all other Buildings; and that after all this they proceeded to Philip Enos's about 3 Miles from Smith's where they made Prisoner of a Lad about 13 Years of Age, who afterwards escaped from them. The Number of Indians that did this Mischief, is said not to exceed 9, who spoke English, and some Dutch. The Quantaty of Grain Destroyed, is thought not less than 2000 Bushels; and the conditions of the Inhabitants is most melancholy, there being in several Houses no less than 30 or 40 Children, besides Men and Women and were obliged to fly for their Lives, without able to bring thing for their support.

SAVANNAH Nov. 17. On Monday the 7th instant, the different nations of Indians that were present at the congress at Augusta, returned their answers to the talk delivered by the Governor, in his Majesty's name, the Saturday before: on Wednesday on the 9th their Excellencies made their reply; and next day a treaty of peace and friendship was signed by the Governors and the Chiefs of the Indians; after which the congress broke up. The Indians seemed well disposed; the Creeks, sensible of his Majesty's beneficence, and his clemency towards them, in forgiving all past offences, of their own accord extended the boundries between their land and the English considerably to the westward.

BOSTON Nov. 21 Extract of a Letter from a Gentleman in New-York, to his Friend in Providence, dated Novenber 7, 1763.

"I am credibly informed that His Excellency Sir Jeffry Amherst, Commander in Chief of His Majesty's Forces in North America, is soon to embark for England; some say, for recovery of his health, while others assert, that it is in consequence of first Information sent him from home; and that he is directed to submit every Thing respecting Indians Affairs, to the Management of the brave Sir William Johnson, who is to have sole Regulation of the Indian Trade for the future. ——— From this Appointment it is not doubted but Peace and Tranquility will soon be restored with those Savages who are desolating our Frontier Settlements and that the Trade with them will revive and flourish."

NEW-YORK Nov. 21. Wednesday last, the Hon. Brigadier General Gage arrived here from Montreal, and is now Commander in Chief of all the British troops in N. America, his Excellency Sir Jeffry Amherst Knight of the Bath, having sailed from hence for England, last Friday, in his Majesty's snow of war the Wesel.

PHILADELPHIA Nov. 24. Extract of a letter from Carlisle November 8.

"Again the savage Enemy have begun to infest our borders, Yesterday Morning about or before Sun-rise, as one James Williamson was going from his House to his Barn, he was fired on by three Indians, who killed and scalped him, and his two young Children, taking the eldest (a Girl above ten years old) Prisoner; the Wife happily made her Escape. ——— Said Williamson lived 16 Miles up the Country, near the Foot of the North Mountain. The Settlement being alarmed, a Party of near Forty immediately turned out, and went in Pursuit of the Enemy; and unless by this means the Indians be intimidated to a hasty flight, we shall probably hear more mischief being done, as the inhabitants on this side of the Hill were in general gone home to their places, and many also of those over the Hill."

P. S. "An account is just arrived of Indians having been seen yesterday in the upper part of Shearman's Valley; and that the people are hasting this side of the Hill. ——— the party that went out after the three Indians, is returned without finding them."

Extract of another Letter from Carlisle, and dated Nov. 10.

"By a Gentleman arrived this Evening from Bedford, we hear the following Account, viz. That the Convoy of provisions for Pittsburgh left that Place on Thursday last, under an Escort of about 60 Men: That on Friday Morning several Indians were seen about or near the Road: That one Man, who had been hunting Horses, was dangerously wounded, but made his Escape, and was brought back to Bedford: That William Keed, and David Glass were found killed and scalped the same day at Dunning's Creek, about three Miles beyong Bedford; and a third was missing supposed to be made Prisoner: And that it was thought there was a large Party of the Enemy in those Parts, as many Tracks had been discovered.

By the same Gentleman we are further informed, That Yesterday in the afternoon, soon after he got to Fort Loudoun, two young men came in there, having fled from Great Cove, and brought advice, that on their hearing several guns fired in the forenoon and imagining it to be a party of Indians, they, and two other were to make a discovery, and soon came up with about 20 of them, as near as they could guess: That the Enemy discovered them, fired at, & wounded one; upon which these two fled; and when they had got on the Hills, looking back, they saw two Houses in flames, the families of which it is feared are all killed, except one Lad who has made his escape. ——— This is all we have yet heard but expect a day or two more will bring us a great deal of melancholy news."

Nov. 15. "Accounts of this morning say, that 4 houses were seen on fire in the Cove, and that families supposed to be murdered."

Extract of a Letter from Bethlehem Nov. 19.

"Yesterday in the afternoon we received advice from Fort Allen, that Job Coillaway arrived there the night before, and brought word that Papunechang, and many more were coming down as friends, from Wyalowsing, having determined to separate themselves from the Enemy Indians; and that he had run as fast as he could two Days before them; because he apprehended the same Enemy Indians would fall on the inhabitants about the same time his company would arrive, which might be laid to their charge: —— He therefore desided that timely Notice might be sent to the People on the Frontiers, that he had certain intelligence that their Parties of Enemy Indians were coming down to fall on this County; Forty of them on the Minisinks; Fifteen toward Allemingle; and Twelve on our Parts. Mr. Erwin is gone out to meet Papunechang and his company.

"We have the melancholy News to send you, that last Night about one o'clock, our watchman discovered our Oil-Mill to be on Fire; a great alarm being given by the discharge of a gun, and the ringing the bells, we were much surprized and first thought Bethlehem was on flames.

"We apprehend, at first it had been done by the Savages, having the day before received the above intelligence. A track being discovered in the snow, over the bridge adjoining to the Mill in the morning, two of our bethren followed it up the Lehi two Miles, where the snow from the bushes fell so thick that no further tracks could be seen, and we could not determine whether it was the track of a white man or an Indian. It is certain the place was set on fire; as there had been no oil made, nor fire in the mill, for a fortnight past. Providently the N. E. wind blew very briskly, and turned the flames from the other houses or they might have been entirely consumed.

"The Oil-Mill was connected with the Mill for grinding the Tanner's Bark, and that for pounding Hemp, and other Mill Work; all which, with several hundred bushels of Flaxseed, are consumed, except the wheel, and that part of the building over it."

SAVANNAH Nov. 24. Tuesday last the General Assembly of this Province met here, when his Excellency the Governor was pleased to deliver the following speech.

Honourable Gentlemen,
Mr. Speaker and Gentlemen of the Common House of Assembly.

The time of our meeting in General Assembly has been considerably delayed by being obliged, in obedience to his Majesty's royal command, to attend the congress with the Southern Governors, Capt. Stuart the Superintendent, and the different tribes of Indians, at Augusta, in order to cultivate and promote a more firm and permanent peace and friendship between his Majesty and the southern nations of Indians.

And I have the pleasure to acquaint you, that, as well as the general benefit resulting therefrom, this province has acquired considerable advantage, particularly, in the existing of our western boundary by a voluntary cession of lands made to his Majesty by the Creek Indians; and I think basis is said for establishing matters between us on a copy of the Treaty settled and agreed upon at the late congress to be laid before you.

Gentlemen, This being our first meeting in a General Assembly since the conclusion of peace with France and Spain, give me leave though late, to congratulate you on that happy event, so glorious to his Majesty and the arms of Great-Britain, and so particularly beneficial to those southern colonies.

We are happy, Gentlemen, in the consequences of this peace, also in the great probability and prospect of a continuance of peace and friendship with the several nations of Indians; for even the Creeks, whose fidelity was most to be suspected, have given the strongest marks and assurances of their pacifick and good intentions; and we are still more happy in a general harmony and confidence amongst ourselves.

Therefore let us consider what measures are in our power which may best promote the general welfare and property of the province, In which I shall always be ready to give my hearty concurrence; and would recommend it to you to consider of and frame a bill for the punishment of vagabonds an other Idle disorderly persons; also a bill to prevent Lotteries and gaming.

Gentlemen of the Common House of Assembly,

I have no demands to make, nor any particular article for expence to desire you to provide for. I shall direct an account of the produce of the last year's tax to be laid before you, and the usual estimate for the service of the current year.

Gentlemen, the season being so far advanced I hope will be an inducement to give dispatch, and I have no kind of doubt but the great unanimity which has hitherto subsisted will still continue.

Savannah, in Georgia Council   James Wright.
Chamber, Nov, the 22, 1763.

BOSTON Nov. 28. The General Assembly of New-York met on the 8th Instant when his Honor Lieut. Gen. Colden, opened the Session with a speech; wherein he represents that —— notwithstanding the Peace which has been settled, the depredation by the Western Tribe of Indians on their Frontiers, made it necessary to make provisions not only for the Defence but also sufficient to chastise those Savages; he likewise says Amherst pressing the Government to furnish a Proportion of Men to proceed early in the Spring with the Regular Troops on this important Service; and his Honor earnestly recommends the Assembly to grant the necessary Supplies for the raising of cloathing and paying a Body of Forces, sufficient with other Troops, to meet the Danger they fear; avenge the injuries they have received; and convince the Savages of their ability to compel them to a Submission.

We hear that the General Assembly of New-York have ordered 200 Men, to be immediately raised, for the Defence of the Frontiers of Orange and Ulster Counties, against the Incursion of the Indians.

CHARLESTOWN S. Carolina Nov. 30. John Stuart Esq; his Majesty's agent and superintendent of Indian affairs in the southern district of North America, arrived here this day from Augusta.

Two Choctaw Indians who were at the congress are come with the superintendent in order to go by water to Pensacola, to which their country is contiguous. The presents for the Choctaws, we are told, will likewise be sent to Pensacola.

DECEMBER 1763

SAVANNAH Dec. 1. Extract of a letter from a gentleman from Mobille, dated Oct. 1763.

"I take this opportunity to acquaint you of my safe arrival at Pensacola the 4th of September, where I found the Spaniards had all abandoned that place, some gone to Havana, others to Vera Cruz, and left a most miserable place in possession of Col. Prevost, with about 300 men; it has a very good bay for ships to ride in, and the whole dependence is from Spanish trade, which may be of great advantage to this place in time. From Pensacola I came here to Mobille with English Troops, who took possession of this place the 20th instant; the situation is well calculated for the Indian trade, the town pleasantly situated on the river Mobille, which divides in two branches, each extending near the middle of the Choctaw and Creek nations, and I am informed the boats drawing three feet may go all seasons of the year; I believe in time we shall have a very considerable trade with the Indians by the change of civil governments; the inhabitants do not seem to like an English military government. The Wolf King, with about 60 of the Creeks Indians, are here, and seem very well pleased with the English; upwards of 2000 Choctaws are to be here in 20 days, to recover their presents from the French Governor, which have been due them upwards of three years. The Spaniards had not one plantation at Pensacola, and the number of French at this place does not exceed 120 men, and much of these very poor, and not above 500 negroes in their whole settlement; they deal mostly in cattle, corn &c. which they use to send to Pensacola; there is very good land up this river, but all near the sea a barren sandy beach; it is a plentiful country for venison, fish, fowl, &c. on which the inhabitants mostly live."

By a gentleman from Philadelphia we are informed, that the brave Major Rogers, who was so serviceable against the French and Indians to the northward in the late war, has been killed in an engagement with a party of Indians.

From Sussex county in New-Jersey, we have intelligence, that on the 17th instant Captain Westbrook with 11 others went over to the Pennsylvania side, in order to bring off some cattle and effects which were left by persons who deserted their habitations: That about 3 miles from the river they were attacked by a body of Indians, who killed Capt. Westbrook and 4 others: That 6 others escaped to Nomeroe, and the other is supposed to be hurried off to give an account of the situation of the forces on the river: That on receiving the news 150 militia immediately went over to Pennsylvania to bury the dead, who found the bodies of 5 of our men unhumanly butchered, and an Indian shaved and dressed in the mohawk manner, who was killed in the engagement; the white men they bro't off and buried and scalped the Indian. The Number of Indians were upward of 40 and 'tis imagined they made a precipitate retreat, as they did not carry off the Indian that was killed, and left behind them the following things, viz. A waggon of smokes beef & pork, 12 lb. tallow, 2 French guns, a Mohawk Indian cap, 4 blankets, 2 strings of Wampum, a scalping-knife, looking glass, leggins and Moquasens, &c.

Extract of a letter from Bedford, Nov. 13,
"The convoy is returned back from the foot of the Aleghny mountains, having discovered several parties of Indians skulking on the road which the commanding officer judged would attack him in some difficult pass: by which as he had not men enough to protect the whole, he feared part of the convoy might fall into their hands. Several expresses who were sent to go to Ligonier and since arrive say that the officer judged right, as they saw several large parties of Indians which prevented their proceeding on the road."

BOSTON Dec. 5. The following was published in last week's Gazette. Several thousand families from Canada are gone to New Orleans, on the west of the Missisippi and many others are following; so that before we have planted a single acre there, they will be in possession of very flourishing Plantations; and what is now alarming, will probably commence intrigues with the Indians, we may find difficult to remove.

Arrived from New-York in the latest post dated November November 18, 1763, Entitled CHARACTERS.

"All Gen. Amherst's disposition were made in the most admirable methods and with that regularity of military arrangement, which makes so considerable a part of the character of that able Commander. And without question his conduct in his last expedition by which he obliged the Town of Montreal to surrender without a blow, and conquered Canada, without effusion of blood, deserves every honour and every recompense a grateful people can bestow. The humanity with which he behaved to the conquered, both French and Indians, tho' the one had perpetrated, and the other had at least conniv'd at the most horrid cruelty on the English prisoners, adds a high lustre to his conquest. His troops set not one house on fire nor one habitation was plundered, nor one man killed.....

"None was more distinguished in this respect than Sir William Johnson. He led into Canada an army of 1000 of the fiercest and most cruel savages which are bred in America, without doing the smallest damage to the country, or offering the slightest injury to the inhabitants. To effect this, he was obliged to exert the most unwearied endeavours, and the whole of those uncommon talents which gave him such power over the minds of all sorts of men, being respected by the regular troops, dear to the provincials, almost adored by the Indians, and possessed of that genius for acquiring popularity and that versatile disposition, which we so seldom see united with disinterestedness and integrity. The great victories, by which he had advanced the interest of the nation, have done him less honour than his conduct, by which he has so greatly advanced its character for humanity and moderation.....

The following remarkable speech is said to have been delivered by the famous Attakulla-kulla, the great Sachem or King of the Cherokees, to Lieut. Governor Bull, of South-Carolina, on being made acquainted with the terms of the late peace.

"I find you are not the warrior I took you for; you have made peace with the French, who are your mortal enemies, and more inveterate than the allegator to the Indian. ―――― You have fought seven years, and given back the fruits of your conquests. Ah! brother these things undo you in the minds of the Indians. ―――― They will conceive you did this thro' fear, and the French will make them believe it. They will deceive and cheat you; they will appear weak, desperate and subdued, till they obtain their purpose. They are treacherous and perfidious; they deceive, and they betray. Their cunning which they practice to your disadvantage, is more than you can conceive, and none but the great Sachem beyond the clouds, can comprehend. How then could you rush into a peace with them, whose interest it is to deceive and destroy you? There are not wanting those of your enemies, who daily represent you among the several nations of Indians, in the worst point of view; your behavior makes them believe it. Take up the war hatchet then, and shew us you are Englishmen, for we doubt it much."

NEW-YORK Dec. 5. Last Monday Capt. Gardiner of the 55th, and Lieut. Stoughton came to Town from Albany. They belonged to a Detachment of 600 Men, under the Command of Major Wilkins, destined for Detroit, from Niagara, but on the 19th of October, at the far End of Lake Erie, 160 of our People being in their Boats, were fired upon from the beech by about 80 Indians, which killed and wounded 13 Men, (and among them Lieut. Johnson late of Gorham's killed) in the two sternmost Boats, the Remainder of the Detachment being ahead about half a Mile. Capt. Gardiner, who was in the boats adjoining, immediately ordered the Men (50) under his Command ashore, and took possession of the Ground from which the Enemy had fired, and as soon as he observed our People landing, he with Lieutenant Stoughton, and 38 Men, pursued the Indians, and in a few Minutes a smart skirmish ensued, which lasted near an Hour, and in which 3 Men we killed on the spot, and Capt. Gardiner, with Lieut. Stouton, and 10 others, very badly wounded. During the skirmish, the Troops that did not follow the Indians, formed on the beech and covered the Boats.

ANNAPOLIS Maryland Dec. 5. Thursday last an Account was brought to Frederick-Town by Mr. James Patten, That on the 8th of November the Indians had done Damage in the Great Cove where they staid about two hours: They killed Christopher Finler, Charles Stewart, and Thomas Query; and burnt William Nox's House, and took himself and Family, eight in Number, Prisoners, The Indians were about 20 in Number, and were pursued by a party of 28 the evening after they had done the Mischief, and followed until Monday evening, when it began to snow, and covered the Tracks. In the pursuit they discovered a Child (one of the eight) which they had murdered on their retreat.

CHARLESTOWN S. Carolina Dec. 7. We have the pleasure to inform the public that as happy an issue had attended the congress at Augusta as could be expected or even hoped for, every thing was conducted with harmony, caution, and decorum, and yet an uncommon dispatch was used by all parties to whom this affair was intrusted. The Chicesaws, we hear, remain steady in their assurance of friendship, with this province in particular has had repeated proof of. The Chactaws declare that as they were in alliance with the Chicesaws they were desirous of being regarded with them as the King's children, and to deserve this protection and favour which they requested, made offers of undertaking, in proof of their sincerity, who were supposed to be the worst disposed, were, in fact, the least friendly; Yet assurances were not wanting on their parts to persuade the Governors and Superintendent, that their future behaviour would be amicable, and in return for the amnesty which, in the King's name, was promised them, they made a voluntary offer of augmenting the Georgia boundaries. The Cherokees seemed very pacifick, and well in their talks to the Governors, as towards the Creeks, who treated them however with a good deal of indifference. The Catawbas are satisfied with their former boundaries, part of which has been run, and have been promised that it shall be fortwith completed. The proportion of the presents, we hear, were determined by the Governors and Superintendent, and the delivery only left solely to him.

PHILADELPHIA Dec. 8. Extract of a Letter from Col. Stephen at Winchester, Oct. 18. 1763

"There has been nothing very material happened of late on the northers frontier. The communication is open with Pittsburgh to some escorts, though several skulking parties of Indians are on the Frontiers. Four men were chased into Harness's Fort and narrowly escaped. John Colvil was killed at Dobson's plantation. On the 5th and 6th of this inst. one man was wounded and another missing, near Fort Bedford. About the 10th Major Campbell intended to proceed to Fort Pitt from Bedford, with 500 horses loaded with flour, and 400 head of fat cattle, under the escort of 400 men. The young men in the frontier counties are very eager to engage in the expedition against the Indian towns.

"One Elinor Ryan, taken prisoner by the Indians the 23d of August last, near Stoney creek, and viz. that she was carried to Capecape, where a scouting party, by talking, discovered themselves to the Indians; three of whom advanced to the road with cocked firelocks, to fire on the party, while two stood by her and her brother, who was taken with her, with their tomahawks ready to dispatch them if they made any noise; the Indians observed the party to be too strong for them, let them pass; and proceeded thro' the woods to the south branch, passing the Forts in the night; when coming on the tracks of some of our scouting parties they were afraid, and turned off thro' the most rugged mountains they could find. After travelling 12 days, they had got on one of the south branches of the Monongahela; and expecting to be tomahawked next day as she was quite exhausted, and unable to march further, she took a resolution with her brother, to attempt an escape that night; and accordingly being sent for firewood, as usual, in several turns to camp, and, under pretence of bringing more, they went into a laurel thicket, and hid themselves until the Indians had given over the pursuit of them, and they then steered towards the sun-rising. After wandering the mountains for 15 days, her brother perished of hunger: and 5 days after she got into Harness's fort almost starved to death."

Extract oF a letter from Capt. William Christian, dated Roanoke, October 19, 1763.

"Being joined by Capt. Hickenbottom with 25 of Amherst's militia, we marched on Tuesday last to Winstone's meadows, where our scouts inform'd that they had discovered a party of Indians, about 3 miles off. ——— as they were on their return, Capt. Hickenbottom marched to join Capt. Ingles, and go down New River. I with 19 Men, and my Ensign, took a different rout, in quest of them. We march'd next day on their tracks, and two hours before sunset, when we heard some guns, and soon after discovered 3 large fires; upon this we immediately advanced, and found they were on an island; being within gun-shot, we fired upon them, and loading again, forded the creek. The Indians, after killing Jacob Kinberlin, a prisoner they had with them, made but a slight resistance and ran off. We found one Indian killed on the spot, and at a distance four blankets shot thro' and bloody. We took all their bundles, 4 guns, 8 tomahawks, two mares, ——— The party consisted of upwards of 20 Indians. By the blood on their tracks, several of 'em are wounded."

PHILADELPHIA Dec. 8. Extract of a letter from Reading, in Berks County, dated November 25.

"The Indians murdered three men on Tuesday the 15th instant, about 22 miles from this place, on the north side of the mountains, in the Forks of the Schuyskill. These unhappy persons were returning to a plantation which they had deserted.

Capt. Kern Immediately upon hearing of this murder marched after the enemy, where he pursued for two days, but a very heavy snow having fallen, and the Indians having fled a considerable time before Kern came to the place where the murder was committed he desisted from the pursuit."

BOSTON Dec. 12. Lately came to Town Joshua Rand, from Detroit, which he left on the 7th of October last; The Indians had withdrawn from the Neighbourhood; the Garrison was in very good Health; and consisted of 400 Men. On the 20th of October at the Mouth of the cut of Niagara in Lake Erie he met with a Convoy of provisions going to Fort Detroit, escorted by 600 Men, chiefly Regulars, commanded by Major Wilkins. As soon as they had delivered their provisions they were to return. ——— This person was taken prisoner in 1757, at the surrender of Fort William Henry, and carried away by a party of Autawa Indians, to a Town of their's beyond Michilimackinac, where he lived with them until the Spring of 1762, when they permitted him to go with them to Fort Detroit, where they gave him his Liberty.

NEW-YORK Dec. 12. We hear from Upper Minisink New-Jersey, that on the 15th of November last, Capt. Silas Park, with 23 Volunteers set out from that Place to go to Coshethton, on Delaware River, in order to bury the dead lately killed there by the Indians, and bring off such of the Effects of the poor people that left said Place as could be found; on the 21st the said Captain, with all his men safely returned to said Minisink in high spirits, having been to said Coshethton, buried 5 Persons found dead there, and brought off all the Cattle and Swine they could find; saw no Indians, but say, that the day they left said Place, they heard sundry Guns fired on the other side said River, supposed to have been fired by the same Party of Indians that did the murder lately committed on the Road near a Place called Lacawse. The said Capt. could not pursue them by reason of the great Quantity of Snow, it being at that Time Knee deep.

A Gentleman who left Albany a few days ago,

informs us, that they were vigorously engaged at that place in building Battoes, and making other preparations for an expedition against the Indians, to be commenced early in the spring.

NEW-YORK Dec. 12. Extract of a letter from Capt. Bowers, to his Friend in Hanover in Morris County, dated Cade's Fort, 32 miles above Col. Van Camp's, on River Delaware, in the frontiers of the province of New-Jersey, Nov. 20, 1763.

"The 15th inst, I received a letter from Ensign Walton, whose station was at Shepecunk, eight miles below mine, informing that 15 or 20 men had that morning been killed and scalped opposite the Normanach, four miles from the river, in the province of Pennsylvania. I immediately sent two men to get the best intelligence I could of the affair; they returned at 10 o'clock at night, and reported that only 12 men went out, of which six were returned. I then marched with 12 men down to my next station, where I arrived at two o'clock in the morning, and at six crossed the river with 19 men, and was soon joined by Capt. Denike of Sumerset, with 21 of his men, and others, to the number of 105 in all. We marched in Indian file, with advanced guards, till we came to the ground where the engagement had been the day before. We found five persons killed, scalped, and butchered in a most unhuman manner, three of whom we buried as well as time and place would permit, the other two we brought down to Normanach, and interred them the same day.

"The persons killed were Capt. Benjamin Westbrook, William Cortwright, Nathaniel Carter, William Duncan, Andrew Decker, (James Wilding, supposed to be made prisoner.) These were going with the six that returned, to a place called Lacawack, 40 miles from the frontiers, to bring down cattle and goods that were left when the inhabitants of that place was cut off, which happened about four weeks before. We found one Indian killed in the above engagement, and concealed under a trunk of an old tree, who was pulled, and soon scalped by a brother of one of the white men that was killed at the same time. We found one Indian gun, two bags of paint, one scalping knife, and a large quantity of dried beef strung on sticks, and left in parcels at the place we found the dead bodies. It appeared to me that the persons killed made a valient defence, and wounded many of the Indians, by the blood found in many of the places at a considerable distance from where the fight was. By the best Intelligence, there must be 40 or 50 of the savages, a number one would think suffiecient to dishearten 12 men,

   I am, &c.   Lemuel Bowers."

PHILADELPHIA Dec. 15. Extract of a Letter from Winchester Nov. 26.

"It was fortunate that the Convoy returned to Bedford, or they must had perished, at least suffered much in the Mountains, from the deep Snow. ——— Major Wilson with 50 Volunteers, has marched to reinforce the Escort at Bedford, and I am sorry to acquaint you, thar the Roads are again much infested by the Savages."

We have since learnt that the above mentioned Convoy had a second Time set out for Pittsburgh, having been reinforced with 150 Men, besides the Volunteers under Major Wilson.

SAVANNAH Dec. 15. Extract of a letter from Mobille, dated Nov. 15.

"The English troops were a week ago to take possession of Tombighie and a party is to be sent from this in a fortnight to take possession of Albama. The French Governor of New Orleans, with the headmen of the Chocttaw nation, have been here for this week past, and many presents have been delivered by the French to those Indians, to testify the great regard they bear their copper friends. The change of government is far from being pleasing to many of the Indians; those who are here are such as have always been strongly attached to the French, and wholly in their interest; none of our party will come nigh the French, and I am informed there are 2 large ____; there is not the least fear of our being molested here, as they are now convinced of it being out of the power of the French to supply them. The plantations and houses here I believe will be sold cheap; of the former there are now about 30 near this place, and these scarce deserving of the name, having few hands on them and their chief dependence being the raising of stock. A Governor is expected here in a few weeks. Rice fell at New-Orleans at nine rials the hundred weight."

At the meeting of the French Governor of New Orleans and the Indians at Mobille, it is said there were 8000 Choctaws, and that most of the presents delivered them were guns, which the English commanding officer took from them, giving them in exchange for three French guns one English, with other presents.

NEW-YORK Dec. 19. The Week before last, an Inhabitant of Minisink, being a Hunting for Deer, on the West Side of the Delaware, fell in with a single Indian: they espied each other almost at an Instant, immediately tree'd and after an exchange of several shots, the Indian imagin'd he had wounded his antagonist and rushed in upon him with his Tomahawk; but the white Man, after receiving two desperate wounds from the Indian, knock'd his brains out with the End of his Musket, cut his head off, and brought it home in Triumph.

Friday last Captain Montresor, Engineer, arrived here from Detroit, in 16 Days, and brought the agreeable News, that the Indians under the command of Pondiac, consisting of Ottawas, Jibbaways, Wyandots, and Powtewattamies being tired of War, (Having lost in the different attacks of the Fort, Vessels and Row-Gallies, between 90 and 100 of their best Warriors) and studying their present Conveniency, being in want of Ammunition, and the hunting Season advancing, had applied to Colonel Gladwin for Peace; which he granted them, upon condition, that it was agreeable to the Commander in Chief of North America, and that they should bring in all their Prisoners, which the Indians immediately complied with and directly sent into the Fort 17 Englishmen.

The Garrison at Detroit was well supplied with every Thing necessary till the first of July next, and the Soldiers, 212 in Number, hearty and well; as there were also at all the Posts on the Road. Major Rogers is arrived at Niagara, with 250 Men from Detroit.

The same Day Major Moncrief arrived here from Niagara: He belonged to the Detachment under the Command of Major Wilkins, destined from Niagara to Detroit, by whom we learn, That on the 7th ult. at 11 o'Clock at Night, 18 of their Boats foundered in Lake Erie, in a Violent Storm at S. E. which came on suddenly, by which Accident 70 brave Men were drowned in which Number was Lieut. Davidson, of the Train, and 19 of his Men; and also Lieut. Paynter, and Doctor Williams of the 55th and a French Pilot. The whole detachment was in danger of being lost, as every battoe that reached the shore were more than half full of water; by which means 50 odd barrels of provisions, all the Ammunition but two Rounds a Man (which the Officers saved in their Horns) and two small Brass Field Pieces, were lost; and that after holding a Council of War, it was though most prudent to return to Niagara.

CHARLESTOWN S. Carolina Dec. 21. The commission and non-commission officers, &c. of the three companies of Royal Americans ordered to replace his Majesty's three independent companies now in this province and Georgia, arrived here to-day in the ship Britannica, John Simblett master, from Philadelphia. The independent companies we are told are to be disbanded, the officers to be on half pay, some of the private men to be draughted, in order to complete the three companies now arrived, and the others to be discharged.

PHILADELPHIA Dec. 22. Extract of a Letter from Fort Pitt, Dec. 1, 1763.

"I Have agreeable News to communicate to you from my wilderness ——— The overlake Indians have sued for Peace and Forgiveness in the most submissive Manner ——— Major Gladwin has refered them to the General, and, in the mean time, granted them a cessation of Hostilities ——— They dare not much boast of, having lost 90 of their best Warriors before Detroit, and a good many here, and miscarried at both Places; They have never appeared before us this Way since our affair, and they seem to vent their Spleen altogether upon the poor defenceless Inhabitants.

"On the 22d October Lieut. Brehm with three

other Officers, and 60 Men embarked in four Row-Gallies to reconnoitre the Camp of the Savages. They fired upon him all along shore, but advancing to the Streights, he found them prepared to receive him with 200 Men in 18 Canoes or Pettiaugers and one Batteau; they came close around the Gallies to hound them, favoured by a continual fire of 150 Savages from the Shore ——— The Batteau with about 30 Men, came up as hard as they could pull under Lieut. Brehm's Stern, who was a little separated from the rest; he kept still rowing, and firing with small Arms upon the Batteau. They advanced with great Resolution all standing upright, until they got within 30 Yards of Lieut. Brehm, who then wore round, and poured his Grape Shot into her which killed or frightened the whole Crew, only one remaining in the Batteau, which he paddled ashore. He might easily have been taken, but the Canoes still coming nearer Lieut. Brehm thought it was better to play upon them, which he did so effectually, that in half an Hour they were all obliged to sheer off, and put ashore. The Victorious Gallies continued to row about insulting them, till the Men being tired with the rowing against the Stream, they went back to the Fort, having only one Man killed and two wounded. The Loss of the Enemy was nor known, but must have been great, in about three Hours firing."

From Fort Bedford we have the agreeable News, that the last Convoy from that Place for Pittsburgh had arrived safe: and that the escort was returned, without any interruption from the Indians.

SAVANNAH Dec. 22. Georgia. By His Excellency James Wright, Esquire Captain-General and Governor in Chief of His Majesty's said province Chanceller and Vice-Admiral of the Same.

A PROCLAMATION

Whereas the twenty-fourth of June last, in obedience to his Majesty's express commands, I did issue my proclamation, in his Majesty's name, strictly enjoining and requiring all persons whatsoever, who might, either wilfully or inadvertently, have seated themselves upon any land reserved to or claimed by the Indians, fortwith to remove themselves, as they should answer the contrary at their peril: And Whereas the Creek Indians, by treaty made at the congress lately held at Augusta, have ceded to his Majesty certain lands extending up Savannah River, from the flowing of the tide to Little River, and along the banks of Little River to the fork of that river, and from thence to the end of the south branch of Brier-Creek, and down that branch to the Lower Creek path, and along the path to the main stream of Ogechee river to the Apalachicola path, just below Mount Pleasant, and from thence across Saneta Sevilla; and it was by the said treaty stipulated that the limits to the south boundary of this province should remain agreeable to former treaties: And Whereas the said Indians have complained that sundry persons frequently build huts, and settle on their hunting grounds, and interrupt and molest them, by hunting on their lands and otherwise, also do carry rum and other things into the woods, and trade them while on their hunts; which practice they complain of as greatly detrimental to them, and which is also contrary to law, and injurious to the province; I have Therefore thought fit, by and with the advice of his Majesty's Honourable Council, to issue this my proclamation, hereby strictly charging and commanding all persons whatsoever, that they do not, on any pretence whatsoever, presume to take possession of, or settle upon any part of the lands so ceded as aforesaid by the Creek Indians, until they shall obtain his Majesty's royal authority for so doing; And further, that they do not trespass on the hunting grounds and lands reserved by the Indians for their own use, either by building huts, or hunting thereon, or in any other manner whatsoever, to the prejudice of the Indians; and also that they do not trade or traffic with any Indians in the woods, or otherwise than at trading houses or stores licenced for that purpose, an they will answer the contrary to either the premisses at their peril.

Given under my hand and the great Seal of His Majesty's said province, in the Council-Chamber at Savannah, the sixteenth day of December, in

the year of our Lord one thousand seven hundred and sixty three, and in the fourth year of his Majesty's reign.   James Wright.
   By his Excellency's command
     John Talley, Dep. Sec.
        God Save the King.
  BOSTON Dec. 26. The Speech of His Excellency Francis Bernard, Esq; Captain General and Governor in Chief, in and over his Majesty's Province of the Massachusetts-Bay in New-England, and Vice-Admiral of the same.
  To the Great and General Court or Assembly of said Province, met at the Court House on Wednesday the 21st instant, being the Day which it was last prorogued.
  Gentlemen of the Council, and Gentlemen of the House of Representatives,
  At the opening of the last Session, we exchanged our mutual Congratulation upon the late happy conclusion of the Peace, and the fair prospect, which it opened, of the extensive Improvement of his Majesty's American Dominion. But this view has been since much over clouded by an insurrection of the Savages, an ungrateful and unprovoked as it has been merciless and inhuman.
  This must create al Alarm throughout all North America. It is not an Attack on this Province; a Dispute about Boundaries or a Resentment of private Injuries: but it is open War, begun indeed by particular Nations only, but avowedly design to be improved to a general Confederacy of Indians against the British Empire.
  To put a stop to these Mischiefs, to punish the perfidious Promoters of them, and to establish a general and durable Peace with the Indians, General Gage, now Commander in Chief, proposes to assemble a respectable Body of Troops at Niagara early next Spring. To effectuate this he finds himself obliged to call up the Provinces North of the River Delaware, to raise Provincial Troops, to join his Majesty's Regular Forces, and carry the War into the Indians own Country upon the Lakes; whilst the Southern Provinces are performing the like Service on the Ohio. The number required of this Province is 700 Men,

to be doubly officer'd, upon account of the Service they are designed for; to be cloathed in an uniform short Coat, and other light cloathing; and to be ready to march to Albany by the first of March next: They are to be provided with Arms and Tents, and furnished with Provisions at the King's Expence; The Time of their Service may be limited to the first Day of November next; but it is to be hoped that they will be dismissed much sooner.

It is surely (to use the General's own Words) consistent with true Policy, Humanity, and brotherly affection, that ev'ry Province should in times of Calamity contribute to the mutual Assistance of each other: I may add, it is also agreeable to his Majesty's royal Instructions to his Governors in America. And therefore the General may reasonably hope from your favourable Reception of this Requisition, when he considers the readiness this Government has shown on former Occasions of forwarding and promoting the public Service. Consider, Gentlemen: If this Flame is not soon extinguished, who can tell how far it will extend? We are at present at a considerable distance from it: and yet if it is suffered to rage much longer, we may expect that it will soon come to our own Homes. But it is not self-interest alone that should dictate to us upon this occasion. The Principles of Humanity, the reciprocal Ties which connect fellow Christians and fellow Subjects, must afford strong incitements for us to assist in putting a speedy end to this horrid War, and inflicting exemplary Punishment upon the abominable Beginners of it.

But Gentlemen, whilst I am recommending to you to assist your Neighbours, I must also desire you to take care of yourselves. It seems to me to be absolutely necessary that some immediate Measures should be taken, for the Security of the Eastern Country. The Indians now having within that part of the Province are not numerous, but enough (even without their being joined by others) to spread wide Desolation through the dispersed and defenceless Settlements of that Country. At present indeed, they profess themselves to be Friends to the English; and it is undoubtedly their Interest to be so. But will you risk so great at Stake as the growing Improvements of that Country upon the Words of Indians? will you put any Confidence in their faith or their Discretion? It has been frequently observed that they always give the first blow, which with them is the best part of the Battle. This may be sufficiently accounted for from their total disregard of public Faith, joined with the Jealousy, Inhumanity and Rapaciousness which mark their Character. But I have sometimes thought, that the Inattention and Remissness of some English Governments have contributed a good deal to the Indian Invasions; they have been as it were, invited to plunder by the defenceless State of the Country. Let not this be our Case; but let Us be suspicious in our Turns, and show ourselves prepared for them before they have formed their Plan for attacking us.

Gentle of the House of Representatives,

The Force I want you to unable me to raise for the Protection of the Eastern Country should not be less than 200 Men, formed in two Companies, with a Captain and three Lieutenants to each, and a Field-Officer to command in chief: They should be made to appear as like Regulars as possible, as Part of their Business is to keep the Savages in awe. They should be inlisted to serve during the Indian War; that, if that should not be determined next Summer, you may not be put to the Expence and Trouble of Reinlistments. With this Force I think that Country will be secured, both from real Danger and Apprehensions of it: without it, I cannot be answerable for the Effects of one or the other. As for the present State of the Forts there, I shall lay it before you in separate Papers, by which you may be enable to judge what is wanting to the proper support thereof.

Gentlemen,

It is ever with great regret that I propose to you any measures that will be attended with extraordinary Expence: A Consideration of what is due to your Honor, and necessary to your

Welfare is always my motive for such a proposal. The present intended Armament will not be very expensive in fitting out, nor, I hope, will be of any Continuance. At least I will assure you for myself, that, such Part thereof as shall depend upon me, shall not be kept up one Day longer than the Safety of the Country shall require.
Council-Chamber, Dec. 21, 1763.

Fra. Bernard.

BOSTON Dec. 26. Extract of a private letter from Montreal, Aug. 12.

"This has been a melancholy place for some time on the accounts of the advices being received from the posts on the country being entirely cut off by the Indians, and all the merchants murdered: but at present we are relieved from our anxiety by the unsuspected arrival of most of the gentlemen who have been most barbarously used, several of them being frequently under sentence to be boiled for soup; four soldiers they actually boiled and eat one night, and obliged some of the gentlemen to eat bread with the blood scraped off the scalps on it. They were relieved by four nations of Indians in our interest, who escorted them to this Place. They have recovered a great deal of their furrs, but are yet considerable losers. The French behaved worse than the Indians."

NEW-YORK Dec. 26. We hear from Philadelphia that on Wednesday the 14th of December last a Number of Armed Horsemen went to the Indian Town of Conestagoe Manor in Lancaster County and without the least Reason or Provocation in cool Blood, barbarously murdered Six of the Indians, and burnt and destroyed all their Houses and Effects. And whereas the said Indians, settled in the Heart of that Province, had during the late Trouble and for many Years before, lived peaceably and inoffensively and were justly considered as under the Protection of the Government and its Laws, therefore the Governor has issued a proclamation requiring the Civil Authority, all the military Officers, and other Inhabitants of the said Province, to exert their utmost Abilities in detecting and bringing the said Offenders to Justice.

The Governor has also strictly forbid all Persons from molesting or any way injuring a number of other Indians lately removed from the Frontier into the Province Island and other places in the neighbourhood of Philadelphia where provision is made for them at the public Expence.

We are told, that the Indian General Pondiac had, to evince his Sincerity in the Overtures for Peace, discovered the Names of near forty Frenchmen some of them Men of Consequence, at Montreal, who were involved in starting the war.

NEW-YORK Dec. 26. Extract of a Letter from Pensacola, October 5, 1763.

"The Spaniards and Indians who lived with them, are all gone from hence to Havannah or Vera Cruz and left Col. Provost with his Battalion of about 300 men in possession of this fort and a few houses. Great part of the lands without the fort are purchased by Mr. Noble who is employed by some great men; he is very busy in clearing the grounds, and has done more already that way than has been done in 100 years before by the Spaniards, who never durst, for fear of the Indians, venture out of the reach of their guns, and depended, for provisions entirely on the French at Mobille. This fort is a stockade standing on a sandy beach, the harbour is very good, we had never less than four fathom coming in, and the bay is fine and large abounding with oysters and all form of fish. Some weeks ago 150 Indians came here armed, demanding presents; they had all their kegs filled with rum, and said they would soon return for more. They always kept the Spaniards in terror, and when they were sparing, the Indians would take a few scalps to put them in mind of their duty, on which the bounty used to be increased. We are in daily expectation of the 35th regiment to relieve the battalion now here, the men will go to New-York, but Col. Provost believes he will be obliged to winter in Carolina. The 22d and 24th regiments commanded by Major Parmer are here bound to Mobille to take possession of the garrison.

Mobille is about 60 miles by land distance from this place, but two large rivers which must be passed, render the journey tedious. The town is situated on the river about 30 miles from the sea, is irregular, but the houses pretty good; the French inhabitants very complaisant, and many of them say they do not intend to remove; they had all their supplies from New-Orleans, and the war greatly impoverished them; and every species of European goods was incredibly high, what that cost only three shillings sterling being sold for thirty dollars, &c. Mobille bar has no more than ten feet water. The fort which they call Conde is strong and is well built of Brick. The lands are very good but they raise only live stock and Indian corn: There is good plenty of fresh fish and game of all kind."

By a letter from Schenectady, dated the beginning of this Month, we are informed, That Sir William Johnson, was then greatly engaged with a large Number of Indians who came to assure him of their attachment to the English, and to make offers of accompanying his Majesty's Troops against the Enemy, wherever they shall be called upon; than which nothing can be more conductive to the security and success of an Army marching thro' an Indian Country, which otherwise would meet with constant Ambuscades and Opposition.

PHILADELPHIA Dec. 29. The General Assembly of this Province, on Consideration made by the Governor's Speech, and the Requisition made by the General, in Compliance with the same, voted a Thousand Men to be employed in offensive Operations against the Enemy in the Spring.

From Pittsburgh we have Advice, that two Messengers had arrived from Detroit, who brings Accounts. That in coming through the Indian Towns, over the Ohio they found about Seventy wounded Men, which had not recovered of their wounds they received in the Engagement with Colonel Bouquet. That Fifty of their Warriors certainly lost their Lives in the Action: And that the Indians, in general, seemed heartily tired of War.

SAVANNAH Dec. 29. The report of Major Rogers being killed in a skirmish with a party of Indians must be without foundation, and no mention made of it in the Philadelphia papers, which we have received to the 8th of December.

JANUARY 1764

BOSTON Jan. 1. By the Hartford Post, we have an Account of the Indian Affairs at Detroit, as follows.

That on the 12th of October last Wappocomoguth, Chief of the Mussisaque Indians, come under a flag of Truce, to Major Gladwin at Detroit, to let him know that none of his Band, had hitherto committed the least Hostilities, and that he was using all his influence, to restore the nations in Arms, to their cession; that he had prevailed on most of them, to listen to his arguments, and that through him (their Mediator) the Chippawas, Outawas, Wiandots, and Pontiwatamies, sensible of their villainous Behavior, begged forgiveness of what was past, and declared it to be admitted to Council, to make their Submission.

That Major Gladwin, not having at this time above fourteen Days Provisions in Store, listened to their Overture, tho' he looked upon it as an Artifice, to lull him for the Winter, and that it was their present Necessity, in the Articles of Ammunition, a desire to go to their hunting Ground, for their Winter subsistence, with the fear of Major Wilkin's Detachment reaching Detroit, that induced them to these measures.

―――― In Council, he told them, if the convince him of their Sincerity, all might be well again; Hostilities then ceased, and many of them went to their Hunting Grounds: Major Gladwin took that opportunity to get Provisions from the Inhabitants, and wood for the Winter.

On the 30th of October, a currier arrived at Detroit, with a Letter from the French Officer commanding at Fort Chartres, on the Missisippi, to all the Indians, advising them to be at Peace, with their Brothers the English, as they were one People; at the same time, it contained an invitation to them, to remove with their Families, to the Western Bank of the Missisippi, where they should have fine Hunting Grounds, with an easy and flourishing Commerce.

A large Party of Indians went from Detroit this Fall, with a great Quantity of Beaver, to purchase Ammunition at New Orleans, and it's tho't their future temper, in a great Measure depends on the talk they may have with the Governor; and the Means they may fall upon to procure Supplies. ——— Major Gladwin continues upon his Guard, and expects the Renewal of Hostilities in the Spring.

The Detachment under the Command of Major Wilkins, in their Passage over Lake Erie met with great difficulty by contrary Winds, and bad Weather; On the 17th of November about 10 o'Clock at Night, they were suddenly surprized by a violent Gale of Wind, within Thirty Leagues of Detroit, at a Place called Point-du Pin: in which they lost three Officers, viz. Lieut. Davidson, of the Artillery, Lieut. Painter, of the PlaToons, and Mr. Williams Surgeon to both Regiments; four Serjeants, forty three Privates, and a Canadian Pilot: All their Ammunition, and a great part of their Provisions lost, and destroyed. ——— in these circumstances Major Wilkins ordered a Council to consider the present Situation of the Detachment, who were of opinion, it was better for the Service to return to Niagara, than proceed to Detroit, without Ammunition, and with very little Provisions: The Major of Brigade Moncriese, who was carrying Orders, from the Commander in Chief, to Major Gladwin, under the escort of this Detachment, being acquainted by Major Wilkins, of the Resolution he had taken, wrote a Letter to Major Gladwin, to acquaint him of it, that he might take his Measures accordingly. This Letter he sent off the 12th of November, by two Hurons of the Village near Quebec; which they delivered with great Fidelity the 18th, and the consequence Major Gladwin reduced his Garrison to Two Hundred and Twelve Men, having the Detachment of the 55th Regiment, Hopkin's Independent Company, and

Roger's Volunteers: Capt. Montrefor left Detroit the 20th of November with these Corps; and tho' they had Intelligence that a large Body of Indians intended to Way-lay them, they arrived safe at Niagara the 17th.

New-YORK Jan. 2. On the 14th of December last a Number of people assembled together and went to an Indian town in Conestoga Manor, In Lancaster County, (Province of Pennsylvania) where, without the least Reason of Provocation they barbarously killed Six of the Indian settled there, and burnt and destroyed all their houses and Effects; the others precipitately fled towards Philadelphia; but 16 of them, being old and infirmed, stoped at Lancaster, and apply'd to Authority for Protection, they were accordingly put into Prison, as the place of most Safety. Their Pursuers soon after arrived, and being informed of the place the Indians were in, demanded the Key, which being denied, they broke open the Doors, and in the most inhuman manner massacred the whole Number. The others about 150 Men, Women and Children fled to Province Island just a little below Philadelphia; and some Soldiers, with several Field-Pieces, were sent for their protection.

The above party, we hear, could assign no reason for their behaving in this manner, except that they were the chosen people of God, and that all the Indians ought to be extipated from among them.

As this inhuman Act, committed in the Heart of the Province on the said Indians who lived peaceably and innoffensive among the Inhabitants, called loudly for the vigor protection of the civil Authotity, ——— Governor Penn has issued a Proclamation, charging all Officers whatsoever within the Government to detect the Offenders if possible. The governor has also signified, at the Peril of Transgressors, that none do molest or injure a Number of Indians lately removed at their own earnest Request from the Frontiers of that Province to the Province Island, and other Places in the Neighbourhood where provision is made for them at Publick Expence.

A considerable number of the principal inhabitants in Philadelphia have had a meeting to consult some measures for the protection of those Indians at Province Island, and was thought they would be transported to Nantucket. Various conjectures were formed of what would be the consequence of the above unhappy transaction; but most were apprehensive that it would produce some ill effects.

PHILADELPHIA Jan. 2. About 3 Weeks ago, 7 Men deserted from a Detachment of the 44th Regiment, posted at Oswegatchie. They were immediately persued by a Party of Indians sent after them by the Commanding Officer, when their Scalps were soon brought into the Fort. A few Days after a Sutler was robbed within a Mile of Oswegatchie, by a Party of Messasagas, and carried off, with his Servant and a Man belonging to the Train of Artillery; on Advice of which a Number of Oswegatchies went in pursuit of the Messasagas, and it was thought would come up with them, and recover the Prisoners.

CHARLESTOWN S. Carolina Jan. 4. On Friday last December 30th in the evening, an Express arrived here in four days from Long-Canes settlement, with dispatch to his Excellency the Governor, containing advices and afidavits of divers murders committed by the Creek Indians, on his Majesty's subjects of this province in thar quarter; whereupon his Excellency immediately issued the following Procalamation, viz.

By his Excellency Thomas Boone, Esq; Captain General and Governor in Chief, in and over the said Province, and Vice Admiral of the same:

A PROCLAMATION

Whereas they are divers weighty and important Reasons for the General Assembly of this Province to meet, with all possible Dispatch, in consequence of Information this Day received, of many Persons being murdered in the Long-Canes settlement, by the Creek Indians, I do hereby with the advice of his Majesty's Council appoint Wednesday the fourth of January 1764 for the meeting; and all persons concerned, are thereby enjoined and required to pay Regard to this Notice, as they value the Security of their Fellow

Subjects in the North West Part of the Province.

Given under my Hand, and the Great-Seal of his Majesty's said Province, this Thirtieth Day of December, One Thousand Seven Hundred and Sixty-three, in the Fourth Year of his Majesty's Reign.   Thomas Boone.
   By His Excellency's command
     George Johnston pro. Secretary.
            God Save the King.
"A letter from Mr. Calhoun to his Excellency, dated Fort at Long Canes December 26, says, that Such a Detachment of the Militia as could be spared from the guarding the women and children, was sent out to bury the dead, and make discoveries; part of them returned the 26th, they found bodies of fourteen white persons killed, only one scalped, but others cut and mangled in a most inhuman manner; several persons were still missing, but the party being small they did not choose to stay out long and had brought in many settlers into the fort. The situation of the poor inhabitants is represented in a very deplorable, fleeing for fear of the Savages with only the cloathes on their backs, helpless women and children exposed to all the inclemencies of a rigorous season, abandoning their habitations and in want of every conveniency and even the necessities of life. An Alarm had been spread through the country, and application made for a detachment of militia from the Regiment commanded by Col. Chevillet at Orangeburgh, which though upward of an hundred miles from Lone Canes was the nearest for relief. Several settlers were come from the Northward and other parts since the congress at Augusta, who with many single men willing to make a stand if they met with speedy and proper encouragement."

By other intelligence we learn, that Moytoy the Cherokee, furnished Arthur Cody with a horse, which enable him to get to the fort at Long Canes, Moytoy said the white scalps which the party of Creeks (first mentioned in Cody's information) had, seven, so that the whole number of white persons scalped by those Indians appear to be twelve, and those killed but not scalped thirteen according to the accounts as yet received. The inhabitants of Long Canes got into two stockade forts, which they built for their own defence; in one were thirty seven men and one hundred and three, women and children. There are likewise forts at Ninety-Six and at Hard-Labour, about 24 miles from Long Canes, whither we hear, many fled for shelter, and all other back settlers, Mr. Calhoun says are moving down to Edisto. The detachment mentioned above, sent out to bury the dead, consisted of only ten men; they went first to Dyer's plantation next to ―――― Lawsen's, and then to ―――― Pawley's, where they found all the families murdered except the three men, one boy and girl, who providentually happened to be gone out.

This day the General Assembly of the province met here, in obedience to the Governor's proclamation, when his Excellency delivered the following Speech to both Houses.

Honourable Gentlemen,

Mr. Speaker, and Gentlemen of the Common House of Assembly,

Without observing to day upon business of various sorts, which well deserve your serious attention, the melancholy incident which shall immediately make you acquainted with will sufficiently justify my calling you so suddenly together. On the 24th of last month a party of Creek Indians, murdered fourteen persons in the Long Canes settlement; an outrage of this sort so soon after the King's forgiveness of all former offences was solemnly declared to them, and every means used to remove their jealousies, and to conciliate their good will, is too plain a proof, I am afraid, that they are not to be reclaimed by good offices, that they Disdain your proffered friendship, and are really dangerous and inveterate enemies; as such they must be treated, and as such guarded against. The consternation and real distress which the poor unhappy back settlers are thrown into reduced to abandon their all, or lose their lives, will I am persuaded excite your compassion, and procure them relief. It would be an insult to your humanity to doubt it, and additional misery, if possible to then be disappointed. I will lay

copies of the information brought me by you and
then rely on your taking such measures as a Love
of your country, and a tenderness for your fellow creatures must dictate. Such assistance as I
could furnish independent of you is ahead ordered. When you, Gentlemen of the Common House
of Assembly are deliberating upon the unhappy
affair, it will be by no means foreign from the
subject to consider how the posts on the frontiers are circumstanced. Augusta which is garrisoned by troops of this province is in ruins;
Fort Moore is repaired indeed, but has not a gun
mounted, or a carriage belonging to it, nor am
I able to convey to either a barrel of Powder,
unless I apply the poor remains of contingent
money to the Service. There is not a month's
provisions in one nor the other nor Prince George
much better supplied, and what is still worse,
the crown no longer allows provisions to the
troops.

   Thus Gentlemen, I have related plainly how
matters are, and have carefully avoided heightening the distress of the frontiers by laboured
descriptions.

   Before I conclude I must acquaint you that in
consequence of representations made to the King,
his Majesty has thought proper to order me to
appoint commissioners to run a temporary line
of jurisdiction, in concert with North-Carolina
commissioners. Governor Dobbs and I have agreed
that they shall begin the first of March, and I
now apply to you Gentlemen of the Common's House
of Assembly to enable me to carry the King's
command into execution.

               January 4th 1764   Thomas Boone.

   A great number of settlers from the northward
have come by land into the western part of that
province during several months past. On the 26th
ult. a number of those settlers with four waggons
arrived at Hard Labour above mentioned, where
they resolved to remain 'til they heard what was
to be done concerning the murders committed by
the Creek Indians.

   [Notwithstanding this present Occasion we hear
the General Assembly still refuses to do any
business with the Governor, who seems equally

determined in refusing, as they in demanding Satisfaction, for the Violations of their Privileges, with which they charge him. Woe be the wrong Side!]

PHILADELPHIA Jan. 5 Extract of a Letter from Detroit November 1, 1763.

"A French Officer, from the Illinois has bro't a belt and Letter to the Savages, with an account of the Peace, which either the French and Indians believe till now. In consequence of this, our most implacable Enemies, the Ottawa's who were the only Nation here disposed for continuing the War (all the others having begged forgiveness for what they have done long ago of our worthy commandant) are now, with the rest, begging for Peace, in the most abject Manner. ——— Mr. Prentice is well at Sandusky, as is Mr. Winston at St. Josephs; and from the present Disposition of the Savages, I apprehend they will bring them as soon; to effect which I will do all in my Power."

Extract of a letter from Detroit November 1.

"Mr. Welch and I were taken Prisoner by the Wyondots the Tenth of May last, about two Miles to this side of your old Grass Guard and carried immediately to Genandot, where poor Welch was killed and was likewise everyone that was with me but Pompey. I have lived ever since, God knows, a most miserable Life, every moment in Danger of being knocked in the Head. Many Midnight Councils they held on me, but God Almighty always prevented them from hurting me. They have now put me into a Family, and I suppose made me as they think, one of themselves. I am in the Place of a Merchant that died last Winter, going to War against the Cherokees, now live with his Brother, who uses me very well and likewise does Mohikas John, and believe there is no danger now of their killing me: and as I hope the war will not last long flatter myself with the hopes of seeing you soon. ——— Mr. Smallman and the two Levy's were taken by the Wyondots, within four Miles of Detroit; One of the Levy's was given to the Chippawa's and Smallman to the Shawanese, and I understand by the Indians here that all the cargo is lost; many a Tear it cost me, to see them divide wear and take the Goods in the manner they did; as it was out of my power to help it. Thought as little of it as I Could."

SAVANNAH Jan. 5. His Excellency our Governor received an Express from Lieut. Banard of the rangers at Augusta, informing, that, on the 24th of December, 14 people, mostly women and children, were killed at the Long-Canes settlement in South-Carolina, by a party of Indians reported to be Creeks. As no accounts have been received from Augusta since this express arrived, it remains uncertain by whom these murders were committed.

On Tuesday his Majesty's royal proclamation, fixing the limits and boundaries of our new Acquisitions in America, was, by order of his Excellency our Governor, declared here, strictly enjoining all his Majesty's subjects to a due observance of the same.

CHARLESTOWN S. Carolina Jan. 14. Extract of a letter from Mobille dated Nov. 12, 1763.

"I arrived at Pensacola the very day that the Spanish troops and inhabitants quitted it, the 3d of September; they might be 1000 of them; the troops went to Mexico, and the miserable inhabitants (rather slaves) for Havana. Col. Provost of the 3d battalion of the Royal Americans, with about 300 men, had taken possession of the place the day before. the bay is an excellent one, would contain all the navy of England, and there is never less than four fathom water at the entrance. In time of Peace a very beneficial trade may be carried on here, and in war, if the spaniards ever break with us again, the trade of Mexico will be subject to great annoyance. The land along the coast is generally low, sandy, dry and barren. At the entrance of the harbour, upon St. Rosa Island, the Spaniards had a small fort, of no sort of use, but the flag-staff there is a good land-mark for strangers, being the first thing they see. The town is situated on a dry sandy beach, about three leagues from the sea, stockaded in the form of a square with bastions at the angles, and composed of miserable houses, or rather huts, and most of them having much the appearance of a Carolina plantation, the Governor's resembling an overseer's house, and the rest negroe huts. By land from Pensacola to Mobille is two days journey, but the road bad there being a wide river and several creeks to cross: By water the distance is about 27 leagues, viz. from the town to sea 3, from that to the point of Mobille 14, and from thence to town 10. The coast from Cape St. Blaize is low, barren, and sandy; and a good way back the land is only fit for stock. The entrance to Mobille extremely dangerous, and the navigation up the river none of the best, occasioned by the extreme width of the mouth and the number of mud and other banks formed by the great freshes, which at some seasons come down with great impetuosity. On the bar there is never more than 12 and a half or 13 feet water, Capt. Bain his Majesty's ship Stag, sounded it six days successively and found that, and he brought up three transports within two leagues of the town; The French never found more than 10 feet but the channels are very difficult to find. This town consists of only a few straggling houses, mostly stockaded for fear of the Indians, some of brick, but has a very good regular built brick fort, with a ditch, covered way, and glacis, which the French call Conde, whereon they had mounted 38 pieces of cannon. Major Termor took possession of this place the 20th of October, with about 500 men, but the garrison is to consist of 1000, from which detachments will be sent to Tombigbee, Fort Thoulouse, and to the Illinois. The cannon that were mounted here are all sent to New Orleans, and in part replaced from our ships. The 6th inst. a lieutenant with 35 men was sent to Tombigbee, Fort in the Choctaw nation, about 200 miles distant. In a few weeks, Capt. James Campbell, with 100 more, will go to Fort Thoulouse (commonly called the Alibamous;) the time is not fixed, because the Creek Indians do not seem in very good humour: And in the spring Major Loftus, with 300 men, is to go to the Illinois on the Missisippi, a very fine settlement, where are about 500 French, who anually supply themselves with necessities for the year. Col. Robertson goes in a few days to New Orleans to purchase boats for conveying the last body of troops to their stations; the French say they will be upward of three months on their passage and go through many tribes of Indians that are settled on the banks of the river, which will make it very dangerous. No place in the universe can be better situated for the Indian trade than this is, as their is water carriages into the heart of the Creek, Chickasaw, and choctaw nations, which last is more numerous than we imagined. There may be about 120 Frenchmen in this Colony, and 500 negroes, the greatest part of which I believe will leave it. The land in generally near the sea is bad. Stock and Indian corn is all the inhabitants used to raise: There may be 12000 head of cattle and a few sheep in it, but, if proper encouragement was given, the land would produce silk, cotton, olives, coffee, and vines in abundance. In my life I never saw so much game and fish as is here; any man may maintain himself and family with his gun. From this to New Orleans the distance is about 70 leagues, viz. to Isle Dauphin the entrance of the harbour, 10: thence to the mouth of the Missisippi 25; and from that to New Orleans 35; there is also an inland passage through the lakes for small craft, but no road by land. The trade to Pensacola and Mobille hitherto is not worth mentioning. An English military government is by no means liked here either by French or English. The Wolf King was here some days ago, pretended to be glad his brothers the English were now so near him, and said he should no more go to Carolina or Georgia; he came a begging, and got pretty well both here and Pensacola. M, d' Abadie, Governor of New Orleans, is now here, delivering presents, which have been three years due, to the Choctaws, of whom they are upwards of 2000 here, and more expected; the whole nation was invited, but only the French party are come, to whom we gave a very good talk, and he really took great pains to reconcile them to the English, which I hope will have good effects, though at present the Indians think it very strange to see the English and French, so lately at enmity, now in so close friendship. I shall conclude this letter with what I heard one of them say. viz. in all their former talks they encouraged and hired us to kill and scalp the English and their Indian friends; now they intreat us to take the English by the hand, and themselves mix promiscuously with them. It is strange, but it looks as if the time is coming when we should be made slaves, as the French told us would be the case whenever we suffer the English to come upon this land."

NEW-YORK Jan. 16. We are credibly informed that, very lately the Chenessies, (upper Castles of the Senecas Indians) have offer'd to make Peace with the English: That the five Nations are ready to declare War against the perfidious Delawares, Shawanese, or other Indian Tribes, who have offensively acted against us. The Canadian Indians have all declared in our Favour; but more especially the Cahgnawagas, who, with other Nations, will commerce Hostilities against all the Savages in Enemy with us. This interesting News must be very agreeable to our exposed Colonies.

We End by the proclamation of the Governor of Pennsylvania, publish'd the 2d instant that besides the barbarous murder of the six Conestogoe Indians, and burning their houses and effects, that on the 27th of last month, a large party of arm'd men assembled, and proceeding to the town of Lancaster, broke open the workhouse, and inhumanly massacred 14 more of the said Indians, men, women, and children, who had been taken under the immediate care and protection of the Magistrates of Lancaster County, and lodged for their better security in the workhouse till they should be more effectually provided for by the government.

The Governor has offered a reward, of 200 Pounds for securing and prosecuting to conviction any three of the ringleaders in this inhuman & bloody affair; and any accomplice not actually concern'd in the murders, who shall make discovery of any of the ringleaders, and apprehend and prosecute them to conviction besides the above reward, that all the weight and evidence of the government shall be employed to obtain a pardon for the offender.

The horrid Massacre committed upon the Conastogoe Indians, settled in Lancaster County, though under the immediate protection of the Magistrates, having greatly alarm'd the other Indians, (who at their request were lately removed from the Frontiers of that Province, and settled by Order of Government, on the Island, and other Places, near the City of Philadelphia) and filled them with Apprehensions of the Fate of the Conastogoes. We hear they are desirous to return to their Friends, or former Habitations, and that on Application, the Government appointed them Guides, and directed their rout thro' the Province of New-Jersey and New-York, giving them recommendatory Letters to their Governments for safe Passage and Assistance; with which, 140 in Number immediately set out and proceeded as far as Elizabeth Town, New-Jersey. But it is reported that no previous Notice having been sent to this Government, Messengers are dispatch'd by Remonstrance, to prevent their Entrance into it, ⸺ and if they persist, to give immediate Notice. Many People apprehend such Consequence, should these Indians at this Time, under such groceded Apprehensions, and with shocking Ideas of Justice, Humanity and protection they may expect in an English Government, return and mix with the Indians now at War with us.

We are told the above Party of Indians are now at Amboy, under the Escort of a Party of Highlanders.

We hear that one Company of the New-York Provincials march'd above a Fortnight ago, another last Sunday, and that the remainder will follow in a few Days. They are all cloathed in the most compleat manner for the Service.

Since the above Accounts came to Hand, we have the following assurance, That the Number which surrounded Lancaster Goal, were 200, well mounted on Horses; that after they had done their Business they rode three Times round the Goal huzzaing, and went off in like Manner to join 300 more who were waiting but a few miles distant to back them.

About Eleven o'Clock last Night the inhabitants of the City was suddenly and greatly alarmed by the Cry of Fire, the striking out of the Fire Bell and all the other Bells in the City; but it was soon after found that a Body of Men [as it is said Royal Americans] had entered the New Goal, and demanded the Keys of Mr. Mills the Keeper, who refusing to deliver them, received several Wounds with a Bayonet. They afterwards forced the Doors and let loose all or most of the Prisoners. ——— It seems their principal Interest was to release Major Rogers, who was a few Days ago come to Town, was arrested, and confined in that Place, which they effected. ——— Part of our Militia were collected together as soon as possible by beat of the Drum; remained under Arms all Night, and have taken six of the Persons. The Particulars of this atrocious Affair could not be obtained at the Publication of this Paper. ——— One hundred and fifty of the first Battalion of Royal Americans came to Town since our last.

A Serjeant of the Highlanders was killed on the Occasion and sundry wounded.

ANNAPOLIS Maryland Jan. 17. On Wednesday the 4th inst. a party of twenty men who went from Mr. Calhoun's Fort at Long-Canes were fired at by a party of Indians, from the house of one Cloud, one man received a bullet in his hat, and another was shot in the shoulder, on which the party retreated, their guns being, wet with snow and sleet. Another party of forty men, headed by Andrew Williamson, has since set out.

Jan. 18. On Thursday last Capt. Lazarus Brown's company of militia, consisting of about 44 men, marched for Fort Moore in Long-Canes; and we hear several other companies are marching for the relief of the distressed inhabitants on the frontiers.

NEW-YORK Jan. 21. Two Companies of New-York Provincials marched for Albany on the 24th of last Month; and a Third Company to go the 8th of this Month; all raised in this City, and places adjacent. They are picked Men, fit for the most alert Service, and are cloathed in a suitable Manner. We are likewise informed, That two other Companies raising in Albany and Dutches County, were lately so near fill'd that there is no doubt they are by this Time completed, and will make a fine Battalion.

A copy from Headquarters, New-York January 5.

His Majesty has been graciously pleased to signify to the Commander and Chief, his Royal Approbation of the Conduct and Bravery of Col. Bouquet, and his Officers, and the Troops under his Command, in the two Attacks on the 5th and 6th of August in which, notwithstanding the many Circumstances of the Difficulties and Distress they laboured under, they repelled and defeated the repeated Attacks of the Indians, and conducted their Convoy safe to Fort Pitt.

NEW-YORK Jan. 23. An Account of the late Riot.
────── Upon the whole it appears that Major Rogers had frequent interviews with a number of those Soldiers, with whom, no doubt, he had laid his plan. ────── That the better to execute it, had singled a set of 15 or 20, who were to do the Job at a certain hour, keeping in reserve at a Distance upwards of an Hundred others to second the riot; but kept in ignorance of the time the Major's release, that the general alarm of the Town might prevent pursuit. This had its effect; ────── For, in half an Hour's time, Rogers was at the front door, and by report, gave one, two and three Indians Yells and afterwards march'd off with himself, ────── At this very instant, Notice was given to the reserve, by those who actually released the Major that they should assist; which they directly furiously bolted in, beat and abused the Prisoners, opened almost every door to the goal in order to find Rogers, and forced every Prisoner out at the point of their bayonets: ────── The greatest part of whom returned the next morning; but the Major (agreeable to logick) major'd up all, for during the uproar he was pushing off with a pick'd-up horse, ────── and Indian like, went the Lord knows where. Two Hundred pounds, however, is offered for apprehending him. ────── To finish the account of this affray, we should be glad to know who would be so desirous of having their

heads broke, and shoulders confoundedly bruised by a stroke directly levelled at them. and afterwards, have it said, no personal hurt was designed them: ——— (a stroke in rhetoric, this, that we are apt to believe most of our readers would rather choose to read than to experience) ——— With Regard to Mr. Rogers saying, Gentlemen you will certainly ruin me, is altogether good; for as he had money about him ——— to put the better face to the matter, it was Indian policy to cry out dread and ruin. And touching his expression of being undone: ——— Take a Bear and chain him ——— let one of the rioters, or any other person break it, and, if the beast could speak (fable like) he would bellow out ——— That fellow has undone me: ——— and that was all Rogers wanted ——— To be undone.

CHARLESTOWN S. Carolina Jan. 23. The following is a genuine and authentic copy of the talk between the commanding officer at Pittsburgh and the chiefs of the Delawares & Shawanese Indians taken by a person, of great integrity, and well skilled in the Indian Languages, who was present.

"At a meeting with Shingas, Teskekemen, Wingeman, Turtle-Heart, Capt. Johnny, and Mulmaleis, principal men and warriors of the Delawares and the Great Wolf, and four other Shawanese: Singas spoke as follows "Brothers, I am glad it has pleased God that we should live to meet and speak together this day in friendship." The addressing himself to his own people "He desired them to observe what was said to them or their Brethren the English."

Teskekeman then taking out a large belt, Spoke as follows;

Brothers, it give us a great deal of satisfaction to have the opportunity of renewing our Antient Friendship, and we are much obliged to you for sending us this small set of colours as a token of your friendship, by which we this day enable to speak together.

Brothers, Listen now with attention to what I am going to say: As it has always been your desire that we should hold fast by the Chain of Friendship, I now assure you that we have always done it, and do still hold it fast, and we hope you do the same; it is now in your power to continue it.

Brothers, On your first coming to these places, We were the first nation you contracted a friendship with; after this you extended Belts of friendships across the country, the end of which reached these nations which are towards the sun setting; then as we were situated in the center between you and them in this country, you requested of us that we would hold fast by the middle of the Belt; this we assure you we have done with both hands, and have holden it close to our hearts, but now I see both ends let loose, and we are now the only people to hold the Belt up by the middle. Brothers, Let us be strong on both sides, and take pity on our warriors, women and children. Let us be sincere and speak from our hearts, and be honest in every thing that now passes between us. —— I now take this Friendship Belt and lay it in the Fort, where we request you will assist us in preserving it. —— Brothers, So not imagine that what I say come from the lips only. I do assure you it comes from the bottom of my heart; we make no doubt but this will give you the same pleasure, if you are as sincere as we are.

Brothers, You sent us word that you were so firmly seated here that you were not to be removed.

Brothers, You have towns and places of your own, you know this is our country, and that your having possession of it must be offensive to all nations of Indians, therefore it would be proper that you were in your own country, whereby our friendship might always remain undestroyed.

Brothers, Some time ago you desired that we would go out of your way, that you might pass to other nations that have disturbed the Chain of Friendship. —— You yourselves are the people that have done it: In the first place, by coming with a large army into the country and building Forts; we were then the first who went to meet you; having no mistrust of your doing, and nothing but good in our hearts towards you, we agreed to every thing you desired, at the same time we requested of you in the strongest terms not to extend your Forts any further than this post [Fort-Pitt] notwithstanding this, you crossed the lakes, and what passed between the nations that way and you, we are unacquainted with, but you see they have slipped their hands from their friendship with us, and as you desire to know who struck you, we take this Opportunity to make you sensible of it, which I believe you cannot help thinking is true, for you have no body whatsoever to blame but yourselves for what has happened.

Brothers, We have endeavoured to stop all parties we saw going against you; some we were able to prevail with, others we were not, who we supposed will prosecute the war against you. Our reason for not coming two days ago to speak with you was, that we received this string of wampum, which I have now in my hands, from all the natios over the lakes, the following is what they said upon it. ———

"Grand Fathers, the Delawares, ——— By this string, we inform you that we intend in a short time to go through your country, with a great large body of men, on our way to the forks of the Ohio: Grand Fathers, you know us to be a foolish people: we are determined to share, eat, destroy and devour every thing that comes before us in our way."

Brothers, Here is the Wampum, you have heard what the desire is, if you go quietly home to your wisemen, this is the furthest they will go, if not, you see what will be the consequences of that, We, by this, desire that you do remove off from hence in peace.
[Gave a String of Wampum]

Brothers, We have now delivered every thing we have to say, Consider on it, and when you have a mind to answer us, fire a gun and we will come over to hear you: We hope when this is done to be able, each of us, to rise up and go to our respective homes."

The following is the commanding officer's answer to the Delaware and Shawanese Indians, delivered at Fort Pitt, 27 July 1763.

"Brothers, you must be certain of our sincerity towards you, as we have never broken our treaties with you or any other Indian Nation since our first come into the country, therefore observe what I shall now inform you of, in answer to your speech delivered yesterday to me.

You complain that we have taken your country and built strong forts: Now Brothers, these forts were built to protect you and your trade, which you have been often told of; with regard to your lands, we have taken none but such as our enemies the French did possess: you suffered them for to settle in the heart of your country without molesting, why would you now pretend to turn us off of it, we who have always been friendly and kind to you.

Brothers, As for the garrison, I now tell you that I will not abandon this post. I have warriors, provisions and ammunition, in plenty, to defend it for three Years against all Indians in the woods, and we will never abandon this place as long as a White Man lives in America: I despise the Ottawaws, and very much surprised at our brothers the Delawares, for proposing to us to leave this place and go home, this is our home; you have attacked us without reason or provocation, you have murdered and plundered our Traders, you have taken our horses and cattle and at the same time you tell us "Your hearts are good towards your Brothers the English," How can I have faith in you, or believe that you are sincere? Therefore now,

Brothers, I would desire you to go home to your towns, and take care of your women and children; when we have occasion to speak to you we shall send for you; if your Chiefs at any time have any thing to say to us, they must go to Fort Bedford, where they will meet our great men and George Grogham: they will be well received, and I will give them letters and copies of the speeches I received of you."

CHARLESTOWN S. Carolina Jan. 23. Extract of a Letter from Mobille, Nov. 24. 1763.

"This place consists of about 120 houses, many of brick. The fort is not very large, but regular, with a ditch, covered way and glacis. The French had 38 cannon 12 and 18 pounders mounted, which are sent to New-Orleans, and we have got some from aboard our ships to replace them. There are barracks in the fort for 600 men. Tombigbee fort, in the Choctaw nation is taken possession of by our troops. ——— Capt. John Campbell is appointed to command at Albama and will soon set out. ——— Major Loftus will set out in january to take possession of the Illinois on the Missisippi, 300 Leagues above New-Orleans. The Governor of New-Orleans has been here for some time with the old French Governor of this place, holding a meeting with the Choctaw Indians, who do not seem at all pleased with the presents the French gave them."

We learn that 500 men to Garrison at Mobille, 100 Tobigbee, 100 Albama, and 300 Illinois.

New-York Jan 16. We hear from the very best authority, that Sir William Johnson was lately visited by above 300 hundred Friendly Indians of the Five Nations; as also by Deputies from the Senecas, who were accompanied by one Hans Fife, a German, formerly taken near Fort Cunberland, and delivered up, with several other Prisoners, to Sir William about two Years ago: But he being a profligate Person, immediately made his Escape to the Senecas whom he has since accompanied, by his own confession to war against the English, and committed several Acts of Cruelty against by the reports of others. ——— On which Information Sir William causes him to be apprehended, and committed to Albany Goal. And has also obtained from a Friendly Village of Senecas, one Gabriel Pilliton, an Englishman, who says he has relation in Bucks County, in the Province of Pennsylvania and was taken in November of 1762, and carried to Canawagan, a castle of Enemy Senecas, from whence he made his Escape to Kanadesago, a Castle of Friendly Indians of that Nation (next to Cayoga) which Indians standing remained neutral the late Hostilities, have now delivered him up to Sir William Johnson's request.

FEBRUARY 1764

CHARLESTOWN S. Carolina. Feb. 1. The transport with the 35th regiment commanded by Maj. William Forbes, which sailed from this port the 6th of October last for Pensacola, did not arrive till December 2d. Col. Provost sailed in the Venus transport for New-York, with several other officers and such of the private men of the Royal American battalion as were not draughted into the other regiments. The French garrison of Fort Thoulouse arrived at Mobille Dec. 16th, the keys of that fort were delivered to the Wolf King of the Creeks, and we are assured no British garrison will be sent thither. Major Loftus is gone to take possession of the Illinois.

A letter from Fort Prince George of the 27th ult. says, "About 20 northward Indians were seen a few days ago, and we just learn, that one MacNamar and another white man are killed, over the hills, either by them or the Creeks."

CHARLESTOWN S. Carolina Feb. 1. Last week Mr. Fredrick Post, who lately arrived here from Philadelphia, sailed from hence to Jamaica. This person has spent many years in endeavouring to convert Indians about the Great lakes and on the Ohio to the Christian Religion: He was beloved and esteemed by them all for his meek, peaceable and primitive deportment, in so much that he went amongst them at the very time they knew General Forbes was marching an Army into their country against them and their friends the French, was of great service to the common cause, and returned unhurt; yet after repeated trials and long perseverance, he is now convinced that the time is not yet come for those Indians to have their eyes opened to receive the Religion of Jesus, and has undertaken his present voyage in order to proceed to the Musqueto shore, and try whether the Musqueto Indians, have hardened their hearts equally with their northern brethren.

NEW-YORK Feb. 2. Yesterday se-nnight came the General Court of this city the trial of the soldiers taken up on account of the late Riot, breaking the Goal and rescuing Major Rogers: We hear five of them were found Guilty, and that they have declared the Major was privy of the Design.

PHILADELPHIA Feb. 2. They write from Burlington of the 25th of January, that Lieut. Shaw, who commanded our detachment at Niagara, after the death of Capt. Johnson, is come down from thence, and says, that the very nations who were at the attack of our people at the north end of Lake Erie were at Sir William Johnson's making their submissions as he passed by.

SAVANNAH Feb. 2. All our accounts from Augusta say, that the murders committed at the Long Canes were done by seven Creek fellows, who have been for some tome amongst the Cherokees. Two other white people we hear have since been killed, thought to be by the same party.

PHILADELPHIA Feb. 5. On Saturday last the city was alarmed with the News of a great Number of armed Men, from the Frontiers being on the several Roads, and moving towards Philadelphia. As their Design were unknown and they were various Reports concerning them, it was thought prudent to put the City in some Posture of Defence against any outrages that might possibly be intended. The Inhabitants being accordingly called upon by the Governor, great Numbers of them entered into the Association, and took Arms for the support of the Government & Maintenance of good Order.

Six Companies of Foot, one Artillery, and two Troops of Horses, were formed, and paraded; to which it is said, some Thousand who did not appear, were prepared to join themselves in case any Attempts should be made against the Town. The Barracks also, where the Indians are lodged, under protection of the regular Troops, were put into a good posture of Defence; several Works being thrown up about them, and eight pieces of Cannon planted there.

The insergents it seems, intended to gather at

Germantown; but the Precautions taken at the several Ferries over the Schuylkill impeded their Junction; and those who assembled there, made acquainted with the Force raised to oppose there, listened to the reasonable Discources and advice of some prudent persons, who voluntarily went out to meet and admonish them and some of the Gentlemen sent by the Governor, to know the Reasons for this Insurrection; and promised to return peaceably to their Habitations leaving only one of their Number to present a Petition to the Governor on Tuesday Evening, and dismissed, and the City restored to its former Quiet.

But on Wednesday Morning there was a fresh Alarm, occasioned by a false Report, That Four Hundred of the same People were on their March to Attack the Town. Immediately on the Bear of the Drum a much greater Number of the Inhabitants, with the utmost Alacrity, put themselves under Arms; but as the Truth was soon known, they were again thanked by the Governor, and dismissed: the Country People being realy dispersed and gone home accordingly to their province.

NEW-YORK Feb. 13. Our advice from Philadelphia so late as Saturday last (not by the Post, who is not arrived) is, That a considerable Number of Persons, who call themselves Paxton Volunteers, had assembled and were on the 5th instant marching down to Philadelphia to attack the Barracks for the Indians who were protected there ⸻ but they were halted at German Town (whithin 7 Miles of that City) on being told, 1000 of the Inhabitants had armed themselves, and were entrenched round the Barracks with Cannon loaded with Grape Shot, to defend it. It appears Philadelphia City was alarmed on the Occasion by 2 o'Clock on Monday Morning last by the Ringing of the Bells, &c. when the Governor and Council were obliged to meet ⸻ Further particulars we have not obtained.

PHILADELPHIA Feb. 16. The following is the substance of a letter from an officer at Fort Penn, in Northamton county dated the 10th inst.

"That on that day, between 6 and 7 in the

morning, a centry and some others observed a great smoke, which appeared to come from the plantation of one James Russel: That he, the officer, likewise seeing the smoke, immediately marched with 20 men to know the cause of it, when he found the barn on fire, and saw a great many Indians tracks, by which he concluded their number must have been 50 or upwards: That in the barn he found a lad and a horse roasted, and imagined another lad was either killed or carried off, as they got his clothes, but could not find the body: That on further examination the tracks of the enemy, it appeared that some of them had crossed Pocono Creek the way they came, and others went towards the New Guiney-Settlement; upon which our people likewise crossed the creek and marched to the head of the Dutch settlement, where it was thought they intended next to strike, and brought off the inhabitants to the fort. That he was afraid the Guiney people were cut off, and he had got but one family from that quarter, and his dispatches were not returned: And that he was to march the next day by day light with a party of volunteers in pursuit of the Indians, which he proposed to continue for three or four days, in order to come up with them."

SAVANNAH Feb. 16. The report of two white people being killed by the Indians, since the murders committed at the Long-Canes on the 24th of December last, we are assured is without foundation. One of the scalps taken at that settlement has been offered by five of these murderers to one of the Creeks, in order to be carried into and accepted by the nation, but absolutely refused; and the nation have promised to give satisfaction by putting to death the authors of this barbarity. By the return of an express lately sent from Augusta to the Cherokees, we are informed, that the Young Warrior of Estatoe, who was suspected to be concerned in these depredations, has denied his having any hand in them, and of this he says he will convince the English whenever called upon to take up arms in their cause.

Notice is now given to all gentlemen belonging

to the first company of foot militia, commanded by Capt. James Deveaux, that they are to appear at the usual place of parade, completely accoutred, on Monday the 5th of March; and as several of the company have refused to pay their fines of non-appearance they must expect to pay for the future. Jeremiah Sliterman and Edward Davidson, Serjeants.

SAVANNAH Feb. 23. By Capt. Sumerville from Mobille we have the following Address, presented at the 21st of January last.

To Robert Farmar, Esquire, Major of the 34th regiment, and commander in Chief of the province of Louisiana.

The humble Address of the British settlers, as well planters and merchants.

It gives us, Sir, being the first British subjects who arrived in Louisiana, a great deal of concern, that we have not found the satisfaction of congratulating you, and the troops under your command, on taking possession of Mobile. We now, though late, do it from our hearts. We likewise, Sir, have long had a desire to lay before you, as commander in chief, some doubts which we cannot clear upon without your assistance, and some grievances we have laboured under, which we imagine you can prevent for the future; but we has not an opportunity given us till Sunday last. This we are willing to attribute to your being hurried with matters of greater moment.

2. By the treaty the French have eighteen months allowed them to dispose of their effects, and whoever of his Britannic's Majesty's subjects that chuse may become purchasers; but having no Lawyers among us, we are at a loss to know if the French titles to their possessions, though good among themselves, will be deemed so under British government. At present, Sir, we should be glad to be informed if you will finally determine what are good, most of us being purchasers, or about to purchase.

3. The Indians trade will be the principal branch for some time; we should therefore take it as a favour that you would inform us if licences are to be granted in the same manner as

in Carolina and Georgia, and whether the French people, after taking the oath of allegiance, will be permitted to trade among the Savages.

4. We have heard, though we don't ascertain it as a fact, that spirits of every denomination are prohibited. In the first place, Sir, we humbly apprehend, that the most effectual method to prevent the running of brandy from New-Orleans would be to allow the importation of rum from our West-India islands; at the same time it would be an encouragement for the planters to make lumber and other articles proper for a West-India market.

5. As to the importations of spirits made in Great-Britain, we cannot help being of opinion, that, without express orders from his Majesty to the contrary, they may be landed and sold to any part of America, and several of us have already commissioned from London.

6. Ever since our arrival here, we have seen the French keep open shops, and as openly sell, not only liquors but other goods that more immediately interfere with the grand staples of England, we mean, Sir, woolens, linens, and iron ware. We know those articles have been brought from New-Orleans since the treaty, we know they have received dollars and deer skins in Payment, which has been remitted there; yet, Sir, we are above being informed, and only hope we shall not see those things again.

7. That we may know upon what footing we are, that we may be enable to write our correspondents in Great-Britain upon what footing the settlers in the province of Louisiana are, that we may order out British manufacturers to supply the inhabitants, and that we may give encouragement for more people to come here, we doubt not you will be pleased to give us a full answer to this address.

8. In case of a war whether with the French or savages, (Which thank God there is no reason to fear) we beg leave to assure you, that we will willingly comply with the orders of the commander in chief in every respect, and that we will risk our lives and fortunes as chearfully as the most loyal of British subjects have in the last

war.
Mobille, Jan. 21, 1764.

Signed
William Irving, Henry Legard.
Joshuah Ward, Alexander Gras.
George Anstrun, Henry Percipcol
William Telfair, Francis Pount.

To the foregoing address the Major returned a very satisfactory Answer.

SAVANNAH Feb. 23. Extract of a letter from a gentleman at Mobille to his friend here, dated Jan. 31, 1764.

"By last account from the Indian country, a war is expected between the Creeks and Choctaws; the Creeks have stopped all goods from coming through their nation either to the Choctaws or Chikesaws, the Chikesaws seem very desirous to have a knock at the Creeks for several injuries they have received from them; so it is the opinion the war will be general amongst themselves, and divert their attention from the white people, to whom they have been menacing wrath."

By a letter from Augusta, of the 14th inst. we are informed, that the day before some people arrived from the upper and Lower Creeks, who said, that three pack-horse men from little Tallassees, with abouy 20 horse loads of leather, on their way to Augusta, near Okmulgees were told by some Indians that the villains who committed the late murders were then at Okmulgee river, and as they could not escape them; if they attempted to proceed, advised them to fly and leave the horses and leather to their care, and they would convoy it safe to Little Tallassees. On this advice, the pack-horse men left all and went to the nation, where they alarmed every white man they saw; and having all met at Maccullulsaw, about nine in number, from thence they went to Pensacola, leaving everything in the nation belonging to the traders in the hands of the Indians. It is as yet uncertain what resolution the Upper Towns will take concerning the late depredations, as very few of them are gone in from their hunts.

Letters from London assures us that the French actually ceded to the Spaniards the island of New-Orleans, with all their lands lying to the westward of the Missisippi.

NEW-YORK Feb. 27. Yesterday morning Captain Magee sailed for Drogheda Ireland. Three Indian men are gone in said vessel, and are bound for a term of years to Hyam Myers, in order to be exhibited by way of show, in the different Parts of England, Scotland and Ireland.

MARCH 1764

CHARLESTOWN S. Carolina March 1. Some intimations having been thrown out by the Creeks, that the Young Warrior of Estatowih was again inclined to go to War against us, and had intimated, if their nation would begin, that he would join them, for, that the approaching spring the English intended to cut them all off, &c. &c. The return of an express from Prince George, Keehowee brings his positive denial of those charges and us positive assurances of his fidelity. In a talk which he gave the 26th ult. he says, that he and his people were all very well pleased with the good talks delivered at the late congress at Augusta, and therefore he is the more surprised at what has been laid to his charge. That the Creeks are lyars and a most perfidious nation. That they have killed Cherokees as well as white people. That he burns with anger, whenever he hears them express their contemptible opinions of the English. by saying, "That they are all women, and they could treat them as no other wherever they should meet them:" by asking, "how they came to make war with the Cherokees? and, if they were any men amongst them, why did they not resent what (the Creeks) had done." That he thought, we could not be strangers to the design of the Creeks, by their behaviours at Augusta & being all of them armed with long knives and pistols, with which he and his people hourly expected they would attempt to massacre both English and Cherokees. That they have sent him a talk since the congress, desiring him not to resent any injury that may be done to traders, but that he was, and always should be, deaf to such talks. ———
He had repeated invitations from the Creeks during the late war, to go and settle amongst them,

and that they have owed him a grudge ever since he refused. That he is very ready to assist in putting the seven murderers to death mentioned in the Young-Twin talk, but they are a very small part of the rogues that have mischief in their hearts, for he has certain information, that the whole nation is resolved on a war with the English; that they design to waylay all the rivers, and particularly the fords, all the way to St. Augustine to the head of the Savannah river; and that they are cutting up all the skins of their winter's hunt for morkasins, to proceed upon the execution of their designs. He desires, that the warriors who are to relieve the garrison of Fort Prince George may have a strict caution to be on their guard, suspecting they may be way-laid by the Creeks; says he shall soon remove his people from Toogouloo to Estatowih; and concludes with the warmest profussion of friendship.

CHARLESTOWN S. Carolina March 1. Extract of a Letter from Mobille.

"My last acquainted you that M. l'Abadie, the governor of New-Orleans was here, had delivered a good public talk, and was giving presents to the Chactah's and some other Indians three years due: I promise to send a copy of his talk, but have been dissapointed of it. Among the Choctah's there was not a man of the English party; tho' they came from no less than fifty-seven towns; those all refused to come, tho' the whole nation was invited. The presents delivered them were very considerable, among them was a great number of guns, and near 6000 lb. of gun powder and balls; every other article they had in proportion. Immense promises were likewise made them; in particular that they should be sent for again in six months, to New-Orleans, to receive more considerable presents there, if they behaved well; and they have all returned pretty well satisfied. Whatever may have been said in public to the Indians, recommending that they should look upon and behave to the English and French as one people, 'tis certain that in private no pains, no arts have been wanting to withhold them from an alliance with us, by telling them,

"That the English only wanted their lands, and would give them nothing, use the women ill, and at last make slaves of them:" and inviting them to settle on the western banks of the Missisippi where they should have lands and hunting-grounds far superior to what they now possesd, and real friends about them. In short, it is my opinion, that the French have some future prospect in view, that cannot tend to our good, for they spare no direct or indirect means to gain and preserve the friendship of every Indian tribe of the nation. Some small tribes that were settled around this place, and were vary useful to the inhabitants, by killing deer, catching fish, &c. have in this manner been withdrawn down to New-Orleans: An attempt of this sort was made while Col. Robertson was here, with a tribe that had a town about 50 or 30 miles up the river, and were going to be carried off in French boats; but the colonel sent for the headman, and gave him assurances, "That if they would remain on their lands, they should have the utmost protection from the English; be always treated as their own children, and never suffered to want any thing," which seemed to have fixed them. ——— The garrison of Fort Thoulouse arriv'd here the 15th instant, accompanied by about 300 Indians, called by the French the Alibamous, and by our traders StinkingLingue, who are also come for presents from the French, with whom they have always lived in friendship, tho' they never would fight against us: Before the garrison quitted the fort, they destroyed all the cannon, and stores they could not bring away; after which they say, they delivered the key to Wolf King, who immediately took possession of it with his family: As there is no message from him yet to put into possession of the English and his intentions are not known, Col. Robertson has determined not to send a garrison there, 'till the Indians ask for one, which I am persuaded they never will. ——— The command sent to Tombigee fort arrived there in fifteen days, without meeting with the least interruption, and the Chactahs have hitherto behaved in a most friendly manner. Major Forbes was here a few days ago from Pensacola, and is returned. Major Loftus is under orders to proceed with the 22d regiment to the Illinois, the 1st of January. The land on the Albahma (or Alibamous) is in general esteemed as good as that of the Illinois."

WILLIAMSBURG March 2. Lieut. Colonel Robinson Deputy Quartermaster General, who was sent from New-York some time ago, with a body of Troops. to take possession of the lands to the southward ceded to Great-Britain by the late treaty, informs, that after having garrisoned St. Augustine he proceeded to Pensacola and fort Conde on the Mobille, at which place he likewise left garrisons and from thence went to New-Orleans, where he was very kindly received by the French Governor there: he then sent the 32d regiment, in batteaus, to take possession of the great fort on the forks of the Illinois, Missouri; and Missisippi, which entirely secures our back settlements and which the French Governor told him would be a voyage of at least 3 months, the navigation being very tedious, owing to the rapid current of the Missisippi, though the distance is no more than 150 miles. Lieut. Robinson says the land about Mobille are light sandy, and barren, that there are some good lands about Pensacola, which are chiefly taken up for a certain noble Family; and that the lands at St. Augustine are bought as private property of the Spaniards, who have grants for the same from his Catholic Majesty. He likewise informs that Fort Halbama is given up to the Creeks, and that no troops are left there.

BOSTON March 5. Extract of a Letter from Philadelphia, February 9, 1764.

"Last Saturday the Governor sent the constables to all the freeholders in the city requesting them to meet him at the State-House: ——— We went, and were informed that his honor had certain intelligence of the large number of Paxton people's coming to town, which was the occasion of calling us. The night before we were called, the Governor sent to the commander of the King's troops at the barracks, to know if he would defend the Indians. He answered No: But if the assembly would pass a riot act, he would defend them to the last. The assembly was then sitting, and the Governor sent them a message on the occasion, when they immediately passed it, the substance of which was, That if any Persons, to the Number of twelve, or more, shall hereafter be unlawfully and riotously assemble together, that then any Justice of the Peace, Sheriff, Constable, or other Peace Officer within his Jurisdiction, shall immediately repair to the rioters, as near as he or they can safely come, and with a loud Voice command silence to be, while Proclamation is making, which shall be dome in a Form prescribed, the Substance is in the King's Name to command all rioters to disperse and peaceably depart to their own homes, under the Penalties contained in the Act. And if the said Officer is obstructed in making Proclamation, or if he makes it, then every person who shall not separate from the Rioters and depart within the space of an Hour from the Time of such Obstruction or Proclamation shall be deem'd a Felon and suffer death without benefit of Clergy, and such Peace Officer or Officers are empower'd to command the Aid and Assistance of all his Majesty's Subjects, of Age and Ability, to seize and bring all such offenders to Justice, and such Peace Officers and their Assistants and indemnified for their wounding, or maiming, or Death of any of the Rioters that may happen in dispersing or seizing them. ——— And for the better regulations, the Governor had papers drawn up for all that were free to sign them, in manner of an association, as we have no laws to compel us. He requested that a number of people would attend him to the barracks, there to stand in defence of the Indians: others he desired to go to ferries of Schuilkill, and sink the boats, in order to prevent their coming over, which was done: 5 field pieces, 18 pounders, were ordered up to the barracks. ——— The above association papers were immediately signed by about 600 people. On Sunday the 5th, at eleven in the evening, letters came to his honour, acquainting him, that a body of Paxtonians had passed Reading, which is 5 miles off, on their way to this city; and that another body was coming down Lancaster road. His Honor called the council, and they sat till one o'clock in the morning, when they ordered a general alarm. Firing one of the field pieces, ringing all the bells, beating of drums, crying fire, &c. Spread a general consternation among the inhabitants, who, not knowing but it was a fire, run to and fro, enquiring the cause. At length was informed the rebels were at hand. ——— I with many others, patroled the streets till day-break. At Sunrise 600 men were under arms, with two troops of horse. We were under continual alarms 'till the afternoon, when some people arrived, and said there was a body of rioters at Germantown, who had sent down to the Governor part of their business, and assured him they would not come any further till they had a conference with him or the council. but threatened the Indians. However on this the companies were discharged till 5 o'clock Tuesday morning, when the alarm was repeated, we all arose to arms and formed the companies as before. The people now began to grow angry, and at 6 sent to the Governor, desiring leave to march to Germantown and disperse them or bring them in; his honor refused, but sent part of the council up to demand the reason of their coming in this hostile manner. The troops were under arms till 4 in the afternoon, when the council returned, and informed us they were dispersing, all but a small number, who were coming to town to lay their grievances before the Governor, &c. ——— The troops were all discharged till 10 o'clock Wednesday morning, when they who had the city arms were to deliver them up; but a fresh alarm was given, there being, as was said 400 of the rioters without 2 miles of the city. To arms, to arms, was the cry; and in less than half an hour near 1000 of the inhabitants were ready, and marched towards Germantown, with cannon, &c. when they met about 40 of those scoundrels, who were coming to see the city; but so exasperated were the people that they would have fired on them had not the Governor's orders been to the contrary. As they had the faith of the city given them. This day they set out for their homes, and the city is again restored to peace. ―――― I believe we shall have a militia law soon."

NEW-YORK March 5. A letter by the last Albany post, of indubitable credit.

"Sir william Johnson hath lately sent out a party, consisting of near 200 Indians of the well disposed nations, accompanied by some rangers and proper officers, in order to cut off the Indians of a large village of Kanestio, who have the greatest inveteracy against the English, and committed the first hostilities. ―――― This party is afterwards to proceed against some Shawanese and Delaware villages: And from the alacrity of our Indians have expressed, there is great reason to hope they'll meet with success; which strikes a terror into the Enemies, in that country. ―――― We hear likewise there are several other parties preparing to go upon the like service; which it is expected will find the destroyers of our back settlements in sufficient work at home, and prove the distruction of many of them."

CHARLESTOWN S. Carolina March 7. By Letters from the country of the Creek Indians, dated the 14th last month, and from Augusta the 28th, we learn that both the upper and lower towns disclaim the late murders though at the same time little is said about giving satisfaction; the Wolf King of the upper Creeks and the Chehaw, Point, and Cossitaw people are very warm in their expressions of friendship and attachment to the British nation. The principal Indians will not return from hunting before March, when they promise to send down their last resolution.

The Creeks that killed the Long Canes people were all of principal families though one only was of that of the Bear, another of them the Nephew to the Young Lieutenant who it is said is the person of most influence that has yet declared for them. Those miscreants are gone from the nation, and gave out it was to hunt, but it is thought their real design is to repeat the horrid tragedy of Long Canes.

Notwithstanding the bad accounts from the country of the Creek Indians, several traders from Georgia has set out for that country, but no conclusion can be drawn from this circumstance against the truth of those accounts, if it is remembered that most if not all the traders to the Cherokees despised or disbelieves every thing that was told them concerning the bad disposition of the Indians before the commencement of the late war, and that may of those traders paid for their temerity with their lives.

BOSTON March 12. Extract of a letter received from Philadelphia addressed to the Publisher of the Boston Evening Post.

Your publishing the following Narrative wrote by a Gentleman at Philadelphia, of the late Massacre in Lancaster-County Pennsylvania, of a number of Indians, Friends of the Province, with some observations on the same: I imagine will be very agreeable to most of your Readers as well as your humble servant. H.

These Indians were the remains of a tribe of six Nations, settled at Conestogoe, and thence called Conestogoe Indians. ——— On the first arrival of the English in Pennsylvania, messengers from this tribe came to welcome them, with Presents of Venison, Corn and Skins; and the whole tribe enter'd into a Treaty of Friendship with the first proprietor William Penn, which was to last "as long as the Sun should shine, or the Waters run in the Rivers."

The treaty has been since frequently renewed, and the Chain brightened, as they express it, from time to time. It has never been violated, on their Part or ours, till now. As their Lands by degrees were mostly purchased, and the settlements of the white people begun to surround them, the proprietor assigned them lands on the manor of Conestogoe, which they might not part with; they have lived many years in friendship with their white neighbours, who loved them for their peaceable inoffensive behaviour.

It has always been observed that Indians, settled in the neighbourhood of white people, do not increase but diminish continually. This tribe accordingly went on diminishing, till now there remained in their own town on the manor, but 20 persons, viz. 7 men, 5 women, and 8 children, boys and girls.

Of these Shehaes was a very old man, assisted at the second treaty held with them, by Mr. Penn, in 1701, and ever since continued a faithful affectionate friend to the English: He is said to have been an exceedingly good man, considering his education, being naturally of a most kind and benevolent temper.

Peggy was Shehaes's daughter; she worked for her aged father, continuing to live with him, tho' married and attending him with filial duty and tenderness.

John was another good old man; his son Harry helped support him.

George and Wild Sue were two brothers, both young men.

John Smith, a valuable young man, of the Cayoga nation, who became acquainted with Peggy, Shehaes's daughter some years since married her, and settled in that family. They had one child, about three years old.

Betty a harmless old woman; and her son Peter, a likely young lad.

Sally, whose Indian name was Wyanjoy, a woman much esteemed by all that knew her, for her prudent and good behaviour in some very trying situations of life. She was truly good and amiable woman, had no children of her own, but a distant relative dying, she had taken a child of that relation's to bring up as her own, and performed towards it all the duties of an affectionate parent. The reader will observe that many of the names are English, it is common with the Indians that have an affection for the English, to give themselves, and their children, names of such English persons as they particularly esteem.

The little society continued the custom they had begun, when more numerous, of addressing every new governor, and every descendent of the first proprietor, welcoming him to the province, assuring him of their fidelity, and praying a continuance of the favour and protection they had hitherto experienced, They had accordingly sent up an address of this kind to the present governor, on his arrival; but the same was scarce delivered, when the unfortunate catastrophe happened, which we about to relate.

On Wednesday, the 14th of december 1763. fifty-seven men, from some frontier townships who had projected the destruction of the little commonwealth, came, all well-mounted, and armed with flintlocks, hangers and hatchets, having travelled through the country in the night to Conestogoe manor. There they sourounded the small village of Indian huts, and just at break of day broke into them all at once. Only three men, two women, and a young boy, were found at home, the rest being out among the neibouring white people, some to sell baskets, brooms and bowls they manufactured, and others on other occasions. These poor defenceless creatures were immediately fired upon, stabbed and hatcheted to death! The good Shehaes, among the rest, cut to pieces in his bed. All of them scalped, and otherwise horribly mangled. Then their huts were set on fire, and most of them burnt down. When the troop pleased with their conduct and bravery, but enranged that any of the poor Indians had escaped the massacre, rode off, and in small parties, by different roads, went home.

The universal concern of the neighbouring white people on hearing of the event, and the lamentations of the younger Indians, when they returned and saw the desolation, and the butchered half burnt bodies of their murdered parents and other relations, cannot well be expressed.

The magistrate of Lancaster sent out to collect the remaining Indians, brought them into town for their better security against any further attempt; and it is said condoled with them on the misfortune that had happened, took them by the hand, comforted and promised them protection. ——— They were all put in the work-house, a strong building, as the place of greatest safety.

When the shocking news arrived in town, a proclamation was issued by the governor, in the following terms, viz.

"whereas I have received Information, That on Wednesday the 14th Day of this month, a number of people, armed, and mounted on horse back, unlawfully assembled together, and went to the Indian town in the Conestogoe manor, Lancaster

County, and without the least reason of provocation, in cold blood, barbarously killed six of the Indians settled there and burnt and destroyed all their houses and effects: And whereas so cruel and inhuman an act, committed in the heart of this Province, on the said Indians, who have lived peaceably and inoffensively among us, during all our late troubles, and for many years before, and were justly considered as under our protection of the government and its Laws, calls loudly for the vigorous exertion of the civil authority to detect the offenders, and bring them to condign punishment; I have therefore, by and with the advice and consent of the council, thought fit to issue this proclamation, and do hereby strictly charge and enjoin all judges, justices, sheriffs, constables, officers civil and military, and all other of his Majesty's liege subjects within the province, to make diligent Search and enquiry after the authors and perpetrators of the said crime, their abettors and accomplices, and to use all possible means to apprehend, and secure them in some of the publick goals of this province, that they may be brought to their trial, and be proceeded against according to the law.

And whereas a number of the Indians, who lately lived near the frontiers of this province being willing and desirous to preserve and continue the ancient friendship which heretofore subsisted between them and the good people of this province, have, at their own earnest request, been removed from their habitations and brought into the county of Philadelphia, and seated, for the present, for their better security, on the Province Island, and other places in the neighbourhood of the city of Philadelphia, where provisions is made for them at publick expence; I do therefore hereby strictly forbid all persons, whatsoever, to molest or injure any said Indians, as they will answer the contrary at their peril.

Given under my Hand and the great Seal of the said Province, at Philadelphia, the twenty-second day of December, Anno Domini One Thousand seven Hundred and Sixty three, and in the fourth

Year of His Majesty's Reign.   John Penn."

Notwithstanding this proclamation, those cruel men again assembled themselves, and hearing that the remaining 14 Indians were at the work-house at Lancaster, they suddenly appeared in that town on the 27th of December. Fifty of them armed as before dismounting, went directly to the workhouse, and by violence broke open the door and entered with the utmost fury in their countenances. —— when the poor wretches saw they had no protection nigh, nor could possibly escape, they being without the least weapons for defence, they divided into their little families, the children clinging to the parents; they fell on their knees, protested their innocence, declared their love for the English, and that, in their whole lives, they had never done them injury; and in this posture they all received the hatchet! —— Men, women and little children — were every one inhumanly murdered, —— in cold blood!

The barbarous men who committed the ferocious fact, in defiance of government, of all laws human and divine and to the eternal disgrace of their Country and Colour, then mounted their horses, huzza'd in triumph, as if they had gained a victory and rode off —— unmolested!

The bodies of the murdered were then brought out and exposed in the street, till a hole could be made in the earth, to receive and cover them.

But the wickedness cannot be covered, the guilt will lie on the whole land, till justice is done on the murderers, The Blood of the Innocent will cry to Heaven for Vengeance.

It is said that Shehaes's, being told, that it was to be feared some English might come from the frontier into the country, and murder him and his people; he replied, "it is impossible: There are Indians indeed in the woods, who would kill me and mine, if they could get at us, for my friendship to the English; but the English will wrape me in their matchcoat, and secure me from all danger." How unfortunately was he mistaken!

Another proclamation has been issued, offering a reward of 200 pounds for the securing and prosecuting to conviction any three of the ringleaders in this inhuman and bloody affair; and to any accomplice not actually concern'd in the murders, who shall make discovery of any ringleader, and apprehend and prosecute them to conviction, besides the above reward, that all the weight and influence of the government shall be employed to obtain a pardon for the offender.

These proclamations have yet produced no discovery; the murderers given out such threatening against those that disapprove their proceedings that the whole country seems in terror, and no one durst speak what he knows; even the letters from thence are unsigned, in which any dislike is expressed of the rioters.

There are some (I am ashamed to hear it) who would extenuate the enormous wickedness of these actions, by saying. "The Inhabitants of the frontiers are exasperated with the murders of their relations, by the enemy Indians! in the present war' It is possible; ——— but thought this might justify their going out in the woods, to seek those enemies, and avenge upon them those murders; it can never justify their turning into the heart of the country, to murder their friends.

If an Indian injured me, does it follow that I amy revenge that injury on all Indians? It is well known that Indians are of different tribes, nations and languages, as well as the white people. In Europe, if the French, who are white people, should injure the Dutch, are they to revenge it on the English, because they two are white people? The only crime of these poor wretches seems to have been, that they had a reddish brown skin, and black hair: and some people of that sort, it seems had murdered some of our relatives. If this be right to kill men for such a reason, then, should any man, with a freckled face and red hair, kill a wife or child of mine, it would be right for me to revenge it, by killing all the freckled read-haired men, woman and children, I could afterward any where meet with. ------------------------------------

Now I am about to mention something of Indians, I beg that I may not be understood as framing apologies for all Indians. I am far from desiring to lessen the laudable spirit of resentment to any countrymen against those now at war with us, so far as it is justified by the perfidy an inhumanity. ——— I would only observe that the Six Nations, as a body have kept faith with the English ever since we knew them, now near an hundred years: and that the governing part of those people have had notions of honour, whatever may be the case with the rum debauchen, trader-corruptive vagabonds and thieves on the Susquehannah and the Ohio, at present in arms against us. ——— As proof of the Honour, I should only mention one well-known recent fact. When six Catawba deputies, under the care of Colonel Bull of Charlestown, went by permission into Mohawks country, to see for a treat of peace for their nation, they soon found the Six Nations highly exasperated, and the peace at that time impracticable: They were therefore in fear of their own persons, and apprehended that they should be killed in the way back to New-York; which being made known to Mohawk chiefs by Col. Bull, one of them, by order of the council, made this speech to the Catawbas:

Strangers and Enemies,

"While you are in this country, blow away all fears out of your breast; change the black streek of paint on your cheek for a red one, and let your face shine with bear's-grease: You are safer here than you were at home. The Six Nations will not defile their own land with the blood of men that come unarmed to ask for peace. We shall send a guard with you to see you safe out of our territories. So far you shall have peace, but no farther. Get home to your wives for there we intend to come and kill you."

The Catawbas came away unhurt accordingly.

It is also well known, that just before the late war broke out, that our traders first went amongst the Piankeshaw Indians, a tribe of the Twightwees, they found the principle of giving Protection to the strangers in full force: for the French coming with their Indians to the Piankeshaw-towns and demanding that those traders and their goods should be delivered up: ———

The Piankasaws replied the English were come there upon invitation, and they could not do so base a thing. But the French insisting on it the Piankeshaws took arms in defence of their guests, and a number of them, with their old chief lost their lives in the cause; the French at last prevailed by superior force only.

  I will not dissemble that numberless stories have been raised and spread abroad against not only the poor wretches that are murdered, but also against the hundred and forty chirstian Indians, still threatened to be murdered; all which stories are well known, by those who know the Indians best, to be pure inventions, contrived by bad people, either to excite each to join in the murder, or since it was committed to justify it; and believe only by the weak and credulous. I call thus publickly on the makers and venders of these accusations to produce their evidence. Let them satisfy the public that even Will Soc, the most obnoxious of all the tribe, was really guilty of those offences made against us which they lay on his charge. But if he was, ought he not to have been fairly tried; He lived under our laws, and was subject to them; he was in our hands, and might easily have been prosecuted; was it English Justice to condemn and execute him unheard? Conscious of his own innocence, he did not endeavour to hide himself when the door of the work-house, his sanctuary was breaking open; I will meet them, says he for they are my Brothers. These brothers of his shot him down at the door, while the word brother was still between his teeth! —— But if Will Soc was a bad man, what had poor old Shehaes done? what could he or the other poor old men & women do? what had little boys and girls done; what could children of a year old, babes at the breast, what could they do, that they too must be shot and hatcheted? —— Horrid to relate! —— and in their parents arms! This is done by no civilized nation in Europe. Do we come to America to learn and practice the manners of Barbarians? But this, Barbarians as they are, they practice upon their enemies only, and not against their friends. ——

These poor people have been always our friends,
Their fathers received ours, when strangers
here, with kindness and hospitality. Behold the
return we have made them! ——— When we grew
more numerous and powerful they put themselves
under our protection, See, in the mangled corpes,
of the last remains of the tribe, how effectually
we have afforded it to them! ———
Unhappy people! to have lived in such times,
and by such neighbours! ——— We have seen that
they would have been safer among ancient Hea-
thens, with whom the rites of hospitality were
sacred, ——— They would have been considered
guests of the publick, and the religion of the
country would have operated in their favour, But
our frontier people call themselves Christians!
——— They would have been safer, if they had
submitted to the Turks; for ever since Mohamet's
reproof of Kbaled, even the cruel Turks, never
kill prisoners in cold blood. These were not
even prisoners. ——— But what is the example of
the Turks to scripture Christians? ——— They
would have been safer, though they had been taken
in actual war against the Saracens, if they had
once drank water with them. These were not taken
in war against us, and have drank with us, and
we with them, for fourscore years. ——— But
shall we compare Saracens to Christians? ———
They would have been safer among the Moors in
Spain, though they had been murderers of Sons:
if faith had once been pledged to them, and a
promise of protection given. But these have had
the faith of the English given to them many times
by the government, and, in reliance of that faith,
they lived among us, and gave us the opportunity
of murdering them. ——— However, What was honorable to the Moors, may not be the rule to us;
for we are Christians! ——— They would have been
safer it seems among Popish Spaniards, even if
enemies, & delivered into their hands by a tem-
pest. These were not enemies; they were born
among us, and yet we have killed them all. ———
But shall we imitate idolatrous Papists, we that
are enlightened Protestants? They would even
have been safer among the Negroes of Africa,
where at least one manly soul would have been

found with sense and humanity enough to stand in their defence: ——— But shall whitemen and Christians act like pagan Negroes? ———In short it appears, that they would have been safe in any part of the known world, ——— except in the neighbourhood of the Christian White Savages of Pectang and Donegall! ———

O ye unhappy perpetrators of this horrid wickedness! reflect a moment on the mischief you have done, the disgrace ye have brought on your country, on your religion, and your bible, on your families and children! Think on the destruction of your captivate country-folks (now among the Indians) which probably may follow in resentment of your barbarity! Think on the wrath of the united Five Nations, Hitherto our friends, but now provoked by your murdering one of their tribes, in danger of becoming our bitter enemies. ——— Think of the mild and good government you have so audaciously insulted: the laws of your King, your country and your God, that you have broken; the infamous death that hangs over your heads: ——— For Justice, though slow, will come at last. ——— All good people every where detest your actions. ——— You have imbrued your hands in innocent blood; how will you make them clean? ——— The dying shrikes and groans of the murdered, will often sound in your ears: their specters will sometimes attend you and affright even your innocent children! ——— Fly where you will, your conscience will go with you; ——— Talking in your sleep shall betray you, in the delirium of a fever you yourselves shall make your own wickedness known.

One hundred and forty peaceable Indians yet remain in this government, They have, by christian missionaries been brought over to a liking, at least, of our religion; some of them lately left their nation which is now at war with us, because they did not chuse to join with them in the depredation; and they shew their confidence in us, and to give us an equal confidence in them, they have brought and put into our hands their wives and children. Others have lived long among us in Northampton county, and most of their children have been born there. These are all now trembling for their lives. They have been hurried from place to place for safety, now concealed in corners, then sent out of the province, refused a passage through a neighbouring colony, and returned, not unkindly perhaps, but disgracefully on our hands. O Pennsylvania! once renowned for kindness to strangers, shall the clamours of a few mean niggards about the expence of the Publick Hospitality, an expence that will not cost the noise wretches Six Pence a piece (and what is the expence of the poor maintenance we afford them, compared to the expence they might occasion if in arms against us) so senseless a clamour, I say, force you to turn out your doors these unhappy guest, who have offended their country-folks by their affection for you, who, confiding in your goodness, have put themselves under your protection? Those whom you have disarmed to satisfy groundless suspicions, will you have them exposed to the armed madmen of your country? ——— Unmanly men! who are not ashamed to come with weapons against the unarmed, to use the sword against women, and bayonets against young children; and who have already given such bloody proof of their inhumanity and cruelty. ——— Let us rouze ourselves for shame, and redeem the honour of our province from the contempt of its neighbours; let all good men join heartily and unanimously in support of the law and in strengthening the hands of government, that Justice may be done, the wicked punished, and the innocent protected; otherwise we can, as a people, expect no blessing from Heaven, there will be no security for our persons or properties: Anarchy and confusion will prevail over all, and violence without judgement, dispose of every thing.

When I mention the business of murderers, in the use they made of arms, I cannot, I ought not to forget, the very different behaviours of brave men and true soldiers, of which this melancholy occasion has afforded us fresh instances. The Royal Highlanders have, in the course of this war, suffered as much as any other corps, and have frequently had their ranks thinn'd by an Indian enemy; yet they did not for this retain

a brutal undistinguish resentment against all Indians, friend or foe. But a company happening to be here, when the 140 poor Indians above mentioned were thought in too much danger to stay longer in the province, chearfully undertook to protect and escort them to New-York, which they executed (as far as that government would permit the Indians to come) with fidelity and honour; and their Captain Robinson is justly applauded and honoured by all sensible and good people, for the care, tenderness and humanity, with which he treated those unhappy fugitives, during their march in this severe season. General Gage, too, has approved his Officer's conduct, and I hear, ordered him to remain with the Indians at Amboy, and continue his protection to them, till another body of the King's forces could be sent to relieve his company, and escort their charge back in safety to Philadelphia, where his Excellency has had the goodness to direct those forces to remain for some time, under orders of our Governor for the security of the Indians; the troops of this province being at present necessarily posted on the frontier. Such just and generous actions endears the military to the civil power, and impress the minds of all the discerning with a still greater respect for national government. ——— I shall conclude with observing, that cowards can handles arms, can strike where they are sure to meet with no return, can wound, mangle and murder; but it belongs to the brave men to spare, and to protect; for, as the poet says ———
Mercy still sway the brave.

NEW-YORK March 12. Our advice from the frontiers of this province, received by way of Express on Thursday last, and by the Albany Post on Saturday, are of as indubitable authority and credit as the extract we gave in our last, relating to the march of 200 Indians sent out by Sir William Johnson against the village of Kenestio. ——— These advises are, That on the 2d Inst. Sir William received an express by an Indian and a white man, from the above party, importing, ——— "That on the evening of the 26th of February, they had reached the great branch of the river Susquehannah, on their way westward, when they received private advices that a large body of the Delawares, our enemies, were at a small distance, determined against some of out settlements," Upon which intelligence our party immediately made all possible dispatch to surprize them, which they happily effected surrounding them in their encampment at dawn of the day of the 27th. ——— Their approach was so sudden that our enemies could make no defence, and were made prisoners to the number of Forty One, with the Chief Captain Bull, (an Indian) Son of Teedyuscung, a person who has been in arms against the English during the late hostilities, leading many parties, and discovering great inveteracy against us. Our Indians immediately bound the prisoners, and sent them under a strong escort down to Sir. William, where expected to arrive a few days after the 3d Instant. ——— We trust this good beginning will be followed by some other successes, and sufficiently prove the importance they are in Indian war, as well as the judgement of the present General who made use of their services.

We are further assured from above, that another party of Indians in out interest, said to be about 400 are preparing to go out against our tawny colour'd enemy tribes, as soon as the weather is somewhat more mild; the whole set in motion by the indefatigable care and industry of Sir William Johnson.

Extract of a Letter from Fort Pitt Feb. 22.

"The Indians have opened the campaign: On Wednesday the 22d inst. a corporal, four men and two waggons, were sent to the hill (the Highlanders encamped on) for wood: whilst they had laid down their arms, and were loading the carriage, a party of Indians attacked them (they saw six) first sending a shower of arrows, and then firing their rifles; they killed one Highlander on the spot, took the whole skin of his head, ripped him open, and took out his heart: Another Highlander was wounded in the breast with an arrow; he was the only man that got to his arms and fired at the Indians, which having done, they immediately run up upon him, and he was obliged to throw himself over the precipice towards the Monongahela, and made his escape with the rest but bruised. The Corporal had several balls thro' his coat. That morning four men came from hunting; they lost one Royal american in the woods, and doubtless the Savages have got him. Its likely several straggling people on the road will fall into their hands."

Other letters mention that the panic occasioned by the above account was very great.

The General Assembly of the colony of Connecticut have voted to raise 265 men for his Majesty's service, to be employed against the Indian Enemy in conjunction with the Troops raised by the Southern Governments.

CHARLESTOWN S. Carolina March 14. By the last authentic accounts from New-York we learn, that the Indians near Detroit continued to sollicit for peace, and that the Senekas had sent deputies to Sir William Johnson on the same errand; but the Delawares and Shawanese still stood out, and had not made any overture of peace: several of the northern tribes of Indians had made offer of their service and assistance to Sir Willian, and it was hoped, by the plan then concerting, the war would soon be finished, even though the Indians who have sued for peace should change their resolutions.

PHILADELPHIA March 15. In a letter from Bethlehem Northampton county, of the 3d of March, it is said, that on Sunday before, as one John Russell was hunting near Fort Penn, he was fired upon by three Indians; upon which he took to a tree where he bravely stood three fires from each of them return'd as many, and oblig'd the Savages to make the best of their way off. One shot went thro' his hat, another thro' the sleeve of his coat, and a third wounded him slightly in the calf of his leg. [Russell is brother to two lads, one which was lately found roasted in a barn, the other either murdered or carried off by the enemy.]

We hear from Carlisle, that on the 5th instant there was a report there of some persons being lately killed at Aughwick by the Indians.

SAVANNAH March 15. From New-York we learn,

that the night of the 15th January last, a body of men entered the new jail in that city, and, on the keeper's refusing to deliver the keys when demanded, wounded him with bayonets; they afterwards forced open the doors, and let out most of the prisoners, their principal intention, which they effected, was to release Major Rogers, who had come to town a few days before, and was arrested and confined there. On the Occasion part of the militia were collected, who took six of the rioters. A serjeant of the highlanders was killed and several people wounded. On the 25th the six rioters were tried at the general court in that city, and five of them were found guilty; they declared the Major was privy to the design.

BOSTON March 19. No doubt many of our readers having for some Time been curious to know the cause of the late Riot and tragical Violence committed in the Province of Pennsylvania especially in Lancaster County, by so large a Number of the Inhabitants: who must have been highly agitated by some general Cause of Discontent or Resentment, which we could not Discover till last Week, when a Declaration and Remonstrace relating to the Affair was published in Philadelphia, of which we shall give our readers a full account, as the Compass of our paper will admit.

The Declaration is in Substance as follows,

That as the killing those Indians at Conestogo and Lancaster, has been, and may be the subject of much Conversation; and by being invidiously represented by designing Men, may incur the severest Censures of others, who are unacquainted with the true State of Affairs; ——— And, as they suppose, that if all Matters were duly understood and deliberated, their Action would appear in a more favourable Light; They therefore make an open tho' brief Declaration of the reasons of their conduct which they confess, could only be justified by necessity, as they appear to fly in the face of authority, and were attended with much Labour, Fatigue and Expence to themselves.

The profess themselves, to a Man, all loyal

Subjects to his Majesty George the Third, firmly attached to his Person, Interest and Government ——— and equally opposite to his Enemies, whether openly avow'd, or concealed under a mask of Friendship, and cheerfully willing to offer their Subsistence and lives in his cause.

They complain, It was those Indians, some of whom were proved to be murderers firmly connected in Friendship with our avow'd and bitter enemies, who by their better acquaintance with the situation and State of the Frontiers, were more capable of doing Mischief, they saw with Indignation, were cherished and caressed as dearest Friends. That the excessive Regard shewn to the Indians, together with other Grievances, had enflamed them with Resentment, and displeased the greatest Part of the People in the Province. The exorbitant Presents made to Indians in former Treaties, and the Severity therein paid them, have long been oppressive Grievances under which they have groaned. That at the late Treaty at Lancaster, with the Indians, the Murders and Ravages they have committed, were timely passed over, the unhappy Captives they had made were abandon'd to Slavery, and a Friendship was concluded with them, allowing them a full and plenteous Trade, altho' a spirited Requisition was made of the Prisoners, &c. But, That notwithstanding these Matters of general complaint, and infatuated Measures, manifestly and mainly partial to the Indians, these Complaints would timely have borne their Grievances, without having Recourse to their late extraordinary Expedient, dictated by Distress, Resentment and Dispair, had it not been for still later and more provoking Causes of the Uneasiness: But that last Summer, when Colonel Bouquet marched thro' the Province, and a Demand was made by General Amherst, of assistance to escort provisions and relieve that important Post, Fort Pitt, on the support of which, and the almost dispaired of Success of our little Army, the standing of the Frontier Inhabitants entirely depended;

Yet that not one Man was granted; but that when a Number of Indians, falsely pretended

Friends, having among them, some proved on Oath to have been guilty of Murder since the War began, together with others known to be enemies, who had been in Battle against Col. Bouquet, and been reduced to distress by distructruction of their Corn at the great Island, and up the East Branch of the Susquehanna, pretended themselves Friends and desired Subsistence, they were openly caressed; and the Publick that could not be indulged the Liberty of contributing to his Majesty's Assistance, obliged, as tributaries to Savages, to support those Villains, those Enemies to our King and country. —— That the Hands which were close shut and refused his Majesty's General a single Farthing against a Savage Foe, were liberally open'd, and the publick Money lavishing prostituted, to Shehaes at an exorbitant Rate, a mercenary Guard to protect his Majesty's worst of Enemies, tho' pretended Friend: while at the same Time, Hundreds of poor distressed Subjects, obliged to abandon their Possessions, and flee for their Lives, (except a small relief at first) in the most distressed Circumstances, were left to share neglected, save what Friendly Hands of private Donations contributed for their Support; wherein those who were the most profuse to Savages, carefully avoided hearing any Part. That last Summer, when the Troops raised for the Defence of the Province, were limited to certain bounds, and not permitted to annoy the Indians in their Habitations; and a Number of Volunteers, at their own Expence, marched to Susquehanna, defeated the Enemy, with the Loss of some of their own number, and several dangerously wounded, the Legislature took not the least Care of the wounded, nor gave them any assistance or Thanks; but that when a Seneca Indian, who had through last War, been an inveterate Enemy, received a cut on the Head in a private Quarrel with his own Cousin; a Doctor was immediately sent from Philadelphia to cure him if possible. That no Premium has been given for Indian Scalps, or any engagement to Volunteers to go against them; yet, when a few Indians, some of whom were known to be fast friends of our Enemies, and Murderers themselves, were struck, by distrest, berest, injured Frontier, a liberal Reward was offered, for apprehending the Perpetrators of the horrible Crime of killing his Majesty's cloaked Enemies, and their conduct painted in the most atrocious Colours; while the horrid Revangers, cruel Murderers, and most shocking Barbarities committed by the Indians, are covered and excused, under the charitable Term, of this being their Method of making War.

But it would tire Patience of Job to recount (say they) the Grievances they sustained from a violent Partiality in the Leaders of a Faction, who for a long Time have found means to enslave the Province to Indians, whose Insolence and Villainy they have encouraged, so that they the Indians of the great Island, and Wyaloosing declared to Conrad Weiser, that these Leaders of the Faction had given them a Rod to scourge the White People, who were settled on the purchased lands: for that Onas has cheated them out of a great deal of Land, in not giving them a sufficient Price; and that the Traders ought also to be scourged for selling them Goods at too high a Price. ——— The Complainants further declare. That in such an unhappy Situation ——— under the Villainy, Infatuation and Influence of a certain Faction who have got the political reins in the hands, and tyranize over the other good Subjects of the Province, to have, in Addition to their former Distresses, the disagreeable Burden of supporting in the Heart of the Province between 2 and 300 Savages, to the great Disquietude of the Majority of the Inhabitants, cannot but awaken the Resentment of a People greatly abused, unrighteously burden'd and made Dupes and Slaves to Indians; And that they hope all well disposed People will entertain, charitable Sentiments of them, who at their own Expence and Trouble attempt to rescue a Labouring Land from a Weight so oppressive, unreasonable and unjust: That this is the Design, which they resolve to prosecute, through which Reluctance, they are compelled to disagreeable Measures, which nothing but their Extremity could Justify.

[The Substance of the Remonstrace we are

oblig'd to postpone 'till the next.]

SAVANNAH March 22. A letter from Mobille, dated the 20th of Frebruary last, mentions the arrival there of the pack-horsemen, 15 in number, who lately fled the Creek nation.

BOSTON March 26. The substance of the Remonstrance, relating to the killing of the Indians in Pennsylvania Government, which we are oblig'd to omit in our last, is as follows. viz.

1. That they think themselves, as Englishmen entitled to Equal Share in the Privileges of Legislation; but that they are unequally represented their 5 Counties of Lancaster, York, Cumberland, Berks and Northampton, having only 10 Members to represent them in Assembly; while the three Counties (and City) of Philadelphia, Chester & Bucks have 26. This they apprehend to be the Cause of many Grievances, and pray that they may have a Number to represent them equal to other Counties.

2. That they understand a Bill is now before the House of Assembly and has actually received the Assent of a Majority of the House wherein it is provided, that Persons charged with killing any Indian in Lancaster County, shall not be tried in the County where the fact is committed, but in Philadelphia, Chester or Bucks. That this would be to deprive British Subjects of their essential Rights of being tried by their equals, of the Neighbourhood where they the Accusers, and Witnesses, were known; and putting their Lives in the Hands of Strangers, who may more justly be suspected of Partiality against them than their Neighbours in their Favour. That it would be casting an eternal Reproach upon the whole Counties, as unfit to serve their counties as Jurymen. And besides, that the well known design of such a law (which never would have passed if the Counties had been properly represented) is to comprehend a Fact committed, before it was thought of —— But they hope the Assembly will not pass an Act of such dangerous Tendency, and so inconsistent with the British Constitution.

3. That Indians now maintain'd and protected by the Government, are Part of the Tribes of our

declared Enemies, in Friendships and Alliance with them, were privy to their Designs and barbarous Cruelties, without giving us any Assistance or Warning, were several of them actually Perpetrators of the Murders and Ravages, and all the Rest of them justly suspected as Principals or Accomplices. That the screening such from the just Resentment of the injured, and the supporting them at publick Expence, while the poor Frontier Inhabitants, ruined by the Savages, are exposed and distressed without Protection or Assistance, fills these Remonstrants with Rage and Tempts them to Action that nothing but the most violent Necessity can vindicate: And therefore, they humbly and earnestly pray that these Enemies of his Majesty may be removed as soon as possible out of the Province.

4. That as Experience has shewn that the Indians are all perfidious it is extremely dangerous and impolitick to suffer any of them to live within the inhabited parts of the Province; Their Claim to Freedom and Independence putting it in their power to act as Spies, to give Intelligence to our Enemies and furnish them with Provisions and warlike Stores. To this fatal Intercourse may be described most of the Ravages and Murders committed during the last Indian War. They therefore pray, this Grievance may be consider'd and remov'd.

5. They lament that no Provisions have been made for the Frontier Inhabitants, who have been wounded in Defence of the Province ⸺ and pray that they may be taken Care of, and cured at publick Expence.

6. They pray that publick Reward may be given for Indian Scalps, in Proportion to the Danger of the Enterprize.

They lament that Numbers of their nearest and dearest Relatives are still in Captivity among the Savage Heathen, to be train'd up in the Ignorance and Barbarity, or to be tortured to Death with all the Contrivances of the Indian Cruelty if they attempt to escape. That as Indians pay no Regard to the most solemn Promises of their Restoration; therefore these Remonstrants Earnestly pray, that no Trade may hereafter be permitted with them, till the Captives are restored.

8. They complain that a certain Society of the People in this Province, in the last War, and at several Treaties, held by the King's Representatives, openly loaded the Indians with presents, and that ———— a Leader of the said Society in Defiance of all the Government, not only abetted our Indian Enemies, but kept up a private Intelligence with them, and publickly received from them a Belt of Wampum, as if he had been a Governor, or authorized by the King to treat with the Enemies. That by these Means the Indians have been thought to despise us, as a weak disunited People. &c. They therefore pray, that no private Subject may hereafter be permitted to treat with, or carry on a Correspondence with our Enemies.

9. They observe, that Fort Augusta, tho' Expensive to the Province, gave little Assistance to our People, or Molestation to the Indians, owing, the suppose Orders given to the commanding Officer. ———— They pray that Measures may be taken to make this Garrison serviceable. ————

A Number of Frontier Inhabitants having by their Deputies presented to the Governor the foregoing Papers, which seem particularly to reflect upon, and be levelled against the People called Quakers. They made application to the Governor, for copies of the said Papers, which they obtained and then drew up an presented to him an Address ———— wherein they vindicated and exculpate themselves from all the reflections Insinuations against them contain'd in the said papers, which they say were evidently intended to render them odious to their Superiors, and to keep up a tumultuous Spirit among the inconsiderate part of the people.

They observe that their Society has been well known throughout the British Dominion, for about 100 years, and was never concern'd in the promoting or countenancing any Plots or Insurrections against the Government, but always manifested a quiet contrary Spirit and Principle, as true Disciples of Christ, and faithful Subjects to his Majesty, who sensible of this, controlled them with many valuable Rights

and Privileges; particularly, that from the
first settling of the Colony till within a few
years past, both the framing and Execution of
the Laws were chiefly committed to Men of this
religious Principles, under who Tranquility and
Peace were preserved among the Inhabitants, and
with the Natives, the Land rejoiced, and every
Man was protected in his Person and Property,
——— but of late, Circumstances are quite
changed, intestine Animosities of War, have taken place of Tranquility and Peace.

That as a Religious Society they very carefully avoid admitting Matters immediately relating
to civil Government into their Deliberations,
any further then to exite each other to demean
themselves at dutiful Subjects to the King, with
due respect to those in authority under him, and
to live agreeably to their Profession in the
Practice of Piety and Virtue, for which Ends
their Meetings were instituted: But that as menbers of Civil Society, Services sometimes occur
which they do not judge expedient to become the
Subject of Consideration in their religious
Meetings, and of Nature in the Association
formed by a Number of Persons of their Profession, of which they think it incumbent upon them
to give some Accounts, as their Conduct is misrepresented in order to reproach and calumniate
them as a religious Society, by the Insinuation
and Slander in the Papers sent to the Governor
&c.

That in the Spring of 1756. The Province being greatly distressed, and an Indian War Apprehended, at the Instant of Conrad Weiser the
Provincial interpreter, and with the approbation
of Governor Norris, some of them attempted to
promote a Reconciliation with the Indians, and
were blessed with Success; the happy Effects
whereof soon appear'd. And that in order to assist the distressed Frontier Inhabitants, they
contributed large sums and exerted their Influence, so that about 5000 pounds was collected
in Presents given at the publick Treaties (always with the Governor's Permission) to promote,
regain and confirm the Peace with the Indians,
and procure the Relief for some of their captive

Countrymen whereby many have been restored to their Friends. That these Measured were made know to the King's Generals, and received their Countenance and Approbation. ———— That the repost of the Indian's Speech to Conrad Weiser, is maliciously and falsely represented, the whole being an idle Tale of second or third Hand, wherein no Person was named.

That the invidious Reflection against a Sect. "That had got the political Reins in their hands &c." tho' evidently level'd against them, yet manifested the authors to be egregiously ignorant of their Conduct of willfully bent on misrepresenting them. For that they have, as a religious Body, both publickly and privately labour'd with, and earnestly desired that their Brethren, who have been elected or appointed to Publick Offices in Government, for some years past, to decline a Task now because so arduous; and that may have voluntarily resign'd their seats in the House of Assembly, and others, by publick Advertisement declining the Service, and requested their Countrymen to choose others in their Places; and that many have refused to accept of Places in the executive Part of the Government. That the Charge, of being profuse to Savages, and of contributing nothing to the distressed Families on the Frontiers, is equally invidious or mistaken, for that they were very early and expeditiously promoted a Subscription and sent them a seasonable Relief of Provisions and Cloathing. ———— That many among them also Contributed by the late tumults. That they ever Sympathized with their afflicted Brethren, and endeavoured to relieve them in their Distress ———— to which End all the Money applied to the Pacification of the Indians has been intended, tho' injuriously misrepresented.

That the malicious Charge of "abetting and keeping a private Intelligence with the Indian Enemies" is entirely false and groundless, a Practice they abhor and disclaim ———— and that the Transaction of a String (called a Belt) of Wampum, was a matter of a publick Nature, which General Forbes and the Governor knew of and Approved. Upon the whole they assert their Innocence of all the Charges and Insinuations against them, contain'd in said Papers, or propagated by Reports; and that they live in the Fear of God, dutiful Submission to the King, are, and have been real Friends to the Government, and steadily desirous of acting agreeable to their Station, as Members of civil Society.

BOSTON March 26. Extract of a Letter from Detroit, December, 3, 1763.

"We have been lately very busy in providing abundance of Wheat, Flour, Indian Corn & Pease from the Country: in which we have so far succeeded, as not to be in danger of being starved out. The approach of Maj. Wilkin's party, had a very good effect, the Enemy moved farther off; 'tis said Pondiac and his Tribe are gone to Missisippi, but we don't believe it; the French have been wonderfully civil this last fortnight, being ignorant of the return of the Troops; in which Maj. Gladwin does not think proper to undeceive them, lest they should bring the Indians upon us, who might harrass us much in our present employ, that of bringing in Wood for the Garrison, as we are obliged to fetch it a great distance. ——— The Wiandots of Sandusky, are much animated against us, they have been reinforced lately, by many Villains from all the Nations concerned in the War, and they are the only Indians that way, that abound in Ammunition and Corn; which they often sell to other Nations that stand in need of it: The Ottawa's, 'tis thought will entirely depend upon them, for this latter article next year."

NEW-YORK March 26. Yesterday Afternoon came to Town under a proper Guard, 14 of the Indians taken by the Party sent out by Sir William Johnson, and lately mentioned ——— They were properly taken Care of by being lodged, and closely confined in separate Apartments in our new Goal with Irons (instead of Leather) Mocasins at Heels: ——— at which they gave a very sneering and insulting call of the Feature ——— The most famous Capt. Bull (Tidyessang's Son) is among the Tribe of Yellow Boys. He has confess'd the killing and scalping abundance of our Black Inhabitants, ———

―――― Quere then, if the Fellow ought not visit the Fresk Water, together with his Brother, ―――― Or Quere 2d. ―――― Whether our Charity, they should not be sent to the Paxton Boys to have their Business done at once? As thereby we shall avoid maintaining such beings, in the manner the Art and Cunning of the Pennsylvanians attempted (some few Weeks ago) to palm on the New-Yorkers.

NEW-YORK March 29, By a Gentleman from Carlisle we learn, that on the 20th inst. at the House of Adam Sims, at Sisney's Gay, about 10 miles from Shippensburg, 5 persons were made prisoners by a party of Indians, one man made his escape on horseback, and got to Shippensburg, where he alarmed the town; immediately 100 Men with Capt. Brady and Piper went to the place where the prisoners were taken, and kept centry that night; but on relieving the Centries, he was fired on and wounded through the body, but not mortally. A party of about 30 went in pursuit of the Indians that had carried off the Prisoners. The same night and next day 7 houses, with a great quantity of grain, which the inhabitants had got ready to carry off on the first alarm, was destroyed by the savages.

PHILADELPHIA March 29. Extract of a Letter from Carlisle, March 23.

"The Indians opened this Summers Campaign the 19th Instant, when they took five young People within nine Miles of Shippensburg, and shot one Man through the Body. There were eleven Indians seen, but their numbers are still not known. About 100 Men are gone out in pursuit of the Enemy. The people are now flying from the frontiers in a most deplorable Condition."

Extract of a Letter from New-York March 19.

"By the Albany Post we received a Copy of the following Paragraph of a Letter from Sir William Johnson, dated the 11th Inst. 'This Moment I received an Account by Express from Augusta of another Party of mine taking three of the Enemy Prisoners, and one Scalp; a Fifth made his Escape; they were going to War."

APRIL 1764

CHARLESTOWN S. Carolina April 4. Letters from Fort Prince-George, Lower Cherokees, say that Salloue, or the Young Warrior of Estatoe, has given information that there were then in the town of Toogaloo a Coweta and Oaksuskee warrior, with sixteen other Creek Indians, one of whom said, "That when he left the Creek nation, the warriors and head-men were assembling in order to concert the proper measures to fall on the English. That the seven Creeks who murdered the people at Long-Canes were in the nation, where they were protected, some of their principals giving out that it should cost the English many sevens before they should have them. ———— That they much blame those seven for the beginning before their project was ready to take place, as they are now obliged to go in large bodies to attack the settlements, the inhabitants being alarmed and on their guard." Salloue was much incensed against the Creeks for their insolent behaviour, he thirst to have revenge for his countrymen who they have killed and is impatient to learn after what manner the English resent the late murders. He says that several Cherokees from Old Chote are going home with the Creeks, he believes to join them, and that he suspects some of his town also, as they caress the Creeks and will not quit the town, which he is about to do immediately, with several others who are removing their corn, &c. to Estatoe on Keowee river.

This intelligence concerning the Creeks seems to give with what was received some time ago from Mobille, viz. "That the most intelligent men, conversant in Indian affairs, had informed the commanding officer that the Indians intended mischief against the province of Georgia." of which notice was given to both governments.

CHARLESTOWN S. Carolina April 4. We hear a proposal has been made by this government, that the Creek trade might be stopped from the four Southern colonies, which has not been concurred in.

We are told application has been made to Capt. Prevost, commanding officer of the three companies of the Royal American regiment, now in the province, to station all the soldiers that can be spared from garrison duty, upon that part of the frontiers most likely to be attacked.

PHILADELPHIA April 5. Since our last we received what follows from Carlisle, viz. "The Distresses of the back Inhabitants are greater than can well be conceived. Two Hundred Miles of an extended Frontier are so exposed to the Incursion of Indians, that no Man can go to sleep within 10 or 15 Miles of the borders, without being in Danger of having his House burnt, and himself and Family scalped, or lead into Captivity, before the next Morning. No Man can tell where the indians will strike the next blow, when they have begun their Murders and Devastations. On the 20th of last Month Agnes Davidson, and her Child of one Year old: Andrew Sims, 14 Years old; Magaret Stephens, 12 Years old, and Joseph Mitchel, 3 Years old were made Prisoners. Seven houses were burnt down on the 21st, and a great Number of Horses, Cows, sheep and Hogs were killed. On the 22d a barn was burnt in the Path Valley, a Horse was killed, and two taken away: About twelve Indians carried off the Captives, and seven or eight tarried, and did considerable Damage. The Capts. Piper and Brady with their Companies did all that lay in their Power to protect the Inhabitants; and Lieut. Charober, and Ensign Asky pursued the Indians, to rescue the Prisoners, but without Success. Some Indians are suspected to be still Skulking about Shippensburg, which seems the more probable, Samuel Rippy's Barn in the Town, was set on Fire, and believed to be done by these Enemies. These fresh Troubles greatly discourage the poor People who intend to return early in the Spring to their deserted Habitations."

The following Paragraph of a Letter from a Gentleman in Carlisle to his Friend in this City may serve to give us some Idea of their Distress, which bears Date March 26, 1764.

"Many of the Inhabitants of the Path and of Shearman's Valley, were proposing to adventure home, but the Affair has quite discouraged their Measures, and the People along the North Mountain are moving further in, especially about Shippensburgh, which is crowded with the Families of the Neighbourhood. Our Country has the Appearance of nothing but Confusion and Distress, which I fear will increase. What shall so many Families do, who have spent the Winter with us, chiefly supported by the Contributions of Philadelphia in hopes of returning to their Settlements in the Spring? Many of them have been forced to sell what few Cattle they saved, to support their Families; and others who, in the Fall, would not apply for a Share, in the public Contributions, are obliged by want to apply now, when our Funds are almost spent. The above seven Families got nothing saved but their wearing Cloaths, so sudden was the Alarm: one poor Woman delivered of a Child, was obliged to remove in about two Hours Time after. Sir, I have but a melancholy Time of it, amidst such Calamity and Woes; I pray God may the Mercy shorten these Days of Misery."

We likewise hear, that on the 26th ult. one Man was killed and scalped, and another carried off from near Fort Bedford: And that the last Messenger that went from Carlisle to Bedford, was pursued by the Enemy for many Miles; but being a good Woodsman got safe in with the Dispatches.

ANNAPOLIS Maryland April 5. We are informed by Mr. Michael Cresap, from Frederick County, that on Monday the 26th of March George Dobson was shot and scalp'd in signt of Fort Bedford, and three other Men are missing, and suppos'd to be kill'd or taken. An Express going from the General, was pursued by Indians on Horseback, who fir'd at him twice, and had almost overtaken him, but he quitted his horse and Gun, & got safe to the Fort, being favour's with the

Night.

SAVANNAH April 5. By the last accounts from Augusta we learn, that the Handsome Fellow and some other headmen of the Creeks were there; that the pack-horsemen who lately fled to Pensacola were returned to the nation; and that the Indians were very quiet.

WILLIAMSBURG April 6. We learn that a party of Indians lately attacked the plantation of an old man on the frontiers of this colony, who at the time at Stauton in Augusta county: They robbed the house of 1500 pounds, in specie, and tore in pieces a considerable quantity of paper currency, carried away his son and 4 negroes, and tomahawked and scalped his wife, who still survived.

BOSTON April 9. It is rumoured, that General Monckton will, at the earnest request of the Colonies be appointed Commander in Chief in North-America.

NEW-YORK April 9. We can acquaint our Readers, from undeniable Authority with some more particulars respecting the Indian War.

Capt. Bull, with his Party of 13 Men were escorted from German Flats, by a guard of Provincials, Bull's Second remains wounded at Aughquage, under the Care of the Indians there, to whom Sir William Johnson has given Five Prisoners, on account of their good Behavior: He has also distributed the rest amongst the Friendly Nations; putting them in the Places of their deceased Relations; which is an Indian Custom they always expect will be followed.

Capt. Bull, with his Party, resided at Kanestie: the Indians of which Village have been all along in Arms. He made large offers of delivering up many English Prisoners on his being set at Liberty.

Sir William Johnson, since the prisoners were bro't to him, have received advice of the success of a Party of 10 Friend Indians, falling in with a Party of 9 Delawares last Month, on the Frontiers of Pennsylvania, directing their Course against some Settlements, and Singing their War Songs; upon which the Friend Indians attacked them, killed the Head of the Party and took three Prisoners, who (with the Scalps) were hourly expected at Sir Williams. This is a lucky Circumstance, the Indians being once engaged in Blood, must carry on the War with a greater Alacrity, as the rest will never forgive them, nor will they probably stop till they have destroy'd these troublesome People who have annoy'd all the Northern Frontiers both last War, and since. Our Enemies are said to be greatly alarmed; and many of them have retired thro' fear beyond the Sioto River, near the lower Shawanese Town. Several Parties are prepared to follow them, as well as to go against the Rest; one of which Parties is to headed by John Johnson, Esq; Sir William's Son.

There were on the 23d ult. at Sir William's above 400 Indians, and some Deputies sent from the Chenussio and other Seneca Castles, to make offer of Peace, as they apprehended the danger from the several Bodies of Friend Indians now upon Service. ——— The Friend Senecas of Kandesago, have delivered up, to Sir William, one Edward Kennedy, of Lieut, Gamble's Platoon, who was taken by the Outawas. After rambling in the Woods, for some Time, he fell in with the above mentioned Indian Town.

ANNAPOLIS Maryland April 12. We have lately received a melancholy account from the westward, of people being killed and taken by the indians, ——— On Saturday last three men were killed near the warm Spring in Virginia, with Indian arrows and afterward scalped. Fourteen Families have left their settlements in a few days.

PROVIDENCE April 14. Extract of a Letter from Charlestown in South Carolina, dated March 20.

"The Creek Indians having suspended Hostilities, many People flatter themselves, that the Measures taken in that Affair have had the desired Effect, and that those Indians begin to be sensible of their Folly in quarrelling with their best Friends."

Extract of a Letter from a Gentleman at Montreal, to another in this Town, dated March 14.

"The Indian War has occasioned almost a total Stagnation of Business in this Quarter and Cash is much scarce here than in the Maritime Provinces.

"We are going to raise a Regiment of Canadians, to be commanded by our own Officers to be sent against the Indians, which must take off all hope of Assistance or Dependence on the French."

BOSTON April 16. An Account of the wonderful fortitude of an Onneyouth Captain, burnt by the Hurons; which is expressive of the savage and brutal behaviour of the Indians who are now destroying some of the frontier Settlements in North-America.

The Hurons who had taken this Captain prisoner and brought him to one of the Villages, made him get upon a sort of stage, where they began to burn him all over his body without any mercy, and he appeared at first as unconcerned as if he had felt nothing; but as he thought one of his companions that was tormented near him showed some marks of weakness, he discovered on this account a great weariness, and omitted nothing that might encourage him to suffer with patience, by the hope of happiness they were going to enjoy in heaven, he had the comfort to see him die like a brave man.

The all those who had part of the other death fell again upon him with so much fury that one would have thought they were going to tear him in pieces. He did not appear to be at all moved at it, and they knew not any longer in what part they could make him feel pain; when one of his tormentors cut the skin of his head all around, and pulled it off with a great violence; the pain made him drop down senseless; they thought him dead and all the people sent away. A little time after, he recovered from his swoon; and seeing no person near him but the dead body of his companion, he takes a fire brand in both his hands, though they were all overstead and burnt, recalls his tormentors, and defies them to approach him. They were affrighted at his resolution; they yell forth horrid cries, and armed themselves some with burning fire-brands, others with red hot irons, fell upon him altogether. He received them bravely, and made them retreat. The fire with which he was surrounded served him for an entrenchment, and he made another with the ladders they had used to get upon the scaffold; and being thus fortified in his own funeral pile, and armed with the instruments of his punishment, he was for some time the terror of the whole Village, no body daring to approach a man more than half burnt, and whole blood showed from all parts of his body.

A false step which he made, in striving to shun a fire-brand that was thrown at him, left him once more in the mercy of his tormentors; and it need not be told they made him pay dear for the fright he had just before put them in. After they were tired of tormenting him, they threw him in the midst of a great fire, and left him there, thinking it impossible for him ever to rise again. They were deceived; when they least thought of it, they saw him ahead with a fire-brand, run towards the village as if he would set it on fire. All the people was struck with terror, and no person had the courage to stop him; but as he came near the first cabin, a stick that was thrown between his legs threw him down, and they fell upon him before he could rise. They directly cut off his hands and feet, then rolled him upon some burning coals; and lastly, they threw him under the trunk of a tree that was burning. Then all the Village came round him, to enjoy the pleasure of seeing him burn. The blood which flowed from him almost extinguished the fire, and they were no longer afraid of his efforts; but yet he made one more, which astonished the boldness: he crawled out upon his elbows and knees, with a threatning look, and a stoutness which drove away the nearest, more indeed from astonishment than fear: for what harm could he do then in this maimed condition? Some time after a Huron took him at an advantage and cut off his head.

NEW-YORK April 16. Our last advices received from above, are dated the 6th Instant, are authentic, viz.

That John Johnson, Esq; Sir William's Son, Has set off with 200 Indians and Whites to destroy the Towns on the West Branch of the Susquehannah, &c. as many of the Delawares who have not retired further South are collecting themselves to have one Tryal for their Country, which the whole Body of that Nation must abandon if repulsed. There are 200 more in the same Service, under Capt. Mentieur and two other Officers: so that when Capt. Johnson joins them, we may expect to hear that the Enemy have received their Defeat.

NEW-YORK April 19. Extract of a Letter from Philadelphia April 12, 1764.

"I have just heard from Northampton County, that one David Owens, deserted from the Regulars some time since and went among the Indians is returned with 5 Scalps having killed 7 out of a Party of nine that he was with; the other two made their escape; he brought in also a white Boy that was their prisoner, ——— He reports that 900 Indians were assembled, and waiting for others to join them in an invasion of this Province.

PHILADELPHIA April 19. Extract of a Letter from Johnson-Hall, April 6, 1764.

"I have now upon service 400 friendly Indians, who will be able to free your province from the incursions of the Delawares, &c. The Senecas have been so greatly alarmed, at the bodies of Indians sent out, That they have begged for peace, and agreed to every concession required of them, tho't this news might not be disagreeable to you."

Extract of a Letter from New-York, April 16.

"Sir William Johnson has concluded a Peace with the Chenosses. They are to deliver up the Murderers of one Hewlick, and two other Indian traders, and for this have left there hostages with Sir William. They are to deliver up all the Prisoners they have, Deserters and Negroes, amongst them. They have ceded to his Majesty the Carrying-Place at Niagara, and some other Posts; have taken up the Hatchet against his Majesty's Enemies; are to send a number of their Warriors to act against the Shawanese and Delawares; and called in their People that are amongst them. ——— Sir William has several Parties out, about 400; one party of 200 commanded by his Son; he expects very good accounts from the Parties, and hopes to bring about a general Peace with the Indians."

Priliminary articles of peace having been concluded and signed by Sir William Johnson Bart. and the Deputies from the Seneca nations; which are as follows.

Preliminary Articles of Peace, and Friendship, and Alliance, entered into between the English and the Deputies sent from the whole Seneca nation, by Sir William Johnson, Bart his Majesty's sole Agent and Superintendent of Indian Affairs, for the northern part of North America, and colonel of the Six United Nations, their Allies and Dependents, &c.

Article 1. That the Seneca nation do immediately stop hostilities and solemnly engage never more to make war upon the English, or suffer any of their people to commit any acts of violence on the persons or properties of any of his Britannic Majesty's subjects.

The Sachens and Chiefs of the Senecas agree fully to this article.

Art. II. That they forthwith collect all the English prisoners, deserters, Frenchmen, and Negroes, amongst them, and deliver them up to Sir William Johnson (together with Indians of Kanestio, who murdered the Traders in Nov. 1762) previous to the Treaty of Peace, which will take place within three months, if they are agreed to; and that they engage never to harbour or conceal any deserters, Frenchmen, or Negroes, from this time; but should any such take refuge amongst them, they are to be brought to the Commanding Officer of the next garrison, and delivered up; promising likewise never to obstruct any search made after such persons, or to hinder their being apprehended in any part of their Country.

Agreed to: and they will assist in apprehending any such in their towns.

Art. III. That they cede to his Majesty, and his successors for ever, in full right, the lands from the fort of Niagara, extending easterly along Lake Ontario, about four miles, comprehending the Petit Marais, or Landing-Place, and running from thence southerly, about 14 miles, to the creek above Fort Schlosser, or Little Niagara, and down the same, to the River or

Strait; thence down the River or Strait, and across the same at the great Cataract; thence northerly to the banks of Lake Ontario, at a Creek or small lake, about two miles West of the fort; thence easterly along the banks of Lake Ontario, and across the River or Strait to Niagara, comprehending the whole Carrying-Place, with the lands on both sides of the Strait, and containing a tract of about 14 miles in length, and four miles in breath, And the Senacas do engage never to obstruct the passage of the Carrying-Place, or the free use of any part of the said tract; and will likewise give free liberty of cutting timber for the use of his Majesty, or that of other garrisons, in any other part of their country not comprehended therein.

Agreed to: provided the tract be always appropriated to his Majesty's sole use: and that at the Definitive Treaty, the lines be run in the presence of Sir William Johnson, and some of the Senecas, to prevent dispute hereafter.

Art. IV. That they allow a free passage through their country from that of the Cayugas to Niagara, or elsewhere, for the use of his Majesty's troops and subjects, for ever; engaging never to obstruct or molest any of his Majesty's troops or any of his subjects, who may make use of the same, or who may have occasion to pass through any part of their country by land or by water, from henceforward.

Agreed to: And moreover (if required) the Senecas will grant escorts of their people: but it is expected they will not be ill-treated by any of the English who may pass through their country.

Art. V. That they grant to his Majesty and his successors for ever, a free use of the Harbours for vessels or boats within their country on Lake Ontario, or in any other rivers, with the liberty to land stores, &c. and erect sheds for their securities.

Agreed to.

Art. VI. That they immediately stop all intercourse between any of their people and those of the Shawanese, Delawares, or other his Majesty's enemies, whom they are to treat as common enemies, and to assist his Majesty's arms in bringing them to proper punishment; solemnly engaging never to be privy to and or assist any of his Majesty's enemies, or those who may hereafter attempt to disturb the publick tranquility.

Agreed to.

Art. VII. That should any Indian commit murder, or rob any of his Majesty's subjects, he shall be immediately delivered up to be tried and punished according to the equitable laws of England: And should any White Man be guilty of the like crime towards the Indians, he shall be immediately tried, and punished, if guilty: And the Senecas are never for the future to procure themselves satisfactions, otherwise then as before mentioned, but to lay all matter of complaint before Sir William Johnson, or his Majesty's Superintendent of Indian Affairs for the time being, and strictly to maintain and abide by the covenant chain of friendship.

Agreed to.

Art. VIII. For the due performance of these Articles, the Senecas are to deliver up three of their Chiefs as Hostages, who are to be well treated, and restored to them, so soon as the same are fully performed on their part.

They agree to leave as Hostages Wannughsila, Seriboana, and Arajungas, three of the Chiefs.

Art. IX. In consequence of their perfect agreement to the foregoing Articles Sir William Johnson doth, by the virtue of the powers and authority reposed in him, in the name of his Britannick Majesty, promise and engage, that the said Indians shall have a full pardon for pass transgressions: That they shall be left in quiet and peaceful possession of all their rights not comprized in the foregoing Articles; and that on the duly performing the same and subscribing to the Definitive Treaty of Peace, to be held in consequence hereof, they shall be once more admitted into the covenant chain of friendship with the English; and be indulged with a free, fair, and open trade, so long as they abide by their engagements. [This Article the Senecas expect will be strictly regarded; and also that trade will be carried on in a fair and equitable manner.]

The following Articles, after being duly and fully explained to the Chiefs, and warriors, Deputies from the Senecas, they have signified their assent thereto, by affixing their marks of their tribes to these presents.

Given under my hand at Johnson-Hall.

    Signed   Signed
Tagaanadie Sayenqueraghta Wm. Johnson
Kaanijes   Wanughsisaue
Chonedagaw Tagannondie
Aughnawawis Taanjaqua

WILLIAMSBURG April 20. The Little Carpenter, the Raven, and several other Cherokees, who lately arrived here, set out homeward this week after receiving some presents. During their stay they had some conferences with the Governor and Council, and the intent of their journey we are told was to solicit a trade for Virginia, the path from their country being spoiled by the Creeks, who had killed several of their people; they say they are determined to go against them, and would be glad to be assisted by their brothers the English, several of whom have lately been murdered by the Creeks also.

NEW-YORK April 23. By an Express arrived here on Friday last from Albany, we have the following authenticated Account respecting the further Success of out Indian Detachment against the Enemy Indians, viz. That in the Evening of the 15th of April Instant, an Indian Express came with a Letter to Sir William Johnson, at Johnson-Hall, acquainted him, That Capt. Montour, after passing several Creeks and Rivers, which were very high and difficult at the Season, arrived with his Party, consisting of 140 Indians, with some Rangers, the beginning of the Month, at the Cayuga Branch of the Susquehannah River, which the Enemy had abandoned with the utmost Precipitation: ——— That they had destroyed two large Towns of well built Log-Houses, with Chimnies and a large Quantity of Indian Corn, and other Provisions; several new Saddles, Kettles, some Arms, Axes, &c. which they had probably taken from the Inhabitants. After this Montour proceeded to the large Town of kenestio, containing 60 good Houses, which he likewise burnt; and there, as well as the other Towns, killed a Number of Cattle, which could not be bro't off; and sent Patties in pursuit of the Enemy, who had fled to the Southward, whilst with the few remaining, he destroyed four other Villages of the Enemy, on the Branches of the Susquehannah, and of the Senecas will now join with the Five Nations (since they have entered into a Peace with Sir William, and made large Concessions, for the performance of which they have left several Hostages) there is great Reason to think, our Enemies will be overtaken, and justly chastised for their Defection.

BOSTON April 24. Extract of a Letter from a Gentleman in Georgia to his Friend here, dated March 20, 1764.

"The Congress lately held with the respective Governors of Virginia, North and South Carolina and this Province, and the several Tribes of Southern Indians, at Augusta at which our worthy Governor presided, appeared to terminate favourably. ——— A Treaty of Peace was solemnly entered into, and certain Boundaries were ascertained between the Creek Indians and this Province; by which we have obtain'd an Addition of a considerable Quantity of Land, that if a late unhappy Affair does not prevent, will soon be settled, and add greatly to our growing Prosperity and Security. ——— Since then, you will learn from the public Papers, that 14 white Persons, all Men and Children (except one Man) have been murdered at a place called Long Canes in South Carolina, which was perpetrated by seven renegade Creeks, who have for some Time harboured among the Cherokees. ——— by the best Information we can yet obtain from the Head Men of the Creeks, they absolutely disavow, and appear very much concerned, at the Villainy. ——— The Governor of Soth Carolina will no doubt demand Satisfaction of the Creeks, agreeable to an express Article in the late Treaty; and if they comply as some say they will, it will give stability to the late Treaty; but if not, we must probably be involv'd with them, as there will be no subsisting under such repeated and unprovok'd Insults. If the Creeks should refuse to do us Justice, it's said the Cherokees, the Chixsaws and the Chactaws, will assist us to obtain it: and the Foremer, I am told, have already declar'd they are ready whenever called upon. However, I hope they will be no Occasion for them, as a War with the Creeks, let the event be ever so favourable, must be attended with the worst Consequences to this young and defenceless Province; and I should be sorry we should be under a Necessity of putting any Confidence in Indian Allies, who under specious Pretence of Friendship may have the most treacherous designs in View. ——— There are near 40 Sail Vessels here and more are daily coming in from different Ports; and if we can attain a tolerable Degree of Security from the too frequent Insults of our Savage Neighbours, this Province must soon become very respectable, in short, it would surprize you to see the business carried on here; and there is so great a demand for all kinds of our Produce that I with the Vessels now in the Habour, and that that are expected, may get duly sypply'd and dispatched. ——— We are certainly informed, that the French have ceded New Orleans and all the Territory on the West Side of the Missisippie River to the Spaniards, which is a very favourable Event for these Southern Provinces, as the latter have no influence with the Indians, and are by no means that enterprizing People which the French are; and in short, we are under no kind of Apprehension of their disturbing our Settlements. ——— By this Cession the French have now no Possessions on any Part of the Continent of North-America.

PHILADELPHIA April 26. We hear that the Indians who have for some time past been under the protection of the King's Troops in the barracks of this City, are, by the particular advice of General Gage, to be detained some Time longer in the Province, as a measure, in the present circumstances of affairs, most conductive to the welfare of the Province, and his Majesty's interest.

SAVANNAH April 26. An Indian Tale, from the Idler.

As the English army was passing towards Quebec,

along a soft Savanna, between a mountain, and a lake, one of the petty chiefs of the island region stood upon a rock surrounded by his clan, and from behind the shelter of the bushes contemplated the Art and regularity of European war. It was evening; the tents were pitched. He observed the security with which the troops rested in the night, and the order with which the march was renewed in the morning. He continued to pursue them with his eyes till they could be seen no longer, and then stood for some time silent and passive.

Then turning to his followers. "My children (said he) I have often heard that there was a time when our ancestors were absolute lords of the woods the meadows, and the lakes, wherever the eye can reach or the foot can pass.

A New race of men entered our country from the great Ocean; they inclosed themselves in habitations of stone, which our ancestors could neither enter by violence, nor destroy by fire; they issued from those places, sometimes covered like armadillo with shells, from whence our lance rebounded on the striker, and sometimes carried by mighty beast, which had never been seen in our vales or forest of such strength and swiftness that flight and opposition were vain alike. Those invaders ranged over the continent slaughtering in their rage those that resisted, and those that submitted in their mirth. Of those that remained, some were buried in caverns, and condemned to dig metal for their masters; some were employed in tilling the ground, of which foreign tyrants devoured their produce; and when the sword and the mines have destroyed their natives, they supplied their place with human beings of another colour, brought from some distant country to perish here under toil and torture.

Some of these are who boast their humanity, that content themselves to sieze our chafes and fisheries, who drive us from every tract of ground where fertility and pleasantness invite them to settle, and make no war upon us except we intrude upon our land.

Others pretend to have purchased a right of

residence and tyranny; but surely the insolence of such, bagains is more offensive that allowed and open domination of force.

But the time perhaps is now approaching, when the pride of usurpation shall be crushed, and the cruelty of invasion shall be revenged. The sons or rapacity have now drawn upon each other and referred their claims to the decision of War; let us look unconcernedly upon the slaughter, and remember that the death of every European delivers the country from a Tyrant and a robber; for what is the claim of either nation, but the claim of the vulture to the leveret, and the Tyger to the fawn? Let them continue to dispute their title to regions which they cannot people, to purchase by danger and blood the empty dignity and domination over mountains which they will never climb, and rivers which they will never pass. Let us endeavour in the mean time, to learn their discipline, and forge their weapons; and then they shall be weakened with mutual slaughter, let us rush down upon them, force their remains to take shelter in their ships, and reign once more in our native country."

NEW-YORK April 30. On Tuesday Night last arrived here, an Express to his Excellency General Gage, with advices from Detroit, the particulars of which have not yet been communicated. ——— We learn from private Hands, that on the 25th of last Month, the Indians, posted near Detroit, had suddenly destroyed their Huts, removed their Women, Children and Effects, called their Warriours together, some say to the Number of 2000, and were marched off; that their Rout and Designs were unknown, some suppose they were gone to the carrying Place at Niagara, to cut off our Communication, others that they intended to besiege Detroit, which is well provided with all Necessities.

"It was never before known, that the United Nations were so unanimous, and hearty, in our cause. They have all, to a Man, taken up the Hatchet, against all his Majesty's Enemies, and are ready to use it, when ever called upon. We daily expect to hear favourable Accounts from Capt. Johnson, who has been gone some time against the Delaware and Shawanese Villains, Living near the Head of the Sources of the Ohio, who, by the last account were murdering pretty strong, and determined to make a Stand. The Chennessies [Upper Castle of the Senecas] have agreed to all the proposals made by Sir William to the New General; and, indeed to Sir William's surprise, have declared they would deliver up the two Kanestio Murderers mentioned in one of the former Gazettes: for the performance which, and many other interesting Articles, they have left with him, three of the Chief Men Hostages."

We hear that in June next Sir William will certainly go to Niagara, to conclude a firm Peace with the Senacas, and the Western Indians, which will effectually serve the Inhabitants of this and the Neighbouring Governments, in the quiet Possession of their Lives and properties. We hear also that Sir William intends shortly to reduce the Delawares and Shawanese effectually, but he has been for 22 Days closely engaged in the most fatiguing Service, of giving audience to 468 Indians in the 6 Nations.

SAVANNAH April 30. To be sold at the printing office.

A Few copies of the following Acts of the General Assembly of this Province, viz.

An Act to prevent the stealing of horses and meat cattle, and for the more effectual discovery and punishment of such persons as shall unlawfully brand, mark, or kill the same.

An Act fort the ascertaining the qualifications of jurors; and for establishing the method of balloting and summoning of jurors in the province of Georgia.

An Act to prevent the bringing into and the spreading of contagious distemper in this province, and to oblige vessels going out of any port within the same first to produce, for that purpose, a passport from the Governor or commander in Chief for the time being; and also to prevent the harbouring of such sailors and of others.

An Act for subjecting and making liable attachment the estate, real or personal of absent debtors, in the custody of power of any person or persons within this province.

An Act to oblige ships and other vessels coming from places infected with epidemical distempers to perfect quarantine,

An Act for the punishment of vagabonds and other idle and disorderly persons, and for erecting prisons, or places of security, in the several parishes of this province; and for preventing trespasses on lands of the crown, on lands reserved for the Indians, and for the most effectual suppressing and punishing bartering with the Indians in the woods.

MAY 1764

SAVANNAH May 2. From New-York we learn, that the expedition against the enemy Indians was going with spirit; the troops in number about 1600, consisting of the 17th regiment of Provincials and a number of Canadians, soon to set out under Col. Bradstreet; besides which, there was a numerous and formidable body of friendly Indians under the direction of Sir William Johnson, His Excellency General Gage, commander and Chief in America, had ordered all officers to join their respective corps immediately. The private men of the 55th regiment to be draughted into the 17th and 27th in order to complete them. The officers of the 55th go to Europe.

PHILADELPHIA May. 3 Extract of a letter from Stanton, in Augusta County, Virginia, March 30.

"The people of these parts are very much alarmed at some late icursions of the Indians in the western part of the country. On the 20th instant a number of them came to the house of one David Cloyd (a wealthy planter on some of the waters of James river) and killed one of his sons, tomahawk'd his wife, plundered his house, and took away above 700 Pounds in cash, besides sundry valuable effects. Mrs. Cloyd, notwithstanding she is a ancient woman, and was very much hacked and mangled, is recovered, and says the number of Indians was ten. Mr. Cloyd and one of his sons were then in this town. ——— it is remarkable that this house is a good way within the settlement, and yet the Enemy found means to convey themselves away undiscovered, ——— It is said several other families are missing.

P. S. Just as I finished writing this account, there came advice, that a party of white men pursued and came up with some of the Indians, killed some of them, and recovered 150 pounds of the cash, all the heavy baggage and four Negroes."

In another letter from the same place, dated the 16th April, it is said that a woman and 3 Children were carried off from the Calf Pasture 20 miles from Stanton, which is the nearest to that town of having any damage done this or last war.

By letters from Carlisle, we learn, that the troops which went to escort a quantity of provisions to Fort Pitt, were returned, without seeing any Indians. ─── That the garrison of that place were in good health and high spirits, being well provided with all necessaries, and not under any apprehensions from the Savages: But on the 21st ult. about 30 or 40 Indians were discovered in those parts, and seem'd directing their course towards Carlisle. ─── Upon the Information Col. Armstrong ordered out a strong party to range in the vallies, while other patties were employed in ranging along the foot of the mountains. ─── The distress and confusion this party occasioned on the frontiers at this season was very great, as they were putting in their spring crops.

NEW-YORK May 7. On Monday last the whole body of New-Jersey Provincials, raised for the present Expedition against the Indians, arrived here on board several Vessels, and the next day sailed for Albany.

Our last authenticated accounts from Albany, dated April 23d are. That two days before, Capt. Montour arrived with some of his party at Johnson-Hall, and brought the scalp, &c. taken some time since. The Indian scalped was a head warrior. ─── Capt. Montour brought with him likewise a lad taken last year at Wyoming (with six others) by the Delawares. And a Delaware who went to Johnson-Hall on the 20th instant, under some specious pretences, was, on discovery of his villainies, apprehended. The Five Nations (except those in pursuit of the enemy) are returned home, to be in readiness for accompanying the troops.

The publick may confide in the following report now in town, viz. That by the articles of peace agreed on by the Five Nations and and Sir William Johnson, they are to cede to his Majesty, all the country from Niagara to above the Great Falls, on both sides of the river; being a tract of 15 or 16 miles in length, and several in breath; very advantageous concessions equally interesting to the Publick.

PHILADELPHIA May 10. From Fort-Pitt that is dated April 26, 1764.

Extract from the examination of Gershorn Hicks (a white man) lately with the Indians, who came in here the 14th instant as a spy. ———

That an English army was expected by the Indians down the Ohio this spring. That he left Hockhocknig about 30 days ago, in company with 7 Delaware Indians, to go to war on the frontier. That they came upon Shearman's Valley, murdered and scalped one James and his wife, and took two boys, their children, prisoners. that they came within a few miles of this post, when he was desired to come in here, under pretence he had made his escape from the Indians, and to enquire into the strength of the fort, ammunition, provisions, &c. ——— and to return to them in two nights. The night they came here, 8 Shawanese came to their sleeping places and had two scalps, which they got between Ligonier and Bedford. That there was 3 parties of Indians then out, consisting of 9, 10 and 13; and one of 30 sent off, for this fort a few days after him. That about the latter end of this month 40 Wyondots, and 100 Ottowaws were to set out for this post, and way lay the communication. In May the Wyondots, Ottawaws, Delawares & Shawanese, in all 800, were to come and attack this post; and should they fail here, to proceed and attack Ligonier and Bedford, which were not so strong. That last winter two Delaware Chiefs, and White-Eyes with them, went down to a large French stone fort on the Missisippi, and took three English scalps, and asked assistance from the French to carry the war against us. They found both French and English in the fort. The Commanding officer, a Frenchman, would not hear them, and ordered the scalps to be thrown out the door; and gave 'em some flints and Powder, and ordered them to return. But that they went to some French people, that lived along the Missisippi, and are great trades with the Indians for ammunition, &c. one of which had 4 or 5 barrels of powder, and lead on proportion. White-Eyes purchased of him 9 horse loads; but in returning, thro' the badness of the weather, they lost a great part of it. And that they entered into agreement with three traders, to send up to Scioto, before the 1st of May, 12 battoes of powder, lead, &c. and he is of opinion they are there by this time. And they are going to pay them with furs taken from our traders in their towns; but should this fail, they will attack us with bows and arrows.

White-Eyes has visited some Indians on the Missisippi, from whom he asked assistance against the English, to which the consented, saying the white men should not live on the Missisippi, and that they would lay on all the narrow passages on the river, & attack our boats and troops as they passed. Those Indians are very numerous, known by the name of Cattahoos, Cawetoos, Warshaes. That the Wyondots, Ottawaws, and Delawares, intended to come here under pretence of peace and to get into the fort, and murder every soul. but if they miscarried, they would fight their way to the lakes, and from thence to the Missisippi, and join the above tribes.

NEW-YORK May 14. Since our last we have been favoured with the following further Matters of Fact, relating to the Indian Affairs, from the above, viz. That Capt, Johnson had returned to Johnson-Hall about the 1st Instant, the Enemy having abandoned the whole Country near the Susquehanna, shortly after the first loss they had sustained. Capt. Montour with 100 Indians, is gone to Niagara on order to secure the Carrying-Place, and Vessels, from any attempt of the Enemy, the Missisagoes, and others, having lately threatened it; and the loss of the Convoys at present, being of too much Importance not to be prevented. The greater part of the Six Nations are only waiting the Motions of the Troops, in order to join them, and proceed on the Expedition. —— Their Appearance with the Army, will its reasonably suppos'd awe any of the distant Nations who may have been disposed to renew war.

The Senecas Indians has delivered to Sir William Johnson, one Samuel Gwin, taken at Minisink last Fall by the Delawares, from whom he escaped to the Senecas. Also a Negro they call Tony, who formerly ran away from Maryland, and lived about 20 Years at an Indian Village on the Susquehannah; amongst which Indians he lately spread many malicious Falsehoods, one among the rest being, that the English designed to destroy all the Indians in a short time; on the news of which, Sir William sent for him; he was brought down Prisoner by the Indians, and is now on his way to New-York.

CHARLESTOWN S. Carolina May 16. Saturday last arrived in town sent down from Fort Prince George by Mr. Price the Commandant, a Creek Indian, who, with another Creek fellow, was concerned in the murder of one Bonnefield, a settler about nine miles above the forks of Long-Canes, on Tuesday the 1st inst. On Monday he was examined before a magistrate, who committed him to the common goal till next general session, when he is to be tried for the murder. His accomplice made his escape from the Young Warrior of Estatoe when he was carrying them to Fort Prince George.

Not one of the populous provinces on the continent, from Massachusetts-Bay to Virginia, have furnished a single man on the expedition against the enemy Indians, Connecticut, New-York and New-Jersey exempted.

Yesterday John Stuart, Esq; his Majesty's agent for and Superintendent of Indian Affairs in the southern district of North-America, set out for East and West Florida, in order to visit the several Indian nations in those countries &c.

PHILADELPHIA May 17. Yesterday a law was passed by the Governor and Assembly, for granting fifty-five thousand pounds for his Majesty's service.

Since our last the following Particulars came to hand from Fort-Henry, in Berk's County, viz.

"That on the 23d inst. the commanding officer there received advice that the Indians had murdered some white people about 3 miles from thence; upon which he ordered an officer and 15 men to go to the place, where they found Jacob Baker's house burnt, his wife and sister killed and scalped, and two boys were killed within 2 miles of the fort, and two other boys are missing: ———— that one of of his reconnoitring parties having discovered 6 Indians at about a mile's distance, he was going out again in pursuit of them, and were to take 6 days provisions with them: That on the 24th a woman was shot through the neck by a party of Indians, they were pursued and fired at by our men, but no account of any of them being wounded or taken. ———— It is likewise said that the Indians in their retreat, met and wounded several of the inhabitants badly."

NEW-YORK May 21. The following Extracts from Detroit may be depended on upon as authentic, viz. Detroit Lan. 4, 1764.

"A few of the Saggana Indians, that never yet took up arms, have lately been here to trade. ———— Flour is now bought here at 50 livres per Ct. and Beef at 16 sols per lb. Most of the French begin to dread that the next blow from the Indians will be upon them in the spring, and and are therefore disposing of many of their cattle. Tho' we have not now any trouble from the Indians, there are still spies in the settlement, who inform their worthy Fathers, (a respectful name gave to the French) that there are great numbers of their dear children assembled in all the hunting villages around. I Imagine this is only a scheme of the French to keep us in the forts."

The following dated Detroit March 25, 1764.

"Col. Gladwin has permitted a few of the Saggana Indians to trade here several times, About 12 days ago, several scalping parties of the Poutewatamies came to the settlement, killed and wounded several of the French cattle, with some belonging to the garrison; and after skulking about 5 or 6 days, went off. We now sleep in our clothes, expecting an alarm every night. We are informed that the carrying-place at Niagara will be beset very early in the spring by the Indians: This I take to be the reason why the French merchants here want to purchase all the goods out of the English stores, in hopes that no more will be here this year. We have now plenty of provisions in the fort."

By a Gentleman just arrived from Detroit, we learn, that all was well the 11th of April last.

CHARLESTOWN S. Carolina May 23. Particulars of Major Loftus's Expedition.

Major Loftus, commanding the 22d regiment, who sailed from Pensacola in order to take possession of the Illinois, arrived safe at New-Orleans, and sailed from thence the 27th of February last, together with a detachment of the 34th regiment which had been employed in reconnoitering the river Iberville, towards clearing the navigation, and was to examine the state of the fort at Natchez. The whole, consisting of about 400 men, were embarked in ten large Battoes, from 16 to 22 oars, and two large canoes of six oars, which rowed from three to four leagues a day against the strong current of the Missisippi till the 20th of March, when, at nine o'clock in the morning, being under the rock of Davion the first high lands on the said river, and about eighty leagues above New-Orleans, the two canoes being a little a-head of Major Loftus's battoe and close to the western shore, which was covered with brush, received a volley, by which, in the first battoe one private man was wounded and three privates killed; in the other, one serjeant and three privates wounded, and two privates killed. The boats going back with the stream, and no possibility of landing on the west side, the river having overflowed its banks, inclined the Major to the opposite or eastern shore, which being observed by the Indians on that side, they fired, at a great distance, about 100 shots at the first fire. The commanding officer, seeing both sides so strongly guarded and the river narrow, returned with the stream, and proposed to take post at the point of Iberville, which is said to be of equal importance with the Illinoise. The next morning early they arrived at Iberville; and a Captain of the 24th, with a party, and Lieut. Pitman the engineer, went ashore to reconnoitre, and

and proposed to clear the point, which the Major on his arrival agreed to. After two hours stay a council was called, and it was carried by the majority of the troops to return from whence they set out, and the whole arrived next day at New-Orleans, where Major Loftus meeting with an English brigantine, went in her to Pensacola, and left the rest of the regiment with the battoes, at Belize. A Captain, the Engineer and twenty men of the 22d regiment, prepared to proceed to Mobille, when M. D'abbaedie, Governour of New-Orleans, was informed that 60 Indians from the eastern side of lake Ponchartrain, intended to intercept their battoes in the narrows between the said lake and the bay of St. Lewis; on which the British officer represented to the French Governour that Major Loftus had departed full of suspicion of his having spirited up the Indians to stop his voyage, and that if any accident should now happen to the party then going to Mobille, that suspicion must be confirmed, and that he (the British officer) would look on any attack by the Indians, (who he know to be submissive to the French) as an assassination: the Governour immediately, replied. That he would send an officer with a detachment to escort them; this was declined, and an interpreter only demanded, one acquainted with the Indians and their lurking places, who should assure them that the English desire to live in peace and in friendship with them, and would behave to them as brethren. The party arrived safe at Mobille on the 5th of April, without any accident on seeing the enemy. M. D'abbaedie called God to witness, that he had no hand in advising or spiriting up the Indians to prevent the English from taking possession of the forts ceded to them by the late treaty; and added, that he had given many proofs, both at Mobille and New-Orleans, of his strong desire to maintain peace and harmony between the two Crowns, and that this was agreeable to the orders he had received from the King his master; and to convince the world of the truth of what he said, he requested the English captain that was to have taken post at Fort Natchez, to remain a few days there at

New-Orleans, and he would send for the Indians chiefs and make them friends with the English by taking them by the hand, and giving them some presents; and would engage they would not only permit the detachment to pass unmolested, but conduct them safe to Natchez; and afford them assistance in their power to establish them there. The Captain resolved to accept the offer if agreeable to the commanding officer who declined it till he shall receive the General's orders.

It is said the Indians that attacked Major Loftus, were the Tonikas, Oumas, Chittimashaws and Yahoos, small tribes inhabiting the shores of the Missisippi from eight leagues below Iberville to about seventeen leagues above it. The whole number of warriors in all the tribes is about 150. The French at New-Orleans say the Oumas, who have 40 warriors, were not at the attack, and say they suspect the Chactaws. Some letters say, the number of Indians, who attacked, was fifty.

PHILADELPHIA May 24. Saturday came to Town a girl about 16 years of age, that had been a prisoner among the Indians of the upper part of the Susquehannah for some years past. She relates that they were concerned about Capt. Bull, not knowing what had become of him and his party and fearing they were killed —— they had not heard of this party's being surprized and made prisoners by Sir William Johnson's Indians. —— She says, that there was a great number of Indians in the town she went at, and many white prisoners. That when they heard of the massacre of the Indians at Lancaster, they were much enraged, the Squaws screaming all night, and tearing their hair, and the warriors promising them revenge. That they began to be very cross to the prisoners, on which she and two others projected their escape. And having, for their subsistence on the way, stolen from the Indians some of their green powder, they left them about three weeks since, running all night, and beding themselves in the day; and when they came to the foot of the hills, the other two left her, to go towards the German Flats, and she came towards hither. She says her name is Sally Wilkins and that she was taken from a place called Guiney, in Northampton county. The green powder, she says, is composed of Indian meal, some dried roots & herbs, and a good deal of salt. That a spoonful of it a day is sufficient for one person, to keep him from hunger; but it makes them thirsty, and occasions their drinking a great deal of water. This powder with some roots found in the woods, they say has been all the substance on the journey, and yet she looks pretty good.

From Carlisle we have advice that about three weeks ago, a man and his wife were murdered by the Indians on the south branch of Potoumack, and a child carried off.

NEW-YORK May 28. We hear that on the 27th of February last, Mai. Loftus was ordered with the 22d regiment, consisting of about 300 men, from Mobille to proceed up the Missisippi, to take possession of the Illinois, 500 leagues distant. That he found the passage up the river very difficult, owing to the rapidity of the current, which retarded their march so much that on the 20th of March, having only got 70 leagues up the river, their foremost boat was attacked by the Indians, and in a few minuted had 6 men killed, and as many wounded; that the other boats immediately attempted to land, but were also very smartly fired upon; that Maj. Loftus having a few days before lost 57 men by desertion, not knowing the number of the enemy, and being then at a place called Le Roche Davoine, about 400 leagues from the Illinois, thought it impractical to fulfil his orders, therefore returned to Pensacola.

CHARLESTOWN S. Carolina May 30. On Sunday last Capt. James Prevost, commanding the Royal American regiment stationed in this province, sailed from hence for New-York, he is succeeded in command by Capt. Garvin Cochran, who arrived here last week from Philadelphia.

The Creek Indians mentioned in our last, who escaped from the Young Warrior of Estatoe, was retaken by him, and delivered by some white men to be brought to Charlestown, and though in irons he found means to get away from them in the settlements, about 30 miles from Orangeburgh.

The house has voted 100 pounds sterling as a reward to Salloue, or the Young Warrior of Estatoe, and the other Cherokee warriors, for the apprehending and delivering up the Creek Murderer now in goal, and made a request of his Honour the Lieutenant Governor to use his endeavours that those, who willfully or through neglect suffered the other murderer to make his escape, may be brought to punishment.

The house has likewise resolved to make provisions for defraying the expences of running a temporary line of Jurisdiction between this province and North Carolina, agreeable to his Majesty's instructions; and to provide pay for six months, for a commanding officer at 25 pounds a month, a serjeant at 18 pounds a month, and 20 private men at 15 pounds a month each, they finding their own horses, arms, and ammunition, and provisions, to be employed as rangers for the protection of the south-west frontiers most exposed to the incursion of the Creek Indians.

PHILADELPHIA May 31. Yesterday a law was passed by the Governor and Assembly, granting 55,000 pounds for his Majesty's Service.

Since our last the following particulars came to hand, that a son of Casper Schnebell's and a son of Nicholas Wolfe's were both killed within two miles of Fort Henry in Berks county; that a day-break an officer went out with 24 men, but could not see the enemy, and by the badness of the weather lost their tracks.

SAVANNAH March 31. To be sold by James Johnston at the Gazette Printing office at Broughton Street, price 12s. 6d.

A Four Sheet Map of South-Carolina and Part of Georgia, containing the whole sea coast, all islands, inlets, creeks, parishes, townships, boroughs, roads, and bridges; also several plantations, with the proper boundary lines, their names, and the names of the proprietors; composed from surveys taken by the Hon. William Bull esq; Lieutenant Governor, Capt. Gascoign, Hugh Bryan, Esq; and the author William D'Brahm.

Notice is hereby given to all the gentlemen

belonging to the first company of foot militia, commanded by Capt. James Devaux, that they are to appear at the place of parade in the savanna, completely accoutred, on Monday the fourth day of June next, being his Majesty's birth-day, and a general muster.
    by order of the Colonel.
                      Robert Bolton. cleck.

JUNE 1764

BOSTON June 4. Extract of a Letter from Montreal May 9, 1764.

"As a well-wisher to this continent, I own that I am particularly inquisitive into every step taken by our Commanders, and Governors, to punish the blind spirit of Rebellion, that has been nursed up in the minds of some of the unthinking and dissafected tribes of Indians, and thereby put an End to the present unnatural war so hurting the Trade & Welfare of our fellow subjects.

"Capt. Claws, the Director of Indian Affairs in this Province arrived here lately from Johnson Hall. Hearing that a numerous congress of the different Nations of Indians settled in this Government, was to be held at Coghnawawa, the 5th Instant in presence of Brigadier General Burton, our Governor; I had the curiosity to follow thither, where he went, attended by all the commanding officers of the different corps in the Government & other Officers of the Garrison. At the approach of his Barge, the Indians, who had hoisted up in several parts of their Fort Union Flags, and Red Flags, saluted him with a discharge of Patararoes, and Vollies of small Arms. The whole village, Men, Women, and Children, shewed the greates Demonstration of Joy, at his Landing, at which time a Company of Warriors, with English Colours flying, and Officers at their Head, formed a double File through which the Governor, attended by Capt. Claws and other Officers marched, and went to the Council-House where after the usual Compliments, I saw, with the highest satisfaction, the chiefs of the different Tribes & Nations assembled, take up the War-Belt, with great readiness, and heartily promise for their tribes to join our Indian Friends, so that Numbers of them are soon to set off for Sir William Johnson."

PHILADELPHIA June 7. Our Advice from Carlisle of the 21st ult. are that Capt. Shelby with a small Party of Volunteers, having been ranging in the Great Cove, heard a Halooing of a number of the Enemy supposed to be about Twenty; upon which he alarmed the Inhabitants, a great many of whom, it is said, were repairing to the Fort.

By a person from Berks county we are informed, that the woman that was shot there is since dead, that the two children of Jacob Baker's were found killed and scalped; that two young men have been since murdered by the Indians; and that the number lately killed by them, amounts to nine.

We learn from Fort Loudon, that one Browne was lately killed at the mouth of the Aughwick by the Indians, and his sister made prisoner; that three men were lately killed near Stanton; and that a considerable number of Indians were between Bedford and Fort Cumberland.

SAVANNAH June 7. We hear from Charlestown, that on Tuesday the 17th ult. a messenger arrived there overland, with dispatches to James Stuart, Esq; from Mobille and the Indian countries. ——— That at a meeting of several of the headmen of the Upper Creeks, at little Talasses on the 10th ult. with Messrs. Germeny, Cornall, Strutchess, McQueen, and other traders, the Indians agreed to send down a talk to the Governor and the Superintendant, which is come down: It is said the Indians complain about their lands; some of the trader's horses stolen by some of their young people, they promise to find out and return, and express their sorrow for the murders at the Long Canes, which they promise to do all in their power to prevent for the future; they claim Fort Albama, now the French have left it, and some of them say intend to live there, but seems satisfied with out taking possession of Mobille, Pensacola, and other French and Spanish settlements in their country.

PHILADELPHIA June 12. Our advices received from Carlisle of the 11th inst. are, That the distress in the Upper Parts of the Country increases daily, the Indians being often heard yelling and hallowing, in their frightful Manner, among the Hills, and through the Settlements dispersed in small Parties of two or three together; that they had fired at several of the people; and some of them were seen not far from Fort Loudoun: That the Country was evacuated briefly (excepting 2 or 3 Families) from the Shippensburgh to Loudoun: And that from the Frontier of Virginia all the Accounts were most melancholy, respecting the miserable situation of the inhabitants there, from the Barbarity of the Enemy.

CHARLESTOWN S. Carolina June 13. Letters from Fort Prince-George of the 8th inst. informs us, that the party of Cherokees returned from their expedition against the northern Indians were those from Toxaway; there was no account of two other parties that had likewise gone out on the same errand, and at the request of the superintendent. The party from Taxaway were attacked near Winchester in Virginia by a number of white men armed, who probably took them for enemies; but by the imposition of some gentlemen of character there the Indians were not allowed to be insulted, which in the present juncture of affairs is a very fortunate circumstance.

Salloue or Young Warrior of Estatoe went out after the Creek murderer that made his escape a second time, but did not come up with him; it is said he went off to the Mortar's new settlement. Salloue offered to bring another scalp, as he could not get the right one.

Two Cherokees who had been about twelve months among the Creeks, having learned that the latter were going to war with their countrymen, set off for their own nation, but were followed by the Creeks, who killed and scalped one, the other got off, and the next day went back, killed a Creek, and carried his scalp into Chote about the 1st inst.

PHILADELPHIA June 14. Indian Affairs. We hear the Indians have done a great deal of damage at Paterson's creek: ——— From Shippensburg that on the 3d inst. they killed one William Crow, and carried off his wife and 4 children: ——— From Fort Pitt, the Indians begin again to show themselves and a corporal and 4 men are missing from thence; on the 27th ult. a Soldier was fired at and mortally wounded; that the same night the garrison heard fourteen death Hallo's on the other side of the Allegaheny river; since which numbers of the enemy are seen every day sculking about the fort, but they are in no fear of attack from them: ——— From Carlisle we hear that a man was found killed and scalped in the road to Fort Loudoun, that at Bedford one man was killed and another was carried off; that at fort Littleton one man was wounded & that the roads are much infested: ——— From Fort Cumberland, on the 26th ult. a large body of Indians fell on a party of white people working in a field, then they killed 15 and wounded 16 more; they then attacked Fort Dinwiddie, and fired six hours on it, but could not prevail; Capt. Ashby and a man were taken prisoners near the south branch of Potomack, also a man, his wife, and child were carried off from Cedar creek, and a negro fellow was taken as he was driving a waggon, the horses killed and the waggon broke; a great number of Indian tracks have been discovered, & the inhabitants are chiefly gone away: ——— From Virginia on the 4th inst. they write, that the situation of their frontiers are truly distressing; that within eight days upwards of 40 persons have been killed; the Indians way laid four families going to a fort, and killed and captured 21; and the day before this letter was dated, six families were cut off near the narrow passage; two companies are gone after the enemy: ——— From Fort Loudon on the 5th inst. we learn, that some of the inhabitants who went to sow corn, were attacked by the Indians, and 1 of them were killed; that on the 2d inst. a man was killed and his wife and four children carried off 6 miles below that post; that 4 miles down the creek, three families were cut off, 13 of whom were killed, and their bodies together with their habitations burnt; a party was sent after these villains, who pursued them so closely, that they killed their prisoners on the flight, being 6 or 7, and then scattered and escaped, one lad who got away, says he saw his father and mother knocked down with a tomahawk before he ran off; the inhabitants are returning in crowds to this and other little posts in the neighbourhood.

PHILADELPHIA June 14. An Extract of a letter from Virginia of the 4th inst. says, "The situation on our frontiers are truly distressing, the Indians killing and capturing daily. About eight days past, upwards of 40 Persons were killed at the pastures, on the frontiers of Augusta county. We are hopeful our troubles were in some measure over, but to our surprize, the Indians came on Friday last, about seven miles from me, and took one Day's wife and four children. Next morning, about sun-rise, four families going to a fort with horses loaded, the Indians way-laid them, and killed and captivated 21, whose names were Lloyd and his family, Clouper, Jones, Thomas, &c. This morning about two o'clock I was informed, that about sun-set yesterday, six families were cut off near the Narrow Passage. Two companies of men are gone after the enemy, to retake the captives if possible, of which there is yet no account."

Extract of a letter form Fort Loudoun June 9.

"Past 10 o'clock, just now news is come in here, that 10 of the party who followed the Indians, and who were detached from the whole (which consists of 40 brave rifle men) had come up with them at the mouth of the Cove Gap, about 4 miles from here; that they counted 16 Indians in the rear of the company, that there were a great many horses, and women and children in the front, that they heard the cry of the children, the Indians fired three shots on our people and called to them "for white sons of bitches to come and fight them now and then they were ready." Our people immediately retreated to join the party behind and will certainly come up with them ('tis supposed) to day; there are provisions and more men sent to join this party, which will consist of sixty when all together."

CHARLESTOWN June 14. The smallpox continues among the Creek Indians, and have carried off a great many in the towns near the Albama Fort. All accounts represent the Creeks as well inclined and peaceable.

Letters from Pensacola and Mobille informs us that they are now convinced none of the Chactaws were concerned in the attack made on Major Loftus; those Indians are likewise very peaceable: some months ago a breach between us and the Creek Indians seemed not far distant, the Cussadaw or Stinking Lingo Indians, who lived under the protection of the Creeks, unwillingly to be brought into a war, left their habitations and went towards the Chactaw country: They are now settled on the branch of Mobille river where Tombigbee fort is situated, on the route from Mobille to that garrison, and have behaved in the most friendly manner to such English as have had the occasion to pass that way, and it is thought will be a great service in awing such as the Frenchised Choctaws as may be inclined to do mischief. On Saturday the first party of French Protestants, who lately arrived here, consisting of 21 men well armed under the command of an Ensign, with a few waggons loaded with their baggage and ammunition; and provisions for the march, in order to begin their settlement and prepare for the remainder, who are to follow in about 3 weeks. We hear that Capt. Calhoun, with a detachment of rangers, have orders to meet them and give them every kind of assistance on their first arrival at the place where their town is to be built.

PHILADELPHIA June 21. From Cumberland county we are informed, that Capt. Lewis, with a party, pursued and came up with the enemy, who lately did so much mischief in Augusta county Virginia, when he engaged them, killed a Frenchman, and two Indians, and retook some of our people they had prisoner; who told them, that there was another Frenchman with them; and from the 22d of last month there had been 100 people killed, or carried off by the Indians. ——— That two of the soldiers, in Shearman's valley saw two Indians, at one they had a fair shot; upon which they went to the officer, and told him what happened, who sent a party to the place, where they found a great deal of blood, and a bit of fat, supposed to come out of with the ball.

We are informed, that Day's wife, (mentioned

in our last to be taken by the enemy) had escaped from the Indians, and was returned; and said the Indians that took her and children were only three, though the party did consist of five, but they imagined the two others to be killed, and they had not seen them for some time.

SAVANNAH June 21. Extract of a letter from Mobille dated May 14, 1764.

"The French at New-Orleans expect the spaniards to take possession of that place in July next. The crop having failed in France last year, they have not been able to send any flour to New-Orleans, which has made the article in great demand here. It has sold from 12 to 14 dollars per barrel by the quantity. We at present under no apprehensions of danger from the Choctaws, and I am of opinion the reports that they intended to break with us came entirely from the French; however I hope when the spaniards come to New-Orleans they will be entirely quiet."

By accounts from Mobille and Augusta, the Creeks seem not to be in a condition to dusturb us, having got the small-pox among them which carried them off very fast.

NEW-YORK June 25. Extract of a letter from Schenectady June 10. 1764.

"Colonel Bradstreet arrived here this day from Albany and sent out from hence tomorrow for Fort Ontario. ———— A letter from Detroit, dated the 14th of May says, that there had been some sculking Indians in the settlement, who fired on soldiers but without doing any damage, and that it was not expected they could make any attempt against the fort this summer; nevertheless, the merchants and their servants do duty at the garrison, in order to prevent surprize.

The Nanticoke Indian and the Fish-Kill Indian, sent to town a fortnight ago by Sir William Johnson, and by the General's order confined in the dungeon in the goal in this city, still remain there. They both say they have always acted as true friends to the English, but that the Mohawks, from private enmity have misrepresented them to Sir William. However, from their close confinement, for which no doubt there is good reason, the truth of their account is much to be suspected.

We are informed that the New-York Independent Companies which has been reduced since the peace, are again to be put in commission on an entirely new plan, to garrison this Province in their former stations.

PHILADELPHIA June 28. By a letter from Fort Bedford, there in advice, that as a party of Indians was flying from a party of our people, a white boy they had prisoner, fell from his horse, upon which they killed and scalped him, cut off his head, and left in the middle of the road.

JULY 1764

NEW-YORK July 2. Extract of a letter from the Little Falls June 18.

"Saturday last 18 companies of Militia, about 1500 men, were reviewed about a mile above Fort Henrick, by Sir William Johnson, who after the review, entertained them with a large ox, and a number of sheep roasted whole, and gave them a barrel of rum to drink his Majesty's health. There was a number of Indians present amongst whom were some of the Senacas; who on their return hence, will tell their people, that the English are coming in vast bodies towards the frontiers; this will undoubtedly have a good effect, in engaging them to keep firm and steady to their late convention with Sir William, fearing that these people should march against them in case of a revolt. And yesterday Sir William set out for Niagara, accompanied by his Son in law Mr. Guy Johnson, and John Duncan, Esq; of Schenectady, with 30 of the chiefs and most noted warriors of the lower castles of the Mohawks, who insisted on accompanying Sir William's person in particular to his voyage. They sang the war songs, and danced, taking Sir William by the hand with the most convincing proof of their attachment."

PHILADELPHIA July 5. By a letter from Comberland there is advice, that on the 13th of June the militia on the frontier of Virginia came up with and killed 5 Indians.

And we hear that in Hampshire, in Virginia, about 16 days ago, the enemy murdered one of our people, and carried off 3 or 4 others.

CHARLESTOWN S. Carolina July 11. From East Florida we learn, that the Hon. John Stuart, Esq; Superintendent of the southern district was set out from thence for West Florida. That the

Long-Warrior and Cow Keeper of the Creeks waited on that gentleman at St. Augustine, and received some presents; those Indians live at the town called Latchewee, which has about a hundred and twenty gunmen, is seventy miles from St. Augustine, and one hundred and eighty from the Creek country, Our advices add, that numbers of Indians are every day coming and going in a very friendly and familiar manner among the English, to the great surprize of the Spaniards that remain, who never durst venture three miles without the lines of St. Augustine.

PHILADELPHIA July 12. Letters from Pittsburgh of the 25th ult. advice that all was well there, that the communication had been quite clear for some time; that a corporal and 4 men who had been missing, were returned safe to the garrison; ant that a Lieutenant with a party, had been down the Ohio, but saw no enemy.

NEW-YORK July 16. On Tuesday Evening arrived the Sloop Success, Capt, Francis Johnson, in 23 Days from Pensacola, by whom we learn, that there has been no loss of any of our people, by the Indians, in those Parts, since the Affair of Major Loftus, in going up the Missisippi, on the 31st of March. So that the report lately circulated here, that many of our people had been cut off by the Indians at Pensacola must have taken its rise from the above affair, or be entirely false.

The People at Pensacola were in the hopes that New-Orleans would be given up the Spaniards, with whom they expect to carry on a profitable Trade; at present the Trade is dull, it being chiefly confined to the Indians, obstructed by two Men of War on that Station, the Princess of 40 Guns, Captain Lucas, and another, who have seized 3 or 4 Vessels going up the missisippi, and prevent Spanish Vessels from Trading, which lately put them in distress, having it is said 60,000 Dollars on board, which they would have laid out to purchase goods.

The Government of Pennsylvania have issued a proclamation dated the 7th inst. declaring war against the Delaware and Shawanese Indians, & have agreed the following rewards for taking and destroying them, viz. For every male Indian enemy, above ten years old, taken prisoner, 150 dollars: For every Female Indian enemy, taken prisoner, and for every male Indian enemy under ten years old 130 dollars. For the scalp of every male Indian enemy, above the age of ten years the sum of 134 dollars: And for the scalp of every female Indian enemy the sum of 50 dollars.

It is not long since we acquainted our readers of the setting off of Sir Willim Johnson, to go to Niagara, in order to compleat a firm peace with the Seneca and Western Indians; his Excellency has since arrived at Oswego, from whence on the third of July he sets out for Niagara. The same day Col. Bradstreet also sets out with 1196 regulars and provincials. There were 608 Indians, of which 300 were Cognawagas, and 180 more were to join at Niagara.

NEW-YORK July 16. The Government of Pennsylvania, has issued a proclamation dated the 7th Instant declaring War against the Delaware and Shawanese Indians, and has offered the following Rewards for taking and destroying them viz.

For every male Indian Enemy above Ten Years old, who shall be taken Prisoner, and delivered to any Fort garrisoned by Troops in the Pay of this Province, or at any of the Country Towns, to the keeper of the common Goals there, the Sum of One Hundred and Fifty Spanish Dollars, or Pieces of Eight. For every Female Indian Enemy, taken Prisoner and brought as aforesaid, the Sum of One Hundred and Thirty Pieces of eight. For the Scalp of every Male Indian Enemy above the age of Ten Years, produced as Evidence of their being killed, the Sum of One Hundred and Thirty-Four Pieces of Eight. And for scalps of every Female Indian Enemy, above ten Years. produced as Evidence of their being killed, the Sum of Fifty Pieces of Eight. And that there shall be paid to every Officer or Officers, Soldier or Soldiers, as are or shall be in the Pay of the Province, who shall take, bring in and produce any Indian Prisoners or Scalps as aforesaid, One Half of the said several respective Premiums and Bounties.

PHILADELPHIA July 19. Letters from Oswego of the 19th of June, advice, that all the New-Jersey forces were arrived safe there. That on the 26th of May the Chippawa Indians came in there, & said, they were empowered to make Peace for four nations, and that seven other nations from above Lake Huron, Mishigan, &c. were willing to make peace likewise, Upon which the Mohawks asked them where the nations were, and why they did not come with them; told them they wanted to see them; that they must meet Sir William Johnson at Niagara and make peace with him there, and that they would take them under their blanket to their bosoms: but that if they refused to come, they would kill them all. Whereupon two or three went off immediately to acquaint the nations with what the Mohawks said, and the third remained at Niagara till they shall return.

Letters from Niagara of the 25th ult. mention that all was quiet at Detroit. That upward of 4000 Barrels of Provisions were on the Carrying Place, viz. Fort Sclosser, Navy Island, &c. and that as there were a great may Carriages employed on the Carrying-Place, it was not doubted the bulk of the Provisions would soon get across.

Another Letter of June 27th, mention two of our soldiers being fired at by two Delaware, one of whom was killed and scalped, and the other got off. And that two of our vessels got off. And that two of our vessels were got into the Lake Erie, and a third would be ready that week.

NEW-YORK July 23. We have advice from St. Augustus, that eight of the Soldiers of the Garrison there, having lately deserted, the commanding Officer sent out 8 Indians in search of them, with directions to take them dead or alive. The Indians came up with, fired upon and killed 4 of them, two more surrendered and two made their Escape: of which one came to Fort Stanwix and deliver'd himself up the other has not since been heard of.

On our last advices from the Lakes and on the third Instant, Sir William Johnson & Colonel Bradstreet, with the Forces under their command, set out from Fort Ontario at Oswego, for Niagara. Col. Bradstreet was so ill, that he was obliged to be carried to the Vessel. The Forces consisted of the following Men, viz.

17th Regt.	243	Tuscararoes	37
55th ,,	98	Ockwagoes	31
New-York	344	Naticokes	22
New-Jersey	209	Stockbridge	17
Connecticut	74	Ottawas from	
Carpenters	9	Machilimakinac	48
	1196	Caughnawagas	
Indians		other Indians at	
Mohawks	74	Niagara	120
Cagnawagas	106	Ossingoes	31
Oniadas	70		778
Onondagoes	68	Whole Army	
Senecas	60	Men	1924
Cayogas	45		

CHARLESTOWN S. Carolina July 25. All the accounts from the Creek country represents those Indians as very well disposed towards the English; but the Jealousies and heart-burnings between them and the Cherokees seem to increase.

The small-pox still continue among the Creeks.

NEW-YORK July 30. Extract of a Letter from Oswego Junr 28, 1764.

"The 26th inst. Sir William Johnson and myself, with about 550 Indians arrived here, and were received on our landing by upwards of 100 Gagnawagas, and others, whom he had sent forward some Days ago. They drew up in two lines, and fired three volleys, as a salute; which was answered by the Indians who came up with Sir William; after which we encamped. We are to be joined this Day by 300 Indians of the Oneida, Tuscarora, and adjacent villages; so that on Sir William's setting out for Niagara, there will be at least 900 Indians to accompany the troops; which with 140 now at Niagara, and those who are expected to join us there, from the Upper Nations, will make a large body than ever been known to take field in our favour. A party of Indians have brought in two scalps from the Shawanese, and our Indians express great desire to go against these people. The Senecas have sent a great number of English prisoners, who are to be delivered to us on our way to Niagara, agreeable to their late engagement."

Extract of a Letter from the Camp at Lake Ontario, dated July 2, 1764.

"We have just received orders to take in provisions for Niagara, and believe we shall set off tomorrow. Sir William Johnson is here with 1300 Indian Men, Women, and children, of whom there about 600 fighting men, who, 'tis said, are to go with us. The Senecas have sent word to Col. Bradstreet, that they will deliver up to him all their prisoners; and last night he sent a boat off, with some Indians and Whitemen, to receive and carry the Prisoners to Niagara. The Hurons and Missisagues are now at Niagara, and we hear several other of the distant nations are to be at the congress there. It is thought there will be a general peace. The Troops are in good health. We have boats which row with 26 oars, but they din't appear to be quite strong enough for the service they are intended for."

AUGUST 1764

CHARLESTOWN S. Carolina Aug. 1. From the Creek country we learn, that at the meeting of all the headmen of the upper towns about three weeks ago, the Gun Merchant and others, on being informed that one of their countrmen was in goal here for murdering a white man, declared their readiness to acquiesce in every step taken in the affair agreeable to treaty; and that, if the fact was proved according to our laws, they had no objection to his being put to death.

Several parties of the Cherokees that went out against the Enemy Indians, are returned, and have brought in both scalps and prisoners from the Shawanese, Twightwies, &c.

CHARLESTOWN S. Carolina Aug. 8. Extract of a Letter from Mobille dated July 1764.

"The Chactaw Indians are at present very quiet: two of those Indians have informed an English trader, that they were accidentally down upon the Missisippi, amongst the small nations there, at the time Major Loftus was attacked, and saw the whole affair: they say those small nations, who have not above sixty gun-men, were led by six Frenchmen who brought them ammunition for that purpose. Whatever credit may be due to this Account of the Chactaws, it is certain, that immediately after Major Loftus's retreat, a large convoy of French goods was sent up from New-Orleans to the Illinois, which could not have been sent if the English could have proceeded. Two of the Creek headmen have lately been here, they say some Cherokees have lately come to their nation, in order to accommodate matters between them and the English, and acquaint us, that two of the murderers have lately been taken by the Young Warrior of Estatoe, and delivered to the commandant of Fort Prince George. They deny that any of the murderers ever returned to their nation, and says their relations and every one else would be glad to hear they are put to death, as they hope to have peace and tranquility restored."

PHILADELPHIA Aug. 9. From Carlisle we have the following melancholy intelligence, that on the 25th ult. a woman named Cunningham, big with child, was met with by the Indians a little way from her own house, who murdered, scalped, and otherwise most horribly abused her, ripping her belly open & taking out the child, the enemy came upon a school-house, on Conecocheauge, 15 miles from Fort Loudoun, in the very heart of the settlement, where they killed & scalped the master and 9 of his scholars, and 4 made prisoners, being all that belonged to that school; this massacre was discovered by a man passing by, who, hearing no noise, went in, and saw the master lying scalped, with his Bible under his arm; that one of the scholars was then alive (but died soon after) who told him there were four Indians, who were not seen till they entered the house; that two of the children then murdered belonged to an unhappy man, who had four other carried off by the savages last war; several parties of Indians have been seen in that settlement; and that a stroke struck so far in the settled part of the country, it was feared, would occasion many of the inhabitants to leave their places.

We likewise hear from Carlisle that one Ensign Smith with 7 men had been out as a scalping party and had travelled 70 miles below Fort-Pitt, till they came to a place called Crow's Town, on the Ohio, which they found abandoned and the houses burnt, that the houses on Beaver creek were likewise deserted but not destroyed, and that they found a few tracks, but did not see but one Indian during the long march, and him they could not come up with.

Col. Bouquet and the troops are expected at Loudoun about the latter end of July, and are to proceed soon after to the Ohio.

BOSTON Aug. 13. Extract of a Letter from Quebec May 30, 1764.

"We have Chief Justice Gregory with some attorneys at Law, &c. lately arrived here, but it is tho't that the civil Government will not take place till sometimes in September, at which time by the Treaty of Peace, all the Inhabitants that do not go to France must become British Subjects; but the Number which we shall lose on the occasion will be very inconsiderable, and we have by every ship from England, French reduced Officers of the colony Troops, and those that have connexions in this Country, coming over to take up their quarters and settle, who are generally very much dissatisfied with with their Reception and Treatment in France. ——— Every thing remains quiet in the Upper Country, tho' it is said by some late Letters that the Savages are making preparations to open the campaign. The 300 Volunteers which were raised and went from hence, and arrived some time at Oswego. The several Nations of Indians about this Place have taken up the War-Hatchet in our favour. 60 Warriors are already gone to join Sir William Johnson, & about 60 more are preparing to set out."

BOSTON Aug. 16. By His Excellency Francis Bernard, Esquire, Captain General and Governor in Chief in and over his Majesty's Province of Massachusetts, in New-England, and Vice-Admiral of the same.

A PROCLAMATION

Whereas in the session of the General Court begun on Wednesday the 21st Day of December last, An Act was passed for the regulating the Trade with the Eastern Indians, and preventing the Abuse therein: Whereby among other things, it was forbid by the Government, shall Truck or Trade with the Indians in any Goods, or shall give or deliver unto Indians any Rum, Brandy or other strong Liquors; and also that any Persons other than Indians should hunt, or take any Beaver, Sables, or other Fur, to the Northward or Eastward of Saco Truck-House, except in the towns or Plantations where they dwell.

And whereas it is absolutely necessary for preserving the Peace of that Country, by preventing Indians being provoked at the Importations of private Traders, being inflamed by spirituous Liquors, or being made desperate by their being deprived of their usual means of procuring their Livelihood, that the said Act should be carried into due Execution.

I Do therefore command, and firmly injoin all Judges, Justices of the Peace, Sheriffs, Constables, and all other Magistrates and Officers whatsoever, that they use their utmost Endeavours that the said Act be duly carried into Execution: And that no one may pretend Ignorance of the same, I have caused an Abstract of the said Act to be annexed to this Proclamation.

Given at the Council-Chamber in Boston the Sixteenth Day of August, 1764, in the fourth year of the Reign of our Sovereign Lord George the Third, by the Grace of God of Great Britain, France and Ireland, King, defender of the faith, &c.   By His Excellency's Command
   With the Advice and Consent of the Council
       A. Oliver, Secr'y.   Fra. Bernard.
            God Save the King.

An Abstract of an Act of Assembly passed the Fourth Year of the Reign of his present Majesty, intituled, An Act for continuing and amending an Act made in the First Year of his Majesty intitled, An Act for allowing necessary supplies to the Eastern Indians, and for regulating the Trade with them, and preventing abuse therein.

Reciting a former Act to the same Purpose, and the Expediency of continuing the same; It is enacted, That Provisions & Supplies for the Indian trade be procured and applied for the Supply of the Indians by such Persons as shall be chosen by the General Court according to Instructions from the General Court or the Governor with the advice of Council in recess of the court, at such Places as are or shall be ordered by the General Court.

Truckmasters shall be appointed by the General Court, and shall be paid for their Service as the Court shall allow: And upon death or removal into recess of the Court shall be replaced by the Governor with the advice of the Council. Such Truckmasters shall be under Oath, shall give Security, shall observe their instructions and shall not trade with the Indians by themselves or others except as Truckmasters. No Officer or Soldier or other person in the Pay of this Government shall trade with the Indians at any Truck-House, or aboard any Vessel. And no Person shall sell, truck, barter or exchange with any Indians any strong Beer, Cyder, Wine, Rum, Brandy or other strong Liquor, Cloathing or any other Thing on Penalty of Forty Shillings, or three Months Imprisonment for each Offence.

The Truckmasters shall sell Goods to the Indians at the Price set by the Commissary, which shall be the same as given in Boston, with a reasonable Advance for Transportation and other Charges, and shall allow the Indians for their Furs and Peltry, as the Price was at Boston by the latest Advice received from the Commissary, who shall send the Prices at least twice a Year, Spring and Fall. The Truckmasters may sell rum in moderate Quantities and with Prudence; and if any Truckmaster shall sell Goods for higher Prices than they are set at, or shall charge any more for Furs or other Goods that he is allowed the Indians therefore, being convicted thereof he shall forfeit Fifty Pounds and be disabled to hold any Office in the Government. And every Truckmaster shall at least once a Year to take Oath that the Goods committed to him have been sold for no more than they have been set at, and that he has charged for the Furs and Goods returned by him, no more than he paid the Indians for them.

The Discovery of Persons selling and Delivering strong Drink to the Indians, to the face of the accused shall be held a legal Conviction of the accused of selling or delivering strong Drink to the Indians, unless the Person accused shall take the following Oath.

You A. B. do swear that neither yourself, nor any by your Order, general or particular, Assent, Privity, Knowledge or Allowance, directly or indirectly, did give, sell or deliver any Wine, Cyder, Rum or other strong Liquors or Drink by what Name or Names soever called or known unto the Indians by whom or whereof you are now accused, So help me God.

Upon Complaint of any other Person for the Breach of this Law, it being probable in the Judgement of the Person complained of is guilty, unless the defendant shall acquaint himself upon Oath, it shall be accounted a Conviction. But if the Defendant shall acquaint himself upon Oath he shall recover of the Complainant double Costs.

To redress the Complaints of the Indians against the English Hunters destroying Beavers and other Furs, and also Beaver Dams, and to prevent the great Mischiefs ensuing therefrom. No Person other than the Indians shall hunt or take any Beaver, Sable or other Furs to the Northward or Eastward of Saco Truck-House, or the Place where the said Truck-House stood, except in the Towns or Plantations where they dwell, on Penalty of Forty Shillings for every Offence, to be recovered by Complaint to a Justice of the Peace in manner aforesaid. And in Case any such Fur shall be found in the possession of any Person who cannot give a satisfactory Account to the Justice of Peace before whom the Trial may be how he came to the same, it shall be sufficient Evidence to convict such Person; and he shall forfeit the Furs and pay the Penalty aforesaid.

The Fines and Penalties shall be disposed one half to the Informer, the other half to the Truckmasters of the District for the relief of Indian Widows and Children.

Persons convicted of false swearing, shall suffer the penalties of Perjury.

It shall be lawful for the Governor with the Advice of Council to grant Licences to persons giving Bond to conform to such Regulations as the Government with the Advice of Council shall determine.

This Act to continue for one Year from the first of May 1764, and to the end of the next Session.

NEW-YORK Aug. 16. Extract of a Letter from Niagara, July 15 1764.

"Last Sunday the Snow Johnson arrived here from Ontario, with Sir William on board; who, since his arrival, has been much busied in holding councils with the Indians, of whom they are now at this place above 1000 of different nations, some to join and proceed with the army, some with peltry, expecting trade to be opened; and others to treat for peace. This morning 105 of the men of the Folles Avoines, arrived here, and are now in council in the fort. The Senecas have been expected for several days past, but are not yet come in: We are informed there are about 900 of them and the Delawares assembled together. It is whispered about that if they don't come in, in a few days, the army will march against them. The Army in the boats were 8 days in the passage from Ontario hither, having met with a violent storm which four of the largest boats were cast away and wreck'd to pieces, but the men's lives were saved and most of the baggage. About two thirds of the army, with the boats, &c. are got over the carrying place, and the remainder will be over in a few days. We have now four vessels on lake Erie."

About the 15th of July a soldier on the Niagara carrying Place was fired at by an Indian, but the ball hitting his haversack, the contents prevented its entering his body, when the soldier returned the fire, and made his escape to one of the little posts.

Col. Bradstreet with his Army left Niagara the 6th of August, on his way to Detroit.

NEW-YORK Aug. 20. Extract of a Letter from Niagara August 2.

"We are here attending the Congress, Day after Day, with about 1300 Indians, of different Nations, some of whom came 600 Miles. They have concluded a peace with Sir William Johnson, except the Dealware and Shawanese, whom we have, near a month waited for, as they are to bring their prisoners, in order to be delivered up. We expect to set off for Detroit in a few Days, having every thing ready for that purpose."

QUEBEC Aog. 20. Extract of a letter to Col. Burton at Montreal, from Oswego, Dated Aug. 7.

"Matters are entirely settled with all the nations who attended the meeting at Niagara; the greatest ever known, being about 2000 Indians.

———— Some reports are spread prevented the Chenussios coming for a long time; at length they came and delivered up prisoners, &c. and gave to his Majesty and his successors forever, the lands on both sides of the strait to lake Erie (or carrying-place) 4 miles on each side, and liberty to post on the north side of lake Erie &c. &c. &c. so that his Majesty will be possessed of all from lake to lake, a cession of near 300,000 acres. ———— They have also given two Seneca hostages for the Shanoese, and Delaware King, whom the Chenussios engaged to deliver up at this post, with all the prisoners among them. ———— There were 22 different nations at the congress, 11 of which were Western Indians. ———— All behaved well, and were discharges in the best humour. ———— The Michilimackinac Indians have engaged to protect the garrison which may be sent there. ———— The Cognawagoe (or Canadian Indians) warriors are gone with the army, and behaved very well. ———— The peace is settled by a solemn treaty of peace and alliance with the Chenussios, and also ratified and conformed in writing, so that every thing is done that could be whished for or expected."

BOSTON Aug. 27. Twenty Dollars Reward.

Ran-Away from Gol. Putnam on the Evening of the 18th of August Instant a Spanish Indian Servant named Charles, about 27 Years of age, about five Feet ten inches high, has long straight Hair, small Eyes, High Cheek Bones, pretty slender made, speaks French well, also a little Indian and broken English; he has a small spot on his Forehead prick't in with Powder, and on one of his Arms has a Cross and the figure of a Cock, also prick't with Powder: He carried with him a blue strait bodied Coat lin'd with red, and a Nankeen Waistcoat, one Pair of Leather Breeches and one pair of red knit Ditto, one white Linnen Shirt, two Tow Ditto, two Pair of mixt worsted Stockings, two Pair of Shoes, an old blue Surtout Coat trim'd with blue with yellow Buttons speck'd with Steel, a yellow Button and Gold Loop in his Hat, he is something pitted with the Small-Pox, he is more than common white, "tis supposed that there is a Squaw part English gone with him and that they carried off two soldiers Blankets with them also a French Fowling Piece, Iron mounted, but has a Silver Sight and Thumb Piece, and likewise a Long knife. He came from Canada and was formerly the property of Col. Lechorn of Montreal. 'Tis supposed he took a forged pass with him. Whoever will take up and convey said Servant to his Master at Pomfret in Connecticut, or secure him in any of his Majesty's Goals and give Notice thereof that his Master shall have him again shall receive the above Reward of Twenty Dollars, and all necessary Charges, paid by me.   Israel Putnam.

  Pomfret Connecticut August 20 1764.

  N. B. All Masters of Vessels and others are hereby cautioned against harbouring, concealing or carrying off said Fellow, as they would avoid the Penalty of the Law.

  NEW-YORK Aug. 27. Extract of a Letter from Fort Scholossor Aug. 12.

  "The schooners, Victory and Boston sailed from Fort Erie for Detroit the 9th, the two others are expected in every day; I shall proceed with them to Detroit & hope to arrive there as soon as the army."

  NEW-YORK Aug. 27. Extract of a letter from from Fort Scholossor, 12 Aug.

  "The morning of the 8th current, the army went off from hence and arrived in the evening at Fort erie, which is on the north shore, about 2 miles above the rapids, at the entrance of the lake; the 6th they set out about 10 o'clock, and proceeded along the north shore about 6 miles where they remained all night, waited for the 17th regiment, which was detained by having lost some of their boats in going up the rapids. Early in the morning of the 10th they stood across the lake to the south shore; I left fort Erie the same day at 10 o'clock since which time have heard nothing from them: tho' we have reason to think they are a considerable way on their journey, the weather being pretty favourable since they went off."

  Philadelphia Aug. 30. Extract of a Letter from Niagara July 26.

  "Provisions are issued out this day for 1717

Indians, and more daily coming in."

Extract of a Letter from Fort Ontario, Aug. 7.
"I sailed from Niagara yesterday in company with Sir William Johnson who has settled matters with the different tribes of Indians to his satisfaction, tho' not a man of the Delaware or Shawanese came near him: but he received letters from them, in which they told him, that as the other nations had condescended to make peace, they would agree, out of pity to their Brethren the English, and not from any fear they were under from them, for in that respect they despised them. ——— They are between 3 and 400 Indians gone with Col. Bradstreet, who threaten these haughty people. ——— The letters from the Indians were wrote by Major Smallman who is prisoner with them."

Our advices from the frontiers are as follows, viz. Carlisle Aug. 13. Last Friday the troops march'd from this place, having with them a large number of waggons and pack-horses, with ammunition, provisions, &c. ——— An Indian was seen and fired at on Saturday about twelve miles above Shippensburg, who it is thought was there as a spy, watching the road. We have had no mischief done since that in July. The woman supposed, some time ago, to be carried off by the Indians, was found murdered in a ticket, a little way from where they took her. The lad found alive in the school, and said to be since dead, is, we hear, yet alive, & in a likely way to recover.

Aug. 14. By a Young man from Conecocheague, we just now are informed, that Indians are seen in that settlement almost every day; and that on Friday last, two men were pursued by four of them, near Justice Dowell's and with great difficulty escaped.

Aug. 17. Some time last week three Indians were seen in the upper past of Marsh creek York county, when one Hugh Dinwiddie fired at and wounded one of them, of which wound we hear, he has since been found dead. A young woman, daughter of one Dysert, going home from sermon at the Big Spring, last Sunday, about 12 miles from hence, was met with and murdered, scalp'd and left her naked, by the enemy. This has alarmed the settlement, who were chiefly gone home to their places, and will we are afraid, make many again fly; especially as there are so many accounts of Indians being seen in small parties almost every day, in one part or other of the country. A number of young men from the upper part of the country are forming a company, to go as voluntiers with Col. Bouquet; and another company is expected to come from the East side of the river.

Aug. 18. The main body of the army left fort Loudoun about the middle of this week; the train is to be here this night.

Aug. 22. A fellow taken at Shippensburg, supposed to be a French spy, and committed to Goal.

Aug. 23. The above mentioned fellow was examined by Col. Armstrong, and some other magistrates, and sent, under a proper guard to Col. Bouquet.

SAVANNAH Aug. 30. Last Thursday night an express arrived to his Excellency from Augusta, by which we learn, That on the 13th inst. the Handsome Fellow delivered a talk to the commanding officer at Fort Augusta from the Mortar, one of the headmen of the Upper Creeks, and who was always strongly attached to the French Interest: The substance of the talk is, That he (Mortar) being thoroughly sensible of the many injuries he had done the English by the outrages and hostilities committed against them, for which he is extremely sorry, now humbly begs forgiveness of the Great King, the Governors, and the Beloved Man; and, as a pledge of his friendship and fidelity for the time to come, presents a white wing, and begs the Great King may be acquainted with his resolution to be for ever his most faithful friend; he likewise presents a string of white beads, for the great men of the nation, who request that the old path between Augusta and the nation may be kept white and clean, and that they may be supplied with goods, &c. by that path, as they want to know no other; and last of all, he desires that the white wing may be sent to Governor Wright, and the string of white beads to Governor Bull as emblems of his attachment to, and everlasting friendship for the Great King.

SAVANNAH Aug. 30. On Monday was committed to prison Nicholas Maloony, a ranger belonging to a party of Capt. Milleges's troop doing duty at Cockspur, for shooting Hillarous Morgan a corporal in the same troop.

SEPTEMBER 1764

NEW-YORK Sept. 3. The Publick will no doubt receive with great Satisfaction the News of Sir William Johnson's safe return to Fort Johnson on the 19th of August, from Niagara; where he has been making Peace with many Nations of Indians: in which, we can venture to assure our readers, he has succeeded beyond Expectation.

Sir William Johnson, Bart, gives this public Notice, that the following Persons have been delivered up to him by the Indians at the late Congress he held with them at Niagara, and that they are now on their Way to his Excellency General Gage, at New-York, where their friends may apply for them. viz.

Benjamin Shepard, of Connecticut. Abigail Chapman, of New-England, but taken at Chushietuck Pennsylvania. An Infant of Abigail Chapman. Sarah Carter, a Girl taken in Pennsylvania. her Sister Elizabeth. John Duncan, a Boy, taken at Leckawechsein. Sarah, his Sister in Pennsylvania. Ezra Trim, a Boy taken at the same place. Peter Up de Grave, and Catherine his Sister, taken at Chushietuck. Abraham Baldwin, a Boy. taken at Wayoming, in Pennsylvania, born in New-England. Sarah Otter and Joannah her Sister taken at Chushietuck. All taken by the Delaware last year and delivered up by the Cheoussios who purchased some, and procured the rest from the Delawares.

Sarah Barnet, Lena Barnet, Hose Barnet, taken at Goblin town, Carolina 7 years ago, by the Shawanese, and delivered up to the Hurons, with whom they long resided.

There are several other Prisoners (some of them related to the foregoing Persons) are yet amongst the Delawares and other Nations, who are to be restored very soon; for the performance of which, the Chenussios have delivered up two of their Chiefs to Sir William Johnson as Hostages.

NEW-YORK Sept. 6. Extract of a Letter lately received from Philadelphia.

"An Express just arrived from Col. Bouquet, Commander in Chief of our Army on the Ohio, which brings we are told the Articles of Peace agreed upon between Col. Bradstreet and the Shawanese and Delaware Indians, who had not come in when Sir William Johnson return'd. The Particulars will be immediately sent to General Gage at New York, from whom perhaps you may get a more exact Account, nevertheless we hear Col. Bouquet intends to proceed with the Army till the preliminary Articles of agreement are fully executed; our provincial Forces are now on the Way to join him and were met by the Express. The Particulars that I can recollect, are as follows. That after Col. Bradstreet with the Forces under his Command had left Niagara, they were met by 25 Indians, who presenting a belt, and desiring to know where he was going and his Design, were answer'd. That the Army was going into the Countries of the Indians who had murder's the English and violated the Peace, in order to scourge them for their Cruelty and Violence. After their dismission, other Messengers were sent with a Belt, desiring the Army might halt till Terms of Agreement might be concluded. This was refused, and the Belt returned. Two other Belts were then presented by the Indian Chiefs, and the following Articles agreed to. Viz. That the English should possess all the Forts that have ever been built by the English and French, and as much land round Each as a Cannon would fly over, with a free Communication between all the said Forts; that the Indians were to bring all the English Prisoners, Black and White, within 25 Days to St. Duskey, where they were to meet the Army and conclude the Peace and that 10 Hostages should be left as a Security for the due Performance."

PHILADELPHIA Sept. 6. We hear that Ten Deputies from the Delaware and Shawanese, Hurons of Sandusky, and other Indians of the Countries between Lake Erie and the Ohio met Colonel

Bradstreet, at Presque Isle, on his Way to there Country, with Forces under his Command and in the most submissive Manner begged for Peace; which he granted on Terms to the most Purport following.

1. That all the Prisoners in their Hands should be delivered to him at Sandusky in 25 Days.

2. That they should renounce all their claims to the Posts and Forts we now have in their Country; and that we shall Liberty to erect as many more as we think necessary to secure our Trade; and that they shall cede to us for ever, as much Land round each Fort as a Cannon Shot can fly over, on which our People may raise Provisions.

3. That if any Indian hereafter kill any Englishman, he shall be delivered up by his Nation and tried by English Laws, only to have half the Jury Indian ——— And if any one of the Nations renew the War, the rest shall join us to bring them to Reason.

4. That six of their Deputies shall remain with him as Hostages, and the other four, with an English Officer and one of our Indians, shall proceed immediately to acquaint those Nations with these Terms of Peace and forward the Collecting of the Prisoners, to be ready at the Day appointed.

"Tis said that the Colonel has told them, that if the Peace is not confirmed by their Chiefs, no other will be granted them; and that if they comtinue the War they shall find the Country filled with Warriors immediately, who will cut them off from the Face of the Earth."

It seems the Motion of the Armies at once towards their Country. viz. That while Col. Bradstreet, from Niagara; and that from this Province, under Col. Bouquet, has greatly Intimidated these People; who at first haughtily stood out, and refused to meet Sir William Johnson at the Congress at Niagara. ——— We wish the easy terms they have obtained, without having suffered from their late Perfidies, or made any adequate Restitutions of Satisfaction for their Robberies and Murders they committed, may not encourage them more readily to engage in fresh

Hostilities, on every little Occasion.

PHILADELPHIA Sept. 6. A letter from Camp Loudoun Aug. 25, 1764.

On the 16th inst. Col. Reid march'd from hence with a large convoy for Fort Pitt, and we hear he arrived at Stony creek the 23d without any interruption.

"An express is just arrived from Fort Bedford, and brings the following particulars, viz. That on the 23d, four pack-horse men going up with good, went after Col. Reid's convoy, and that when they came to the Shawanese cabins, near the S. E. foot of the Alleghany mountains, the saw some Indians, who fired on them; on which they made off thro' the woods to the camp. leaving one horse loaded behind them; and on their return, they saw the body of Isaac Stimble, killed and scalped on the road, and perceiv'd the tracks of Savages (having horses with them) pointing towards Denning's creek. On this alarm Captain Lens, with a few men of the garrison and some inhabitants, went out, and found the body, but could not prevail on the inhabitants to pursue the enemy.

"Swine the grand suttler was encamped at the foot of the Alleghany, and two of his men are missing.

"We are also informed by a person arrived from Virginia, that some men were killed a few days ago twelve miles above Winchester."

PHILADELPHIA Sept. 6. A letter from Fort Loudoun of the 25th ult. says, "By an express just arrived from Bedford, we are informed, that the Indians have been harrasing, in small parties, some of the suttlers following our convoys too great a distance, and have taken some of their horses and goods. One Man Isaac Stimble of Ligonier, has been killed and scalped near Qurry's bridge."

CHARLESTOWN S. Carolina Sept. 6. From the Cherokee country we learn that the two last parties of those Indians that went out to war against the enemy Indians are returned. We are assured that they met with some Frenchmen among the enemy, whom they killed, and brought four of their scalps to the town-house of Chote. About the middle of this month Oucconstota, Attakullakulla, Kittagusta, and most of the headmen, are to set out for a congress which they are to hold at a place upward of 400 miles down the Cherokee river, with the Chickesaw and Chactaw Indians, to renew the ancient friendship among them; we are told none of the Creeks are to be present, and we hear the Superintendent will have a deputy there.

The Cherokees have a great many traders amongst them, against most of whom they complain very heavily, and beg the trade may be put under some settled regulations to be observed by all the traders, from whatever province they come; till that is done, they say, they always will be cheated.

By letters from Fort-Boone at Long-Canes we are informed, that on the 24th past Capt. Calhoun of the Rangers received information from two Cherokee Indians that they had discovered some Indians which they took for Creeks, with two horses, at some distance. Capt. Calhoun immediately dispatched his Lieutenant with a party, accompanied by one of the Indian informants as a guide; they soon came up with the Indian camp, round which as there was no body in it, they placed themselves in ambush, in order to seize the Indians on their return, which happened soon after, when the Lieutenant made a prisoner the head of the gang, who to his great surprize proved to be a Cherokee from Toogoloo, and were likewise the seven with him: The Lieutenant took the horses, which knew to be the property of one of the inhabitants near Long-Canes. ——— We are told a very shameful traffick has been carried on with the Indians for horses which they are induced to steal in the settlements.

The Delawares, Shawanese, and Other northern tribes of enemy Indians, continue their incursions on the Cherokees; two of the enemy were lately killed in the upper Cherokee towns.

From New-York we learn, that Col. Bradstreet is building a fort on the south shore of Lake Erie, to be garrisoned by fifty men, with stores capable of containing 4000 barrels of provisions. We are told the operation to be carried out during the remaining part of the present campaign, against the Indians in those parts, were not finally agreed upon when the last advice came away.

We hear the civil government of East-Florida will be established with all possible expedition, and that lands will be granted there to settlers as fast as they apply for them.

CHARLESTOWN S. Carolina Sept. 6. The Mortar the principal head man of the Creeks, who has always been in the French Interest, has broke up his settlement on the Coosaw river and gone back to his old town of Oackehoys, in the Creek country. He now professes himself a true friend of the English. The Handsome Fellow, and several other principal Creek Indians from Oaksukee, were sent down lately by the Mortar to Fort Augusta where they delivered on the 13th past, a talk from the Mortar, addressing to the Governours of South Carolina and Georgia, and the Superintendant, in which he says. "I am thoroughly sensible of the many outrages and hostilities which I have committed against the English, while I held the French fast, and I beg forgiveness of the Great King, the Government and Superintendant. ——— I present you with this white wing, as a pledge of my firm friendship and fidelity for the time to come, and I beg the Government and Superintendant may acquaint the Great King, that I am determine to be ever his most faithful friend. ——— I likewise present you with this string of white beads, at the request of the great men of our nation, to show that it is their desire that the good old path between Augusta and the nation may be kept white and clean, &c." As we have not received an entire copy of the talk, we cannot be more particular; our letters add that the Handsome Fellow was the Spokesman; that the Mortar desired that the string of white beads might be sent to our Governour, and the white wing to Governour Wright, as true emblems of his firm attachment and everlasting friendship to the Great King, and that he intended to go to Mobille to wait upon the Superintendant in person.

NEW-YORK Sept. 10. The Persons delivered up

to Sir William Johnson at Niagara, by the Indians, arrived in this City last Monday, where their Friends may apply for them.

Benja. Sheperd, one of these persons was taken the 4th of Sept. last at Wyoming, in Pennsylvania, by the famous Capt. Bull, now in our goal, in the company with Daniel Baldwin and Jane his wife, Abraham Baldwin, John and Daniel Howell, and his wife died of hunger at the Jenesee town last winter; John Howell attempted to make his escape, but was found dead in the woods, having lost his way; Daniel Howell got off; Abraham Baldwin was murdered, & Sheperd would have been murdered also, had not Capt. Bull persuaded the Indians to the contrary; however, Bull with his own hands, gave him a severe whipping. ——— Shepherd says, there are yet a great many prisoners at the Indian towns, and among them a daughter of one Conpla, who was taken the war before last.

NEW-York Sept. Extract of the Speech of the Honorable Cadwallader Colden, Esq; his Majesty's Lieutenant Governor and Commander in Chief in and over the Colony of New-York, and the Territories depending thereon in America.

To the Council and General Assembly of the said Province.

Gentlemen of the Council and General Assembly,

Desirous to consult your case I have called you together at a season, represented to me as the most convenient to yourselves.

Your enabling me to place guards on the exposed part of the frontier hath been attended with the most salutary effects, the people having remained entirely free from incursions of Indians, who seldom attack those they find prepared for defence.

With great satisfaction, I congratulate you on the peace lately concluded with the several nations of Indians at Niagara, through the ability, experience, and zealous efforts of Sir William Johnson. ——— The army collected to chastise them, while it facilitated this happy measure, must, by impressing on the minds of the Indians a high sense of our power, render their submission more firm and lasting. It will give you particular pleasure to be informed, that his Majesty graciously distinguishes and approved your conduct, in providing for the troops now in your pay; who have greatly contributed towards the general service.

PHILADELPHIA Sept. 13. Camp at Loudoun Aug. 29.

A large convoy of waggons and pack-horses will march tomorrow with the remainder of the Army, under the command of Col. Bouquet excepting a garrison left at this Post.

The 27th Instant an Express brought letters from Presque Isle, giving an account that the Indians had sued for peace in their usual abject manner, at the same time those Savages continued skulking on the Frontiers and Murder every defenceless Person they can catch in an unguarded minute.

Yesterday we received the following copy of a letter directed to the commanding officer at Fort Cumberland.　　　　Winchester August 22.

"I have just now received certain Intelligence by Thomas Smith, baker, of this Town, who says, that about Twelve o'clock this day, Bodies of John Miller, and three others of his Family lie dead and scalped and mangled, within a Mile of George Bowman's and about twelve Mile distance from this Town. I am apprehensive that there are several small parties of the Enemy near our Quarters, and by this Intelligence you may probably fall in with some of them in their return. You will please to forward this, by Express, to the Commanding Officers of Hampshire, not omitting shewing it to the Commanders of the several posts as they pass.

P. S. Just now I received an accounting of three more, taken from Slover's Town, and two others fired at by the Indians.

As this Express set off, another Man killed at Slover's Town, and three made prisoners."

A Letter from Carlisle of the 29th ult. mentions there having received certain advice there, of seven Persons being killed, near Winchester, on the 23d of that Month, by Indians; That the Enemy had been lately seen in different parts of Cumberland County: and that two of them are said to have appeared within a Mile of Carlisle on the 26th of last Month.

Another letter from the same place of the 4th Instant, advises, that the first division of our Army was arrived safe at Pittsburgh; the Rear received a few random Shots from the Enemy near the Fort.

WILLIAMSBURG Sept. 14. Extract of a letter from Fredericksburg, dated Sept. 3, 1764.

"Lieutenant Colonel Reid, of the Highland Regiment, got as far as Fort Ligonier, with the first Division of the Troops under Col. Bouquet's Command, the 29th ult. without any Loss from the Enemy; and Col. Bouquet marched from Fort Loudon, in Pennsylvania, on the 31st, with the rest of the Troops. A Party of 4 Indians killed several People near Strasbourgh on the 22d ult. and took one Mary Dillester Prisoner, but the Activity of the Militia employed at the advanced Posts, they intercepted the Indians, scalped one, on the 26th, and retook the Prisoner. Several small Parties are down, conducted by white Men, who have lived with the Indians, and turned as savage as they; but such dispositions are make for pushing and intercepting them, that it is hoped they will not have an Opportunity of committing any Outrages.

Sir William Johnson has sent some Northern Indians to Fort Pitt, to reclaim the Ohio Indians, and a general Peace is soon expected."

NEW-YORK Sept. 17. On Monday last nine of the Indians who have been for some time past been confined in the New Goal, were sent to the several Goals on Long-Island, least any infectious disorder should arise from the confinement of so many persons together. The other five still remain in the Goal in this City.

PHILADELPHIA Sept. 20. Extract of a letter from Fort Cumberland Aug. 28, 1764.

"On the 22d inst. a party of Indians in Virginia at Stover's Town, took three scalps, and two prisoners, being a woman and a child of four years old, which they tomahawked and scalped after carrying them two days. On the 24th a party went off to cut them off on their return. Lieut. Stinson with 25 men also set out on Braddock's road, and came up with two Indians, one of whom they killed and mortally wounded the other, who was found dead the next day; they likewise retook two horses, and all the Indian baggage, also the wearing apparel on one Mrs. Gibbons, whom they killed the 25th, within a mile of this garrison. The Lieut. also fell in with ten Indians returning from the Inhabitants, but being discovered by them immediately took to Laurel swamp and escaped. Our party retook a white woman and all the Indian baggage, and returned without making any further discoveries."

Extract of a Letter from Fort Cumberland of Sept. 3, 1764.

"A great number of Indians have been seen upon the south branch of Potowmack, and done much mischief. Capt. Macdonald is gone with his company of militia to way-lay them when they go back, and I hope to send you good news within 8 days."

PHILADELPHIA Sept. 27. Extract of a Letter from Carlisle, dated Sept. 17. 1764.

All appears quiet at present along the Frontier, except about Bedford, where there are according to Intelligence from thence, some of the Savages laying in wait for Opportunity of doing Mischief. They attempted very lately to take a man that was fishing, but he got off. The People are returning over the Hills to their Places, which we are afraid, is yet to soon."

A letter from Fort Bedford, dated Sept. 14.

"Yesterday Col. Bouquet marched from hence with a large convoy of provisions and communication, on Pack-horses, for Fort Pitt, and lay last night at the Shawanese cabbins. Tomorrow a convoy of 60 or 70 waggons is to follow, under the command of Capt. Hay of the royal artillery. And next the last convoy of pack-horses under the command of Capt. Ourry with the rear of the Troops.

"It is hoped that these convoys will get up with very little difficulty, as Capt. Williams, chief engineer, procedes them with workmen to repair the roads, He has with 200 Pennsylvanians, completed in four days, a most excellent waggon road round the Sidling Hill.

OCTOBER 1764

NEW-YORK Oct. 1. Extract of a letter received from Philadelphia.
"Letters from Fort Pitt of the 16th of September bring advice, that an express that set out from Fort Pitt with dispatches to Sandusky, in answer to letters sent with advice of the late negotiation at Presque Isle, was discovered about 45 miles from thence to have been murdered by the Indians, and his head stuck on a pole in the middle of the road: It is supposed that a man who accompanied him, is carried off by the Indians. From hence its very apparent, that the design of the Villains has been to over-reach and impose upon us, in the late negotiation, by gaining time to dispose of their wives and children out of reach, should they be attacked; and endeavouring to make so late in the season, that no offensive operation can be carried out on against them."

ANNAPOLIS Maryland Oct. 4, On Wednesday last marched from Fort Frederick, under the command of Capt. William M'Clellan, a company of Volunteers, consisting of 43 brave woods-men, besides officers, all of them well equipped, with good rifles, and most of them born and bred in the Frontiers of Frederick county. They leave without pay, and intend to meet Col. Bouquet at Fort Pitt, and go against our enemy Indians. — May success attend them.

CHARLESTOWN S. Carolina Oct. 5. The express sent to the Cherokees is returned, and we hear the Indians cannot possibly at present go out against the Enemy. They say they have been naked a great while, that the white traders had trusted them with a great many goods which they have no way of paying for them, but by hunting, which they were just going about when the messenger arrived. —— We must hunt very strong, (they say) for the white people or they will never trust us again. If we had received a talk that our debts to the traders were to be paid, then we could all go out, but we cannot see our wives and children naked. —— If we are supplied with ammunition we will certainly go against the northward Indians in the Spring."

Attakullakulla or the Little-Carpenter returned from Virginia the 13th of August. The Seed formerly of Settiquo, three other Cherokees, and one James Brennom, a half-breed that talks English tolerably, part of Attakullakulla's retinue, remained in Virginia to bring some of Col. Chiswell's miners to make trial of the lead-mine discovered by him on the Tenassee river.

About ten days ago Oucconostota and several others were to set out for the great meeting with the Chickesaws and Chactaws, which the Indians last named had been informed of by runners dispatched about three weeks before.

PHILADELPHIA Oct. 11. Our last advices from Pittsburgh are, that all the forces had got safe there; and that Col. Bouquet, with 400 men, had crossed the Ohio, where he encamped, waiting of a number of volunteers from Virginia, hourly expected.

CHARLESTOWN S. Carolina Oct. 12. We hear that Capt. Cochrane, commanding his Majesty's troops here, who is set out to visit the out posts and garrisons in this province and Georgia, has been requested by his Honour the Lieutenant-Governor to look out for a proper situation on or about Stephen's creek for building a fort instead of Fort Moore, for defraying the expences whereof assembly hath made provisions.

PHILADELPHIA Oct. 18. Extract of a Letter from Carlisle, Oct. 3, 1764.

"A few Hours ago came to Town a certain De Haven from Conogoching, who informs us, that on Monday morning two Sons of William Armstrong, near Loudon, were plowing and being called home to Breakfast, they left a Boy in the Field with the Plows. As they came in sight of the House they observed Indians about it, upon which they tacked about to return to their Plows, and take off the Boy, but found that he was gone; that hereupon they fled to Loudon. He further says, it was reported that the rest of said Armstrong's Family were missing; and that 19 Indians had been seen in three parties in the Settlement, ten in one body, seven in another, and two in another. ——— As many of the Over-Hill Inhabitants were gone to labour for a fall Crop, this report if it is proven true, (and Generally these reports are found so) will greatly discourage the poor People, and I am afraid prevent many from labouring for their next years Bread.

BOSTON Oct. 22. The following item in a London Newspaper lately received, Dated Aug. 15, 1764.

WANTED.

By one of our American colonies, for the better protection of the frontier inhabitants, and more effectual pursuit of the Murdering Indians. Fifty couple of true Blood Hounds.

As the Indians make their attacks by surprize, on single families; and having murdered men, women and children escaped thro' unknown ways, and their traks in the woods is soon lost by the pursuers: It is tho't if the breed of true Blood Hounds could once be obtained there, they would be of great use in such pursuits; and by discovering the enemy in their retreats, give our people frequent opportunity of coming up with them, and recovering the captives and plunder, and thereby more effectually discourage their attempts, and induce them to sue for, and more faithfully keep peace with us; and that during the war, such Hounds, by discovering the Indian ambuscades, may be a means of saving many lives of our poor countrymen.

It is therefore hoped, that Gentlemen who have dogs of that kind, which they know to be good, will be kind enough to spare them on this occasion: It is intended to furnish every scouting party of soldiers, appointed to guard the frontiers, with some of these Hounds. Two persons skilled in breeding and management of Blood Hounds, are wanted to go over with them to whom, being well recommended, good encouragement will be given. Those who are disposed to sell or give such Hounds for the service aforesaid, are desired to give notice thereof to Richard Reave and Son, of St. Lury-Hill, London.

NEW-YORK Our last Advice dated Sept. 28. from Col. Bradstreet, with the army under his command, was still at St. Dusky, waiting for the arrival of the Indians to execute the articles of accommodations, according to the stipulated terms. —— The Indians had been for some time past, very quiet in those parts. —— yet many people doubt their sincerity, and think if they can gain time to get in their winter stores, and find pretence to delay the operations against them till the season is past, and all our expensive preparations, and the difficult, painful services of the year, render'd entirely useless. That they will show themselves as inveterate, and as destructive enemies as ever; and that our easiness in admitting a reconciliation after suffering the most pervoking and and cruel expressions of their implacable malice that they could possibly invent, will probably give them reason to suppose they may treat us in the same manner again with impunity.

PHILADELPHIA Oct. 25. Extract of a letter from Fort-Pitt Oct. 3.

"Our army, consisting of 400 regulars 400 Pennsylvanians, 100 light-horse and 250 Virginia Volunteers, begin its march this day, towards the towns of the enemy Indians. We go across woods, and cut the road for pack-horses; this may make our march a little tedious, but as the woods are pretty clear, they may perhaps, not require much cutting. Our people are all in high spirit, and seems desirous that the enemy would meet us. In a week hence, you may reckon that we shall be at or near the first town being the Tuscarora, but it is abandoned; and from thence it about 170 miles to the lower Shawanese town, which we are also to destroy, but there are several little towns and habitations to burn, before we come to that. It will take 25 days to go; and we may reckon to be back again to Pittsburg about the first of December."

NOVEMBER 1764

PHILADELPHIA Nov. 1. A letter from Fort Pitt mentions, that they had a good store of provisions there, without the least interruption.
―― Ant that two soldiers, one of the 42d and the other of the 60th regiments have been shot for desertion. ―― By another letter of the 10th ult. we learn that a company of 60 Volunteers, from Maryland, had arrived there, in order to join our army.

CHARLESTOWN S. Carolina Nov. 2. The petty jury were discharged on Tuesday the 23d, having found Solomon Hughes and Wholanawidzie, alias Evil-Doer, alias a Creek Indian guilty of Murder. the court adjourned to Wednesday the 24th, when Solomon Hughes was sentenced to be hanged on Wednesday the 31st.

On Wednesday Solomon Hughes and the Creek Indian was executed pursuant of their sentence. The Indian had four interpreters at his trial; he was one of those taken by Salloe or the Young Warrior of Estatoe in the Cherokees, and by him delivered to the commanding officer of Fort Prince George; he was convicted of having murdered a settler named Bennefield near Long-Canes.

CHARLESTOWN S. Carolina Nov. 9. The number of new settlers who have had warrants for land granted them in this province for ten months past, amounts to upwards of eight hundred and seventy.

NEW-YORK Nov. 12. Extract of a letter from the Camp, near the Carrying Place, Sandusky late, October 5, 1764.

"I hope before now to have been on our passage towards home, agreeable to what I wrote from Detroit. ―― We are halted at Sandusky. ―― We all expected we were come here to finish the peace with the Shawanese and Delawares, which our Colonel had begun at Lance aux Fuilled, instead of that consequence of some orders just come, we are to attack them, and destroy them root and branch, or they must give up ten men to be put to death. ——— We have different reports every day in the army, and this may be as void of truth as many others that I know of: ——— We were going on very cleaverly, and should have finished the peace with the Shawanese, and the Delawares, if these orders, whatever they are, had not come; for they were bringing in 200 prisoners, and would have ratified the peace, and then we would have jogged home, after having restored tranquility to all this part of the world, open the trade, & give our poor miserable country one more chance of extricating herself from the load of debt she now so heavily labours under. ——— I have heard there are wheels within wheels; it may be so now. I am not connisieur enough to penetrate it. ——— I know we have been ordered to attack the Shawanese and Delawares. ——— The impracticability of a march into that country, 300 miles from hence without any horses, is well known; and the incapacity of the troops, to attempt it, is to evident; if you but look at them, more than half are in condition of Sir John Falstaffe's. ——— Our boats are the most excellent that ever formed for the service of this country, but the river which we are to go up in order to get to the Shawanese and Delawares have not water in the sufficient for an Indian canoe; and I assure you we have no contrivance to sail on dry ground. ——— We brought from Niagara, Indians of the five Nations; and expected great things of them, they were ordered to go with the army to attack Miamis, no, they said they would not; they were now desired to go against the Shawanese, but they stand like stocks not one of them will bulge. You see what our dependence ought to be on those dear friends of ours. ——— We shall see if example has any force on them. Our new acquired subjects the Ottawas, Chepawas, and Hurons, are gone against the Shawanese, &c. with a blood belt, they last night took up the hatchet and sung the war song. I hear we are to stay here till November. God forbid! my heart already akes at the apprehension of snow and ice. I have somewhere read of frost being so intense, as to freeze the words coming out of people's mouths; should it so happen here, the air would be full of curses from the lake of Coeytus, even to New York. Farewell, &c.

NEW-YORK Nov. 12. By the following letter we have further a further account of the progress of the Army under Col. Bouquet. From the Camp near Tuscaroras, October 20, 1764.

"Our little Army reached this Place after a March of ten Days without haulting, thro' a hilly Country, and many Streams to pass which gave some interruptions to out Pack-Horses: The Savages terrified, and astonished to find their Woods will not protect them, are coming in the most abject manner, to beg our Mercy and ask for Peace, or they must immediately fly away, and abandon their Country. We have had some meetings with their Chiefs, wherein our Commander unbraided them in severe Terms for their cruelty and Treachery; and particularly for their perfidious Behaviours in amusing our Forces at Lake Erie, with a fallacious Peace, and the notorious Lye that they had recalled their Mutherers from our Frontiers, whilst their Parties were committing the most cruel Murders, and continued their Massacres almost to this Time. They acknowledge every Thing, and begged Mercy and forgiveness. We march again to the middle settlements, where they are to bring all their prisoners to be delivered up, and there, it is said, we shall make peace with them."

PHILADELPHIA Nov. 15. In a letter from Stanton, in Virginia, Oct. 26, it is said, that on the 29th of September the Indians killed one Crawford and his wife, and burnt their house and barn, with a great quantity of grain in it. And the first of October they burnt the house of William Patton, and carried off a boy.

Our Advice from Carlisle are, that all is quiet there, our people in general returning to their places, and that fifty or sixty volunteers from the frontiers, marched with Col. Bouquet against the enemy.

Our intelligence from Pittsburg is, that that post enjoyed a perfect calm. not an Indian is to be seen on the communication, by which people with loads of butter, cheese, &c. arrive daily.

SAVANNAH Nov. The following intelligence was lately received from Charlestown dated Nov. 3.

"On Wednesday the 17th past the Court of General Session for the province began, when the Honourable Charles Shimmer, Esq; Chief Justice with Robert Pringle, Esq; assistant judge, attended by the officers and ministers of the court, the grand and pitit jurors & went from the State-house in procession to St. Philip's church and heard a sermon preached on the occasion by the Rev. Mr. Wilton; and being returned his honour delivered his charge to the grand jury. On Monday evening 22d, the Grand jury returned their presentment and were discharged, having found thirty three bills of indictment and thrown out twenty. The petit jury were on Tuesday the 23d having found Solomon Hughes, and Wholanawidzie, alias Evil-doer, alias a Creek Indian guilty of Murder; Josua Gin, James Wright, Sarrah Kelly, Eleanor Kelly, and Catherine Campbell of Petit Larceny: also verdicts on some indictments for assault.

The court adjourned to Wednesday the 24th, when Solomon Hughes was sentenced to be hanged on Wednesday the 31st.

The court adjourned ne die in diem, to Monday the 29th, when Wholanawidzie, received the sentence to be hanged the 31st.

BOSTON Nov. 19. The following received from Charlestown S. Carolina, dated Oct. 29, 1764.

On Wednesday last arrived the ship Friendship, Captain Samuel Bull from London with about 120 tons of ordinance and stores on board, for St. Augustine (consisting of near 60 mortars, &c. and 23 heavy cannon, &c.) and about 60 passengers, 40 of which were going to Florida. Among the passengers are Arthur Oneal, Esq; appointed his Majesty's ordinance storekeeper in West-Florida, with his family; Henry Lloyd, Esq; going to the settlement forming by Denys Rolle, Esq; at St. Mark's; Lieut, Funston of the royal Artillery, and Rev. Mr. Forbes, to Augustine.

PHILADELPHIA Nov. 22. Since our last a gentleman arrived from Mobille, who favoured us with the sight of a letter, which he receiv'd after he left that place, dated the 10th ult. in which was the following paragraph.

"I have no news to offer you from this place, only that it is now certain the Spaniards are coming to New-Orleans, which is mentioned in a letter from the King of France, to the Governor of the above place. It was ceded in the year 1762, and the Spaniards are said to be bringing out a garrison of 4000 men, to take possession of it."

And this gentleman received another letter from the same place in which was said, that some of the Spaniards had actually arrived; and that the French General had given notice to the inhabitants, that those of them who were inclined to remain under a Spanish Government, were at liberty to stay; and any who had a mind to remove, vessels should be got ready to carry them off.

NEW-YORK Nov. 26. On Monday Night last, an officer arrived Express from the army to the northward from whence we have received advices that Colonel Bradstreet had broke up his Camp at Sandusky, on the 18th of October; having first engaged many of the Upper Nations, with whom Peace has been concluded, to declare against the Shawenese and Delawares, and to send parties against them. That about 70 Miles from Sandusky, the lake rose in the Night, on a sudden, and the Surf beat with such Violence on the shore, where the army had landed, that between 20 and 30 boats were beat to pieces, notwithstanding the efforts to save them: The Night was very dark, and little than the small quantity of Provisions that were in them could be saved. The army proceeded to Grand River, about 70 Miles farther, which they entered in a Storm: The tempestuous weather having the appearance of continuing, and the boats being deeply laden, by receiving the additional men from the boats which were last; a number of the best marchers marched along the Lake Side, and the Indians took to the Woods. ——— The men who marched, were for a time relieved by other men from the boats: but provisions being out, and a Snow Storm upon the lake; about 200 men pushed for Fort Erie, in which they suffered greatly, and would have suffered more had not most of the advance being relieved with provisions and boats from Fort Erie, in consequence of Col. Bradstreet's directions, sent by express. The Remainder, except a few Missing, were taken up by boats, on the 2d instant, and the army arrived at Niagara; from whence, the Regular Troops and some provincials, sailed in the vessels on the 9th inst. The rest of the army were left to follow in boats under Lieut. Colonel Putnam. The vessels arrived at Oswego on the 11th instant, in a great Storm, in which the Snow Johnson, was lost going into the Oswego River; by this accident some baggage and arms were lost, but the men are happily saved.

PHILADELPHIA Nov. 29. Our advices from Fort Loudoun of the 22d inst. are that all was well in the frontiers; and that they expected soon to hear of the arrival of the army at Pittsburgh, from the Indian country.

NEW-LONDON Nov. 30. The following letter was wrote by Col. Putnam, at Sandusky, to Maj. Burke in Norwhich.

Camp at Sandusky, near Carrying-Place, Oct. 7.
Dear sir,
"According to your desire I have wrote to you several times, but have had no answer from you, not any body since I left home; nor don't know but you are all dead. I think you and Mr. Parke was to meet us somewhere hereabout; but believe you had better let it alone; for I can tell, the land is good eno', and suppose you would think it strange if I should tell you, that, in many places in this country, there is 10 or 20,000 acres of Land in a place, that has not a bush nor a twig on it, but all covered with grass so big and high that it is very difficult to travel; —— and all as good plow-land, as you ever saw; any of it fit for hemp; but there is too many henp-birds amont it, which will make it very unhealthy to live among.

Detroit is a very beautiful place, and also

all the country round about it. We sent out an officer and three Indians to the Delawares and Shawanese from Priskeal, to returned and were illy used. We sent the like number from Sandusky, and from the Moamme River, but all before any returned.

"From Sandusky we sent Capt. Monteur and Capt. Peter; from Moamme we sent Capt. Morris, of the 17th, and one Thomas King with three Indians, Capt. Morris returned some time ago, and was much abused, and strip'd and whip'd and threaten'd to be tomahawk'd, but had his life spar'd, in case he would return. Capt. Thomas King and three of the Conawawas proceed, ——— This Capt. King is one of the chiefs of Oneida Castle; and about ten days ago, King came in to Detroit, almost dead, and had left all the Conawawas; who gave out, for want of provisions, and could not travail: he supposed they all perished in the woods. And three days ago he arrived here, and yesterday he had a conference with the Indians: and when all assembled he made a speech to them, after some talk with them he expressed himself in this manner,

——— Friends and Brothers, I am now about to acquaint you with the facts too obvious to deny: I have been since I left you, to Monsieur Pontuck's Camp, and waited on him to see if he was willing to come in and make peace with our brothers the English. He asked me what I could mean by all that; saying you have always encouraged me to carry on against the English: and said the only reason you did not join me last year was for want of ammunition: and as soon as you could get ammunition, you would join me. King said, there was nothing in it, at which Pontuck produced six belts of wampum, that he had last year from the six nations, to join with them to carry on the war against the English. King said he did not know what to say about that; but said, he knew nothing of it. Pontuck said, that the six nations said, the English were so exhausted that they could do no more; and that one year's well push'd, would drive them all into the sea. King then made a stop for some time ——— Brothers, you know this not to be true, and you have always deceived me. ——— At which the six nations were all angry, and this day are all packing now to go off; and what will be the event I don't know, nor don't care, for I have no faith in an Indian peace, patched up with presents.

"Yesterday Capt. Peter arrived, which is the last party we have out. Capt. Peters says, the Windots are all coming in: but the Delawares and Shawanese are not coming. nor durst to come, for they are afraid, if they should come here, Col. Bouquet will be on their towns and castles; for he had sent to them to come to make peace; and on the contrary, if they should go to him, we should be on them. And they intend to lay still, until Bouquet comes first to them; and then send out to make peace, if possible, if not, to fight him, as long as they have a man left. But believe they wait to get some advantage of us, before they try for peace: But Capt. Peters says, Bouquet is within 30 miles of the towns; and believes, it to make no peace with them, for Col. Bradstreet had orders, from Gen. Gage, eight days ago, to make no peace with them, and to march to reach Bouquet. But, on calling a council of war and examining the Indians, and Frenchmen that was acquainted with the road, found it to be 50 leagues to travel by land, and nothing to carry any provisions, but on men's backs, which, allowing for hindrances, must take 40 days days to go and come; and four large rivers to pass, two of which must be crossed by rafts, and very difficult, and considering the season of the year, it was judged impracticable. And here we are, and for what I know not; nor when we are to leave it.

   I am, &c.   Israel Putnam.

DECEMBER 1764

NEW-YORK Dec. 3. On Tuesday last come to town 4 Officers, and a Company of Grenadiers from Detroit.
We are credibly assured, that Sir Willian Johnson proposes calling down the chiefs of every nation this winter, to his hall, on business of great importance to England and the people of America. A great number of Indians came to Sir William's the 6th of last month. The whole, we hope, will terminate to the honour of his Majesty, and the general benefit of his subjects.
HARTFORD Dec. 3. The Troops that were raised in the Colony las Spring and went out under the Command of Col. Putnam, have lately been disbanded, and are return'd to their respective Homes; they were remarkably healthy the whole of the Campaign.
NEW-YORK Dec. 6. We have no accounts from authority from the army, but it is rumoured that the famous Pondiack, finding the other Indian nations had made peace with the English, had sent a message, whith a string of Wampum, desiring to be included in the treaty; that col. Bradstreet broke the wampum, and sent back the messenger to acquaint him that he must come himself or send his Son; but that he found pretence to decline both, however that the last peace was concluded with him.
PHILADELPHIA Dec. 6. On Monday last arrived here Major Small, in his way to New-York, with dispatches from Col. Bouquet to General Gage, our advices by the gentleman are as follows.
That he left the Army in high Spirit, encamped at the Fork of the Muskighan, on the 18th ult. That the Expedition into Indian Country has had the desired Effect, the Mingoe, Delaware and Shawanese Indians, after a long Struggle, having

at last submitted in the Terms prescribed to them, viz.

1. To deliver up all the prisoners without exception.

2. To give fourteen hostages, to remain in our hands, as a security for the strict performance of the foregoing Articles; and that they shall commit no hostilities against his Majesty's subjects.

That upon these conditions they are permitted to send deputies from each Nation to Sir William Johnson, to make peace. That the Mingoes, have given two of the abovementioned hostages, the Delawares six, and the Shawanese six. That from the humble disposition of the savages, it was thought our frontier inhabitants might return to safety to their deserted plantations. That the Indians had brought in above 200 prisoners before the Major left the camp, and above one hundred more were daily expected. That the Delawares and Mingoes have not only delivered all the prisoners but even their own children, born by white women. That the Shawanese had been very obstinate, but were forced to submit to the same conditions as the other nations. That the enemy were said to be in the greatest distress, having neither Provisions, clothing, nor powder: their women, we hear, being covered with skins only, and the men in still worse condition; and that it was generally believed they are now sincere, and the peace will be lasting, as they are convinced, at last, that even their woods could not protect them, when followed by so brave and judicious a Commander, at the head of a gallant, though but small Army; that the whole of the troops on the expedition have behaved in the most regular manner, and shown the greatest activity and resolution; and it is particularly mentioned, that the men from this province have carried on the service with great Zeal and cheerfulness, and that their conduct does them honour in every respect. That the troops from this Government were to be sent immediately to Carlisle, and with them the prisoners belonging to it. That the Army have been very healthy, and had met with no loss since they had left

Pittsburgh, only one of the light horse who was killed by some Indians, supposed to be Wyondots, but that there were other Indians out after them, who promised to bring them in, if possible. And that the Colonel, with the Forces it was expected, would be at Fort Pitt on Sunday last.

NEW-YORK Dec. 10. Thursday last two officers came from our army to the southward, under Col. Bouquet, who they left encamped at the Forks of the Muskingham the 18th ult. by these Gentlemen we have the following intelligence, viz. That the army arrived there on the 28th of October, being in the centre of the Delaware towns, and near Wahatamike, the most considerable settlement of the Shawanese; & matters had been so managed with the savages, that we remained masters of the conditions we had to prescribe to them; first insisting on the delivery of all their prisoners, before any terms of peace should be proposed: The Delawares, Mingoe & some broken tribes of the Mohikons and Wyondots were first reduced, and submitted to the restoring all the prisoners, even to their own children born of white women, which was peremptorily insisted upon, and may be considered as a strong proof of their sincerity and humiliation, they had likewise given fourteen of their chiefs as hostages into our hands, for security of the performance of their engagements, and that no hostilities should be committed; and likewise agreed to send deputies from each nation to Sir William Johnson. properly authorized to make peace, engaging to ratify all the conditions that should be imposed upon them. The Shawanese were more obstinate, and refused to submit to the same conditions, shewing a particular aversion to the giving of hostages, the army was on the point of coming to extremities, but meeting with a firmness that staggered them, and being properly talked to, they found themselves obliged to stoop to the same conditions as the other nations. They immediately delivered up forty prisoners, and have given six of their principal chiefs as hostages, for the delivery of the remainder of their captives. Parties were sent to their towns, to assist in collecting them &

bringing them to fort Pitt. The number of prisoners already delivered exceed two hundred, and many more are expected from the Shawanese: Several of them remained so many years with the Indians as to become as savage as themselves, and the Indians were obliged to tie them to bring them to the army.

CHARLESTOWN S. Carolina Dec. 14. They write from St. Augustine, that the gentlemen there have subscribed upwards of 200 guineas towards making a road for carriages from that town to Fort Barrington in Georgia, whereby a communication will be opened for all sorts of carriages between East Florida and all the provinces in America to the Northward of it.

HARTFORD Dec. 17. Governor Penn, has publish'd a proclamation, ordering a suspension of hostilities between the province of Pennsylvania, and the Indian nations of Delawares, Shawanese and Senecas on the Ohio, till further orders.

His Honor Cadwallader Colden, esq; Lieutenant Governor of New-York has issued a Proclamation for the like purpose between the Goverment and the above Indians.

NEW-YORK Dec. 20. Last week Mr Levie Ashen belonging to Lancaster in Pennsylvania Government, who was taken prisoner at Pittsburgh about 4 Years ago by the Seneca Indians, and return'd on the late Treaty, to Sir William Johnson, came to town, and set out on Sunday last for Pennsylvania.

NEW-YORK Dec. 27. By a Letter dated the 8th Instant, from Mohawk River, of the best Assurance,

We are inforned, that by the strange conduct of some, Sir William Johnson will have infinite Work to do with the Indians. —— The distressed, struggling Army are now crawling homeward. —— Many left their Cacases in the Woods, and along the Lake Side, a Prey to the Wolves and the other Vermins, thro' merr Fatigue, and want. Some Indians and a few of the Indian Officers, are arrived in a shocking Condition; having been in the Woods 26 Days, without a Morsel, but what they killed, which was but a trifle for their number. The main Body of them with Capt. Montour,

Johnston, Lieut. Preston, &c. are expected in a few Days at Sir William Johnson's. They are detained carrying some sick Indians on their Backs through the Woods. [If the advice of Sir William had been attended to near three Years past, in all Probability we should have had no Indian War: for at that Time it was demonstrable that he could have form'd upon the surest Basis, such a Constructure of amity, with the Nations, as would no doubt have been productive of the most sensible Advantage to the Inhabitants here, as well as those at home: but he was abridged of a poor 7000 pounds which if properly applied then, would have prevented all the Calamities of a scalping War.]

Since our last the Captains Rea, Byrn's, Dawson, White, and Grant, of the Provincials, returerd to this city from the Expedition under Col. Bradstreet.

BOSTON Dec. 31. Extract of a Letter from St. Augustine.

"Believe me, the English Papers have greatly exaggerated in their favourable Accounts of this Place. I never saw in my life a more unpromising Spot, though I have been a Sojourner in both the Indies. The whole Province of East Florida is little better than a sandy Desert, parch'd and dry; the very Cattle can hardly subsist. God knows how we should live here, if Provisions were not brought us from the Northern Colonies: New-England cheese at 16. per pound: Butter. or rather putrefied oil. a vast price and every thing dear in proportion. Our common Currency are Spanish Piasters and Dollars, the latter of which does just purchase a Dinner notwithstanding, if it were not for some turtle from Providence and the Misquito Shore, we would hardly be said to eat; Judge then, if out of my 60. pounds per annum I can save money, Such is the place we have wisely exchanged for the Terrestrial Paradise of Martinico, I shall be home in December next. Adieu."

NEW-YORK Dec. 31. A Letter from Detroit dated the 12th ult. says "Yesterday some of the Indians belonging to this Place, who had been out on a Scout against the Shawanese, returned with the Scalp of one of the chiefs wives: They were extremely well received by Col. Campbell, our Commandant, who made them several presents, which they seem well contented.

We hear there are some late advoces come to town from the army at Fort Pitt, but have not time to get the particulars, or any authenticated accounts. It is said the 6 hostages given by the Shawanese Indians, had made their escape, but being pursued, had been all retaken, except one, who was shot.

JANUARY 1765

CHARLESTOWN S. Carolina Jan. 4. Major Loftus was preparing in November last, to go up the Missisippi to take possession of Fort Natchez, the Illinois and other posts.

CHARLESTOWN S. Carolina Jan 11. The 32d regiment goes to Mobile, instead of the 22d, Captain John Ormsby of the 35th is appointed Major there of Major Forbes appointed Lieutenant Colonel.

CHARLESTOWN S. Carolina Jan 11. The last account from West-Florida are of November 30 when every thing was in a fair way of being adjusted with the Indians, in regard to the extent of British settlements there.

Our last advices from the Cherokee country informs that every thing continued quiet amongst those Indians, Ottassite who went out with a party some time ago to intercept the supplies which it was expected the French were sending to the enemy Indians, was not returned.

Last week a number of waggons arrived in town, by direction of his honour the Lieut Governour, in order to carry up some of the Germans lately arrived here with their arms and other necessaries, and accordingly about fifty of them are set out for the lands allotted them on the Long Canes settlements, about 20 miles W. N. W. from the French settlement of Hillsborough.

HARTFORD Connecticut Jan. 21. Extract of a letter dated London Oct. 24, 1765.

"It is said a scheme is on foot for the more regularly relieving of the several British regiments now stationed in the West-Indies and North-America, by which such troops as are order'd abroad, may have an opportunity of returning again to their own country, without being condemned to spend half their lives, in the torrid Zone.

CHARLESTOWN S. Carolina Jan. 31. Letters from the country of the Creek Indians inform us that the Hon. John Stuart, Esq; Superintendant of the southern district of North-America, has summoned all British traders in the country to meet him at Pensacola on or about the 1st of March next, when he is to hold a congress with the Creek Indians. The last Advices from West Florida informs us, that the Superintendant was then holding a congress at Mobille with the Chickesaws and the Choctaws Indians, and that his Excellency Governor Johnston was with him.

FEBRUARY 1765

CHARLESTOWN S. Carolina Feb. 2. Letters from West-Florida of the 17th of December advice, that a peace has been made with all the Induan nations upon the Missisippi, as high as Fort Natchee: That the only enemy above that post, are the Arkansa's, who had promised to meet Lieut. Campbell at Point Coopee the next full moon: a safe navigation is now opened from the Missisippi, the rivers Iberville and Amit to Lake Maurepas, a passage of great consequence to that province; that a fort is to be erected on Point Iberville, now Point Richmond, about 36 leagues from New-Orleans, which will completely command the river, and greatly facilitate the gaining possession of the Illinois. The 34th regiment is to go to the Illinois, and the 22d home, and a great number of French and German emigrants are soon expected at Mobille, to settle the fruitful banks of the various rivers in that province.

BOSTON Feb. 4. In the Southern Papers there is a list of the Names, &c. of Ninety-one Virginians, and one Hundred and sixteen Pennsylvanians, who had been taken captive by the Indians, and were delivered up to Colonel Bouquet, by the Mingoes, Delawares, Shawanese, Wiondots, and Mohecons, at Tuscarawas and Muskigum, in November last.

His Excellency James Grant, Esq; Governor of his Majesty's Province of East-Florida, has issued a Proclamation, to make known to all Persons that they may, on Application to him in Council, at St. Augustine, obtain Grants of Lands in said Province, on Condition specified in said Proclamation.

CHARLESTOWN S. Carolina Feb. 6. Letters from West-Florida, dated 14 days ago, informs us, that the Hon. John Stuart, Esq; Superintendant of the southern district of America, was then in Mobille, where the headmen of the numerous nations of Choctaw Indians were to meet him on the 15th inst. A congress is likewise to be holden at Pensacola with the Creeks next month, and an other with the same Indians at St. Augustine as soon as the Superintendant can leave West-Florida: A proper boundary between the two Floridas and the Indians, we are told, is one great objects of these negotiations. The small nations of Indians on the Missisippi who stopped Major Loftus's progress, seem now better affected to the British nation, The Superintendant having sent a deputy amongst them. The 34th regiment commanded by Major Farmer, is preparing to set out to take possession of the Illinois: the Superintendant sends out two gentlemen well acquainted with the Indians on that route, to go before the troops and make the path straight. The Spanish troops, were not arrived at New-Orleans but were hourly expected, and are said to be in number 4000.

Mr. D'Abadie the French governor gives the strongest assurance of his readiness to facilitate every measure necessary for our taking possession of the Illinois, and other posts on the Missisippi. His Catolic Majesty has appointed M. Istassi first, and M. Villemont second in command, in the new acquired country of Lousiana.

LONDON Feb. 12. By a letter from the Hon. major general Gage, commander in chief of his Majesty's forces in North America, to the Earl of Halifax one of his Majesty's principal secretaries of State, dated at New-York the 13th of December, 1764, the following advice have been received.

The perfidy of the Shawanese and Delawares, and their having broken the ties, which even the Savage nations hold sacred among each other, requires vigorous measures to reduce them. We Experienced their treachery so often, that I determined to make no peace with them, but in the heart of their country, and upon such terms as should make it secure as it was possible. This conduct has produced all the good effects which could be wished or expected from it. Those Indians have been humbled, and reduced to accept of peace upon the terms presented to them, in a manner as will give reputation to his Majesty's arms amongst the several nations. The regular and provincial troops under Col. Bouquet, Having been joined by a good body of volunteers from Virginia, and others from Maryland and Pennsylvania, marched from Fort Pitt the beginning of October, and got to Tuscaroras about the 15th. The march of the troops into their country, threw the Savages into the greatest consternation, as they had hoped their woods would protect them, and had boasted of the security of their protection from our attacks. The Indians however found the troops during their march, but despairing of success in an action, had concurred to negotiate. They were told they might have peace, but every prisoner in their possession must first be delivered up. They brought near twenty, and promised to deliver the rest; but as their promises were not respected, they engaged to deliver the whole on the 1st of November at the Fork of the Muskingum, about 150 miles from Fort Pitt, center of the Delaware towns, and near to the most considerable settlement of the Shawnese. Colonel Bouquet kept them in sight, and moved his camp to that place. He soon engaged the Delawares, and soon broken tribes of the Mohikons, Wiandots, and Mingoes, to bring in their prisoners, even to children born of white women, and to those who were grown as savages as themselves, and unwilling to leave them, must bring them bound to camp. They were then told that they must appoint deputies to go to Sir William Johnson to receive such terms as should be imposed upon them, which the nations should agree to ratify: And for the security of their performance of this, and that no further hostilities should be committed, a number of their chiefs must remain in our lands. The above nations subscribed to these motions; but the Shawanese were more obstenate. They did not approve of the conditions, and were particularly averse to the giving of Hostages: But finding their obstinacy had no effect, and would only tend to their destruction, the troops having penetrated in the heart of their country, they at length became sensible, that there was no safety but in submission, and were obliged to stoop to the same conditions as the other nations.

They immediately gave up forty prisoners, and promised the rest should be sent to Fort Pitt in the spring. This last not being admitted, the immediate restitution of all the prisoners owing the fine qua non of peace, it was agreed, that parties should be sent from the army into their towns, to collect the prisoners, and conduct them to Fort Pitt. They delivered six of their principal chiefs as hostages into our hands, and appointed their deputies to go to Sir William Johnson in the same manner as the rest. The number of prisoners already exceeds two hundred, and it was expected that our parties would bring near one hundred more from the Shawanese. These conditions seem sufficient proof of their sincerity and humiliation of those nations: And in justice to colonel Bouquet, I must testify the obligations I have to him; and that nothing but the firm and steady conduct, which he has observed in all his transactions with those treacherous savages, would ever have Brought them to serious peace.

I now flatter myself, that the country is restored to its former tranquility, and that a general, and it is hoped, lasting peace is concluded with all the Indian nations, who have taken up arms against his Majesty.

CHARLESTOWN S. Carolina Feb. 27. Letters from Cherokee country informs of the return of Ottassite or Judd's Friend, who went out at the desire of the superintendant in order to intercept the supplies said to be going up the Missisippi from the French to the enemy Indians, and that he had brought in two French prisoners who were speedily to be sent to Fort Prince George. Fourteen Cherokees, five men and nine women and children were lately killed by some Indians who live near the Missisippi.

MARCH 1765

CHARLESTOWN S. Carolina March 9. Several white men from the western parts of this province and North Carolina, have lately gone into this province and killed beaver, which occasions some uneasiness, as it is expressly contrary to the treaty; and we hear the Cherokees have complained of it; but in the same modest terms have adopted for two or three years past.

BOSTON March 11. Extract of a Letter from New York.

"The Delaware Deputies, who by treaty with Col. Bouquet were to meet Sir William Johnson in order to enter into a Peace, on behalf of their Nation, are arrived at Johnson Hall, having been greatly obstructed by the great snow. The Delawares who fled last Winter from the party of Indians sent out by Sir William, are likewise on their Way to Johnson Hall, with several prisoners, so that his Excellency will be sufficiently employed for some Time.

CHARLESTOWN S. Carolina March 16, Just now an account has come from Keeowee, that five of the Lower Town Cherokees were killed, about the 25th past, by some of their own colour but a different nation.

CHARLESTOWN March 20. The Honourable the House of Assembly of this province hath voted 7000 pounds, towards building a new fort (instead of fort Moore) on Savannah River, near the mouth of Broad-river, about 15 miles above Hillsborough township, which will be of great use to the three settlements of Irish, French, and of German protestants.

The following is the most particular account we have been able to procure of the expedition of Ottassite or Judd's Friend, (the Cherokee headman who was about three years ago in England) undertaken at the desire of the Hon. John Stuart, Esq; Superintendant of the southern district of America.

Ottessite went out in October last in order to intercept the supplies which it was said the French were sending up the Missisippi to the enemy Indians at Detroit, &c. When he got to the fort Assumption, which the French had evacuated, he received information that several loaded boats had gone up the river about 12 days before. In consequence of which information he took the route for several days; but finding it impracticable to come up with them, his party being weak, and doubting a little the truth of his Intelligence, he returned, and after some days marched down the river perceived two boats, which he followed, keeping out of sight till they should come to an anchor, which one of them did two days after at the fort, when Ottassite and his party seized the boat with two Frenchmen in her; the other boat pushed to the opposite shore, and the people escaped. He carried his prisoners into the fort, which he took possession of in his Majesty's name, made a fire, and out of a keg of brandy the Frenchmen had, drank the health of Great King George and Queen Charlotte, and obliged his prisoners to do the same, the 13th of January he arrived in the Overhill Cherokees with the two prisoners, and delivered them to the Superintendant's deputy in the nation, who intends sending them down to Mr. Price commander of Fort Prince George, Keowee.

Ottassite and his party having lost their Hunting season by this expedition, expect a reward so as to enable them to purchase as many necessaries as those that brought in skins or furs instead of prisoners.

The two Frenchmen above mentioned appear to have been furnished with a pass from the governor of Fort Chartres, to hunt and kill buffaloe in order to carry down the river to New-Orleans. Fort Chartres, is built of stone, and has a garrison of fifty men with an officer, who expects the arrival of the English troops every day. The French planters live there as formerly and carry on their farming.

The prisoners left the Illinois on November last, and acknowledged that several boats went up the Missisippi, agreeable to Ottassite's Information, but say, they were loaded with all sorts of Indian trading goods except ammunition, and that they all belonged to the merchants residing at the Illinois and were escorted by four Frenchmen. Five Englishmen, forty Delaware and fifty Shawanese. They further say that several large parties of Delaware and Shawanese came to Illinois last fall, but were refused any ammunition by the commanding officer, except as much as was sufficient to carry them back; and that they thereupon went away very angry. This, however was contradicted by the Cherokee Indian, who being in one of the parties sent out by the Superintendant last summer, was taken by the enemy and made his escape, as mentioned in this paper of the 5th of October last: he told the Frenchmen that he had told lies, for he himself saw the French officer distributing great quantities of arms and ammunition to the different Indians, bidding them, use them against the English and Cherokees: the prisoner had nothing to say for answer but that he did not see any such thing.

PHILADELPHIA March 27. An extract of a letter from Carlisle, dated March 14, says, "An affair has lately happened in the upper end of Cumberland, which has given us, and the best thinking people of the country, much uneasiness. Some time ago Captain Calender employed several waggons to carry Indian goods to Mr. Pollan's, in Canogochig, to be carried then by pack horses to Fort Pitt. Unhappily the head came out of one of the barrels which was full of scalping knives, (say the people) pruning knives say others, the news of this alarmed the upper end of the country, and the neighbouring parts of Maryland and Virginia, upon which advertisements were posted up, inviting all to join and prevent the carrying ammunition and such things to the Indians, by which the frontiers had suffered so much before, (This we in Carlisle heard by the Pack horse masters who came down to the settlements.) Our next news was, that a number from Maryland,

Virginia and Conogochig, had followed and overtaken eighty-one horses loaded with goods, and killed the horses, fired at the drivers, and burnt the goods, which alarmed us very much. Hereupon Mr. Calender rode thither, by whom on his return we learned, that four or five horses were shot; and sixty one horse loads of goods were burnt; eighteen loads of rum, and two of match coating were saved; we understood likewise, that Robert Alison, dispatched from Loudoun, with a number of Highlanders to the place where this happened, viz. near Sidling-Hill, and upon their return to Loudoun took up two or three people whom they suspected, and brought to Loudoun, upon which we are informed, several parties appeared in and about Loudoun, and demanded the men to be enlarged upon bail, which was accordingly done, and that Mr. Calender returned to Carlisle.

We are further informed, that another party, supposed mostly from the border of Maryland, meet Pollan's alias Howe's and examined the remainder of the goods, and searched for ammunition, but finding none, went to Maxwell's, where they found and burnt some casks of powder. This, Sir, is the truest account we could learn. ——— It gives us much concern that an affair of this nautre should have at all happened and the rather as the innocent will share in the reproach; but this is not to be omitted, which gives us a good deal of satisfaction that few, if any, of the principal inhabitants of Conogochig, were concern, and that upon understanding there was a design of this nature carried on by some hotheaded, stiff people they used their utmost endeavours to discourage and disswade them from such an undertaking; and that particularly William Smith, Esq; and John McDowall, strove with all their might to crush it.

We make no doubt, Sir, from the temper that seems to prevail with some, but that the body of Conogochig settlers will be represented as concerned, and from the disposition which some are already discovering, we are ready to apprehend, that endeavours will be used, and innuendos given, that the whole county will be traduced as privy, and accessaries to a fact which we heartily condemn; we therefore must humbly request, Sir, that you will inform our friends of the true state of affair, and we hope that the most thinking and virtuous of every society will not easily admit innuendos and indiscriminate reflections, which men may too liberally pour out on the whole county in general."

An extract of another letter from the same place, dated March 19, says, "Some few days ago we transmitted you an account of the Conogochig affair, according to the best information we could obtain, and thought we have had latter accounts, yet nothing contrary to what I gave you. A few days ago William Smith Esq; came to Carlisle, from whom we have had a very Circumstantial narrative, viz. That upon the first report of goods being upon the road, the country was alarmed, hearing that a vast quantity of ammunition and scalping knives were carrying out; that many of the people had applied to him, complaining that, before there were any confirmed account of a peace being established with the Indians, ammunition should be sent them; Alleging, that if it had been by authority, either some of the King's troops would have escorted the ammunition, or the General's orders had been known, and hence concluded it must be the mere notion of some merchants who wanted to catch the benefit of an early commerce with the savages. So reasoned the people. Mr. Smith advised them not to raise any disturbance, and to satisfy themselves by enquiring on one Whiston who accompanied the said goods; the young man was not condescending enough to honour the people, which increased their suspicion and raised their indignation. A part of the goods at length set off, and as the carriers were passing into Great Cove by the house of said William Smith, they were overtaken, by a considerable body of men armed, who seemed much enraged; but by the endeavours of Mr. Smith, and the fair words of Elias Davies and Robert Alison, who were employed to carry out said goods, were persuaded not to stop the horses, and a good many went home, but still a great number of the party suspecting that there was ammunition among the goods, followed into the Great Cove, where said Davies and Alison opened such heads that was suspected, and convinced them that there was no ammunition; at this the people seemed satisfied, and next morning as Elias Davies, who was to go no further than the Cove, returned, the greatest part of the people returned with him, he thought they had all come back, and as they had passed Mr. Smith's house, Mr. Smith believed this to be the case, and all danger was over. but Mr. Smith thinks a few, not above 15 or 16 [the carriers in their affidavits say about 20] according to the best accounts he could get, had parted that evening from the rest and privately followed the carriers, and near Sidling-Hill did the mischief, viz. Shot six horses and burnt about 60 loads of goods. Mr. Smith was for some time of the opinion that it was done by a company from Virginia, as a report prevailed among them that the Virginians on the Frontier had so threatened.

"As to the consequence burning of seven or eight casks of powder at Mr. Maxwell's our opinion that it was by a company from Maryland is more confirmed by a deposition made this day before John Holmes Esq. by Volgomet in Maryland, near Potomack, who being occasionally here, was taken up on suspicion by Mr. Calender, who was threatened to be put into goal unless he would give bail for his appearance; he deposed that on the 10th instant, a number of armed men rode by his house towards Pennsylvania, he inquired whither they were going, but gave him no other answer, but up the road.—— and further said, that on that or next day one Prector told him that said company had destroyed the powder at Maxwell's. —— And we are of opinion, that the greatest part of the people who first followed the carriers were mostly about the line.—— I would only add, that however unseasonable the carrying out of goods, especially ammunition to to the Indians (before there is a certainty of peace) appears to many, yet all the sensible thinking people I have conversed with condemn the conduct of those who seized and destroyed them."

APRIL 1765

CHARLESTOWN S. Carolina April 3. The last letters from West Florida informs us, that the Hon. John Stuart, Esq; Superintendant of the southern district of Nort-America, was then in Mobille, and that the Wolf King, the Mortar and all the headmen of the Upper Creeks, had sent down runners to acquaint him of their intentions to meet him there last month.

PHILADELPHIA April 4. On Saturday before last his honour the Governor set out for Carlisle, attended by some gentlemen, in order to enquire, we hear, into the cause of a quantity of goods being destroyed by a number of men near Sidling Hill.

WHILMINGTONTON N. Carolina April 10. We hear that a party of Cherokees, who lately went to hunt on the Missisippi, have lost 5 men and 9 women, killed by a nation of savages hitherto unknown to them.

BOSTON April 22. The Board of Correspondence in the Colony of Connecticut being called together on the 12th Day of March 1765, to examine a Number of Students, in the Charity-School in Lebanon, under the Care of the Rev. Mr. Wheelock, in order to their being authorized and sent forth as Missionaries and School-Masters, out amongst the remote Indian Tribes of Indians; at the very instant when the Commissioners were coming together, came in Gwedelnes Agwerondonewas, a Man noted for integrity and Religion, and of distinction and great Importance among his Tribe on Susquehanna River, and who was principal Actor in taking the Delawares, who were sent to New-York Goal, last Year; and with him Dawet Shagorakaongo, Son of the chief Sachem of that Party; and bro't with them a Boy designed for this School. And at the same time came in

Mr. Elisha Gun, an accomplished Interpreter; who had heretofore for several years resided in the same place with these Indians, and contracted an intimate Acquaintance with each of them. The three Parties though from places so very remote, all met together at this favourable Juncture within the space of half an Hour, without any previous Notice or Appointment. By Mr. Gun, they were enable in the best manner to communicate, and we to receive the Message which they brought, and which was the first thing the Commissioners attended to, and was as follow.

"Brothers, I received Intelligence from this Minister here, (meaning Mr. Wheelock) that he desired I would visit him at his School. After I had considered of the affair, I informed the Indians; they called a council; in which I told them, I had concluded to accept of his offer. At which they said they were very glad, as they wanted to send a Speech to their Brethren the English, and had no white man to write for them. They thanked me for my Understanding, and delivered me a Speech to be delivered to out Brethren the English as follows.

"Brethren, We thank you greatly that you love and regard us. Brethren you say, that you love God's News; likewise, that you love the Indians, that you love God's News above every thing; that you desire we should be happy as well as you. We are exceeding glad Brethren that we hear such Things from you. Brethren, you say, that you would be glad if you had our children, that you might learn them to read. It is a very difficult Thing for us to send them now; the most of them are from home. Another Difficulty is, we hear they have the Smallpox, on the Road, and we are concerned about that. We expect, Brethren, that you will find us a Minister this Spring; and that and that we shall have Opportunity to send our Children by him, as he goes backwards and forewards.

Now. Brethren, Concerning your sending a Minister among us. We have had many Ministers; that come and stay among us a little while; and we just begin to love them, and they go away and leave us. Now we want you should send us a

Minister who is a Man of Courage and Resolution; and who will correct his Children (meaning his People) when they do amiss. When Fathers (for so they call Ministers) are gone Children will often behave themselves imprudently.

When our Fathers were gone, we took up the Hatchet, against the Delawares, in defence of our Brethren the English; and cut a piece of their Flesh. And since this, our Brethren have left us exposed, without any means of defence. It has been a Time of Difficulty with us; but now we think it almost over: We think it will be Peace.

Now, Brethren, We should be exceeding glad of a good Minister among us. We are poor miserable Creatures, left all alone, destitute of a Minister. We give our hearty thanks that our Brethren for your love to us, and the Care you take of us."

After the Board immediately proceeded to the Business for what they were called, and how directly and agreeable they pursued the Thing requested of them may appear by the Votes then passed, which is as follow.

This Board having examined Mr. Titus Smith, and Mr. Thropbilus Chamberlain among the Indians, do approve of them as qualified for that Business.   Voted,

And it is further agreed by this Board that Mr. Titus Smith and Mr. Chamberlain, be separated and set apart to the Work of the Gospel Ministry, and a Mission among the Indians, by fasting and Prayer, with laying on of Hands, on Wednesday the 24th of April next.

Voted, That nine of the Indian Scholars, now at the Charity-School, under care of Rev. Mr. Wheelock, return to the Indian Tribes for a seaon. Three of which, viz. Joseph Wooly, David Fowler, and Hezekiak Calvin are recommended by this Board to be improved as School-Masters among those Tribes, having been examined for that purpose. The others, though well instructed and educated for the Time, yet considering their want of age, are to be employed by the English Missionaries, and under their Care and Direction in such service an Employment, as shall be found most serviceable and useful for them, and those Tribes where they shall reside; and in special to present themselves in Languages of their Tribes. The School Master also to be employed under the Visitation and Direction of the English Missionaries while they reside there.

Hereupon, Answer was returned by this Board to the following Request, that a Missionary was appointed for them, provided Support for him may be obtained.

And as there is no Fund nor any Provisions made, for their Support on their Mission; and a wider door then ever is now opened, by late favourable Occurrences to carry the Gospel far into the Indian Country; and the Advantages thereof at the present Juncture, likely to be greater than ever to the Crown of Grear Britain as well as to Enlargement of the Great Redeemer: So it is hoped and earnestly desired, that the Christians of every Denominations, who love our Lord Jesus Christ and wish well to our King and Country, would shew their Liberality upon this Occasion, and that in Proportion at there expence, in such a Situation, where an Assistance from the Savages, is to be expected, must need be very considerable; though they neither ask or desire more than to be supported, whole in that service, so as to be able to perform the important Business, and answer the great End of their Mission.

And we hope such a Pattern and Example of Charity towards the perishing Creatures as they herein shew, will be a further Motive to excite Largeness of Heart, in the People of God, sufficient to feed and cloath them, while they are thus jeoparding their own Lives, and risking every worthy Interest, to serve our King and Country, and especially save the perishing Souls of Men from eternal Death. Signed by Order of the Board of Correspondence.

                        Elizr. Wheelock, Secretary.

MAY 1765

CHARLESTOWN S. Carolina May 6. A letter from Augusta, dated 1st. inst. informs us, that some traders lately arrived there from the Creek country say, that three hundred Chickesaws, and fifteen hundred Choctaws are lately dead of the small-pox; and the Creeks say, the Indians always catch some dreadful disorder when they go to meet the white people.

Letters from the Cherokee country informs us, that Salloue or the Young Warrior of Estatoe, who set out with a party in pursuit of some of the Northward Indians who had scalped and taken eight Cherokees, was returned with success.

SAVANNAH May 9. Mr. Simpson is appointed third Lieutenant in the first troop of rangers in this province, by Capt. John Milledge in the room of Lieutenant Joseph Butler, who has resigned, and Doctor John Perkins is appointed quarter-master of said troop.

A Letter from Mobille, dated 12th April last, says, that 200 French Families from Cape-Francois arrive lately at New-Orleans, which makes it doubtful whether that place is to be given up to the Spaniards or not. Capt. Hughes, who arrived here on Monday last in 21 days from Mobille, informs us, the day he sailed a report was current there, that several Spanish vessels, with troops on board, were arrived off Fort Bulise, one of the mouths of the Missisippi. His Excellency Governor Johnston and the Hon. John Stuart, Esq; superintendant of the southern district lately held a congress at that place with about 2000 Indians of different nations, which lasted three weeks; and we hear they will soon be another congress at Pensacola.

NEW-YORK May 20. We can assure the Public. That Sir William Johnson at his Seat at Johnson

Hall, on the 4th Instant was surrounded by upwards of a Thousand Indians of different Tribes not in a hostile Manner, all Friendship: and that every Thing went on well in the Negotiation greatly in satisfaction of his Excellency, as tending to the good of his Majesty's Subjects.

NEW-YORK May 20. Monday arrived from the Westward, six companies of the first battalion of the Royal Americans, and next day set out for Albany: We hear they are to be posted at Albany, Mohawk river and Lake George.

CHARLESTOWN S. Carolina May 22. The following is the most particular account we have been able to procure of the late expedition of Salloue or the Young Warrior of Estatoe: ——— "On the 30th of March last a hunting party of cherokees, ten were attacked in their camp by thirty Shawanese, Delawares, &c. who killed and scalped one young man, and made two young men, three boys and two women prisoners; two young men got off and gave information to their people, on which fifty men were detached the next day to march with the greatest expedition, in order if possible to retake the prisoners, and revenge the insult; the command of the whole being given to Salloue.

April 9th, late in the Evening, the scout discovered the enemy, of which Salloue being informed, immediately called a council of war, when it was agreed to dog them in their canp, there surrounded and attack them early in the morning; accordingly on the 10th, about Daybreak, the Cherokees poured in about the enemy, some whereof mending their mockasins, and others not got up: they released their own people, who were lying in stocks, killed and scalped four of the enemy, two of whom were warriors, and wounded a great many, took almost twenty guns, twelve tomahawks, and a number of wampum belts, some gorgets and all their cloaths, which last were of very little value. The Cherokees had one man killed and three wounded, one with a Tomahawk, another with a spear, and the third with an arrow. Notwithstanding the surprize, and what the enemy suffered, they carried off one of their prisoners: upon receipt of the news, on the 24th past, three of the great guns were fired at

Chote, and the party, with their brave leader, were received with all the honours could give them."

Letters from the Cherokee country likewise inform us, that the Mortar of the Creeks had sent a talk about the middle of last month to Oucconnostota or the Great Warrior, which was said to have come from some Frenchman about New-Orleans, inviting Oucconnostota and some other Cherokee headmen to accompany the Mortar to meet him and five other French warriors some where above Albama fort; But Oucconnostota refused the invitation, though accompanied with a present of rum saying, "The French now talk for nothing."

CHARLESTOWN S. Carolina May 22. Extract of a letter from Mobille in West-Florida April 3 1765.

"On Tuesday the 26th, ult. the conference with the Chikesaws and Choctaws were opened: they are favourable and friendly as can be conceived. There are here above two thousand Indians, and so orderly, that they are hardly heard in town. The superintendant [John Stuart, Esq,] is much carressed by them, and is this day to received a beloved name from them with great solemnity; he has sent Peter Acton Sinnot, Esq; up the Missisippi to the Illinois, who is accompanied by Mons. De La Gauterais, now a British Subject, and intimately acquainted with the tribes on that river. He has likewise sent Lieut. Charles Stuart to Point Iberville, where Capt. James Campbell commands, to settle all matters with the small tribes round the post. In short, every thing here thus far promises peace, and we shall soon know what humour the Creeks are in, as they are to be with us in about a month or so."

CHARLESTOWN S. Carolina May 29. Letters from Pensacola, in West-Florida, of the 4th instant advise, that the congress with Hon. John Stuart, Esq; Superintendant of the southern district of America, had been holding for some time with several nations of Indians, was ended much to the satisfaction of the said Indians, who had consented that British subjects might settle and possess any part of their country within 40 leagues from the sea.

SAVANNAH May 30. The following newspaper was

received with the London Head of February 26.

"Last week 47 young women were engaged on high encouragement, to embark for Pensacola and Augustine; after the expiration of the term agreed, they are to have free passage to England, should they chuse not to remain longer here in America.

JUNE 1765

NEW-York June 3. Governor Fauquier of Virginia, has issued a proclamation offering a reward of 100 pounds for apprehending the ringleaders of a gang of villains that fell on a party of Cherokees as they were coming down to Winchester, and killed the chief and four others of the said Indians, and wounded two more.

The six nations, with the Delawares, arrived at Sir William Johnson's the 6th and we are assured have agreed to the particulars recommended to them by the King's orders. The Delawares of Ohio and Susquehanna, has subscribed to a treaty of peace which must prove very advantageous if duly observed; the latter have left their two chiefs, as hostages, until they bring down some prisoners, and the Senecas have done the same. The number of Indians assembled on this occasion exceeded 900. They were to go to their respective homes in a few days after the 16th of May, and the prisoners were to be delivered up within 40 days, in which time there is reason to expect they will be punctual, as there are so many of their chiefs hostages at present in Sir William's custody, whose enlargement must be greatly desired by the several nations.

PHILADELPHIA June 6. From Virginia we learn, that a party of Cherokee Indians had arrived at Stanton, in Augusta county, in the way to Winchester, having a pass from Colonel Lewis for that purpose, but on their way thither, they were attacked by upwards of Twenty Men, when the Chief, with some more of said Indians, were killed, and two others wounded; upon which a Proclamation was immediately issued offering a Reward for the murderers.

CHARLESTOWN S. Carolina June 12. Extract of a

letter from Mobille, in West-Florida, dated May 6, 1765.

A gentleman is just returned from the river Manchak or Iberville, about thirty eight leagues from New-Orleans on the east of Missisippi, a very pleasant situated and a good soil, abounding with fish and game. The neighbouring Indians are very peaceful and seem to be inclined to live peacefully with us, and they themselves say, while we are at peace with the French. There vicinity to the people has naturally attached them to the French interest, and low mercenary individuals make it their study to keep them blind to their own; but the disposition of the superior and more powerful nations toward us has already begun to open their eyes. Capt. Campbell has given them some trifling presents; but their permitting him to do what he had done has been greatly owing to the just, though kind representation of Mr. Aubry, who commands at New-Orleans since the death of M. D' Abbadie. Capt. Campbell's opperations are not yet completed; the middle of last month the river was greatly uncommoded with logs, stumps, canes and rubbish, and the season so dry that numbers of fish died for want of water: a great deal of work has been done and a great deal yet remains to be done. A large spot is cleared for building a fort on the point of Iberville; the standing wood with the rivers Manchak or Iberville and the Missisippi form a sort of triangle, near it lies the Nautilus frigate, Lockee, and two sloops laden with artillery, stores and materials for erecting the fort, for which purpose an engineer is likewise there.

"The convoy which the Superintendant sent from New-orleans to Illinois was on Easter Sunday nine leagues above Fort Natchez, in good health and spirit. They had on board some Illinois chiefs, who came down to consult the French governor what they had best do in the present state of affairs. He gave them some small presents, and advised them to receive the English as friends and brothers. The Superintendant's deputy gave them greater presents, and honoured the principal with a medal, which he received with great satisfaction, and promised to carry a letter, which the deputy gave him, to Col. Bradstreet or officer commanding the army, together with the calumet of peace. They were highly pleased with the honours they received from Capt. Lockyer of the Nautilus, when they paid him a visit on board.

"Major Farmer sailed yesterday with the 34th regiment on the second expedition up the Missisippi, and we flatter ourselves that by the prudent steps taken to facilitate his passage, he will succeed, though some doubt if he will get further than Natchez this year.

"The Honerable John Stuart, Esq; Superintendant, has now finished with the Chactaws to mutual satisfaction, and the whole it is hoped will meet with the approbation of our superiors. He has been great trouble. There is not one French commission, medal or gorget left in the Chactaw nation; the last party of those Indians that arrived was to a man French, yet we think they returned English to a man: they chearfully accented to the treaty, and took their leave the 4th instant. The Superintendent, after his immense fatigue, is gone for a few days into the country, and propose to set out for Pensacola in about a week, there to meet the Creeks, who have been sending repeated messages to him for some time past, being impatient for the departure of the Chactaws, Chekesaws, &c. as he had absolutely refused to receive any of them before he has finished with the others. —— The Creeks have lately killed some Chactaws, and it is not doubted but revenge will be taken this summer."

Letters from Fort Prince-George informs us, that Ouconnostata or the Great Warrior was then there on a friendly visit to Mr. Price, the commandant, being the first time of that chief's trusting himself in our hands since 1759; he was very friendly, & gave the strongest assurance of his attachment to the English nation and interest.

Capt. Garvin Cochrane, commanding his Majesty's troops here, has ordered a party from Fort Moore to take post at Fort Charlotte. Fort Moore is to be entirely evacuated, the artillery, stores. &c. being ordered to the new fort above mentioned.

CHARLESTOWN S. Carolina June 12. The last advice from Pensacola are dated the 22d past, informs us that the congress with the Creeks was to be opened there about the 28th. The important affairs transacted at the great congress, which was opened at Mobille the 26th of March last, necessarily took up so much time that the congress with the Creeks could not be beholden any sooner, as it was never intended to assemble the Creeks till the said congress was concluded.

PHILADELPHIA June 13, Extract from a letter from Stanton, in Virginia dated May 29, 1765.

"On the 12th Instant, two of the Party of Cherokee Indians who escaped from the white People went to the House of a blind man, about ten miles from hence, where the tomahawked him and his wife, and took a very small scalp of the man, but did not disfigure the woman. The same day, about 4 miles from thence, as they were lying behind a log, a man on horseback came up, and his horse starting, threw him, when one of the Indians seized and struck him in the Cheek with his tomakawk, and imagining he had done his business, left him, and went to assist the other in catching the horse, but in the mean time the man escaped, putting his hat under his wound, to catch the blood, that they might not track him."

NEW-YORK June 17. Thursday last Capt. Dobson arrived here from the Havannah in 10 days; he says that it was very healthy at Pensacola, but was beginning to grow sickly at Mobille, whence he came away; that the 35th regiment under the command of Major Farmer, set out to take possession of the Illinois the 1st of May, but that it was suspected the Indians would impede their passage up the Missisippi notwithstanding their pretentions of friendship.

CHARLESTOWN S. Carolina June 19. By letters from North-Carolina we learn, that about the beginning of last month a party of Cherokee Indians, ten in number, were on their way through the western part of Virginia kindly entertained by Col. Lewis, who kept them two nights, and on their departure furnished them with a pass and a pair of colours; but in a little time after, they were set upon by a much superior number of lawless people, who murdered five of the Cherokees; what became of the other five we are not informed. Col. Lewis, immediately on receiving the information of the barbarous and more than savage outrage, dispatched expresses to his Honour Francis Fauquier, Lieutenant-governor of Virginia, who laid the advices before the assembly of the colony, then sitting at Williamsburg, and the house of burgesses came to the following resolutions, viz.

"Resolved, That the Killing of the Cherokee Indians, as mentioned in a letter of Colonel Andrew Lewis to his Honour the Governor, which he has been pleased to lay before this house, is a flagrant violation of the treaties of peace established and subsisting between his Majesty and the said Indians, and of the laws of this colony, and that the offenders ought to be prosecuted with the utmost severity.

Resolved, That an address be presented to his Honour the Governor, to desire that he will be pleased to offer a considerable reward for the apprehending the said Assassins; that he will cause the resolutions of the house to be transmitted to the Cherokees, and to assure them every proper step will be taken to bring the offenders to Justice.
                              John Randolph, S. H. B."

Lieutenant Governor Fauquier accordingly issued a proclamation offering a reward of one hundred pounds for apprehending each of the two principal ringleaders, and fifty pounds for each of the others concerned in the said murder who will make discovery that the rest may be brought to justice. Col. Lewis had apprehended two of the murderers, and had sent two messengers to the Cherokees to inform them of the whole affair; and we hear from Fort Prince George, that an express was arrived there with letters from Governor Fauquier, which Mr. Price the commandant had sent by an Indian to the Superintendant's deputy, then in the upper towns where the relations of the murdered Indians live, and

and are said to be of great interest.

PHILADELPHIA June 20. By a gentleman from Bedford we learn, that all was very quiet on the communication between it and Pittsburgh; that a large quantity of goods had lately got up there; and that a white man, named M'Clure, was killed at that place by an Indian, occasioned by some difference betwixt them, when the Indian took an opportunity of dispatching him by a knife. He afterwards escaped, but some Indians had gone out to endeavour to catch him, and bring him in.

SAVANNAH June 20. Last Friday was brought to town, and committed to goal, one William Procter, who had been for many years among the Cheokees and, during the last War with these Indians, as head of several parties, barbarously murdered many families of white people. He was taken near Augusta about five weeks ago, and it's to be hoped will now meet with his just desert.

NEW-YORK June 24. Extract of a letter from Detroit, May 19, 1765.

"Since the arrival of the Charlotte, we have been informed that Maisonvelle and Andrew the Huron, who you may remember, were sent from this to Fort Pitt, were sent from thence with some Englishmen to Illinois, whom it is suppos'd are burnt; as Pondiac's Nephew arrived at the Miamees from thence the 9th Instant, and told the Indians that Pondiac had seiz'd 6 Englishmen, one Frenchman, and three Indians, that had been sent from Fort Pitt to that place, and carried them to Ouittanon, where they were all burnt, except which they intend to bring to the Miamees for a present.

"Pondiac is now raising the St. joseph Indians, the Miamees, the Mascoutins, Ottanons, Pians, and the Illinois, to come to this Place, the beginning of next Month, to make what effort they can against us, for which purpose he had procured a large Belt for each Nation, and one larger than the rest for a Hatchet for the whole: They are to be joined by some of the Northern Indians, as is reported. This, this they say, is to be an understanding of their own, and they are not to have any assistance from the French."

"When Pondiac left the Miamees, he told them to remain quiet till he came back, and it should then be all Peace or all War.

"I make no doubt of their Intentions to perform what we have been informed of, tho' I don't think it will come to any head; and I am likewise well convinced if Pondiac can be made to believe he would be well received at this Place, he would desist from any Intentions he may have; but it will be impossible to convence him of that, while there is such a Number of traitorous Villains about him. You can't imagine what most infamous Lies they have made even since you left this. Some of them Fellows who came from the Miamee last Spring, upon whom we had a Court of Enquiry are run away, and have made some very insolent Speeches to the Indians." ———

We hear from good Authority, that on the 3d Inst. Sir William Johnson had just finished with 900 Indians; that his House was then full of Ottawas, Chippiwaes, and the Indians of Ohio and Sandusky. &c. were then on the way to his House, so that he is not likely to have a Moment's Leisure this Season.

We hear from Albany, That on Sunday the 16th Instant six Indians in a Bark Canoe, attempting to cross the Ferry at Green-Bush were overset by which Accident four of them were happily drowned.

Niagara May 30, 1765.

The following accounts received last Night from Detroit, from the Commanding Officer and Col. Vaugh in order to be made publick.

Sir,

"——— I received Intelligence lately of Pondiac's raising a great many Nations of Indians, who are to assemble at this Place the beginning of next Month, to make what Efforts they can against the English. Tho' I give little credit to this Information, yet am determined to be upon my Guard: The same Informers acquaint me, that Six Englishmen, a Frenchman, a Huron, a Mohawk, and a Delaware, arrived at Illinois from Fort Pitt, a short time ago, and that they were apprehended by Pondiac's Orders, and carried Prisoners to Ouatanon, where they were burnt except two, which Pondiac is carrying along with him to give to the Miamies. Whether this be true or not, can't say." ———

CHARLESTOWN June 26. From Fort Prince George we learn, that the messenger mentioned in your last arrived there the 4th Instant from Virginia with copies of the resolutions of the house of burgesses, and a letter accompanying them from Governor Fauquier to the chief of the Upper towns. The five murdered Indians belonged to Chilhoe and Settico, and has here powerful friends in the nation, who it was thought might be exasperated; the dispatches therefore were sent to the Superintendant's deputy by an Indian, as in all likelihood the express would have been knocked in the head. The Young Warrior of Estatoe having a great deal to say in the towns before mentioned is set off to try to reconcile the friends of the party who went out till they can be more particularly informed; and we are not without hopes that this unlucky affair may blow over though another of the like kind was the original cause of the late Cherokee war which cost this province and Virginia, as well as our mother-country, such immense sums.

CHARLESTOWN June 29. One William Procter, who was an active robber and murderer at the head of several parties of Cherokees, during the last war with the nation of Indians, is at last taken, and confined in Savannah jail.

JULY 1765

NEWPORT Rhode Island July 1. The following intelligence received from the southward. His Excellency the Governor of West Florida, and the Hon. John Stuart, Esq; Superintendant of Indian Affairs for the Southern District of America, on or about the 30th of May held a Congress at Pensacola, with the Mortar, Headman of the Upper Creeks, and about 600 other Indians, consisting mostly of Creeks, with some Chickesaws, Chactaws, &c. which terminated to mutual Satisfaction. The Indians made a Grant to the English of a large tract of Land.

CHARLESTOWN S. Carolina July 6. Extract of a letter from Mobille, May 10.

"By some late discoveries it appears, that the commerce carried on between the French at New-Orleans and the Illinois was the true cause of the obstruction which Major Loftus met with in attempting to get up the Missisippi last year. This commerce in the company which had a monopoly of it. Our taking possession of the Illinois puts an entire stop to this lucrative trade, but, as the Hon. John Stuart, Esq; Superintendant, had engaged the Chotaws to send an embassy to the small tribes, to prevent their attempting any thing against Major Farmer, we hope they will be quiet. The Superintendant has likewise engaged the Chicesaws to give peace to the Arkansas, the most powerful of those tribes, and with whom they were at war, on condition of their assisting the troops; both the Chikesaws and choctaws have used threatnings as well as promises to induce those tribes to behave as they ought. The Superintendant has likewise sent one hundred Choctaw warriors to accompany the troops on the eastern banks of the Missisippi, also a hundred Chickesaws, which the leader of that brave nation has promised shall meet them at the place where Mons. Dartaquet was defeated and burnt by the Chikesaws. Those two strong flanking parties will be of great service.

"These are some of the good effects of the late treaty concluded with the Choctaws and the Chickesaws, which was carried on and finished with great regularity, as well as dispatch. The Choctaw chiefs delivered up all the French medals, gorgets and commissions to the Superintendant, who having engaged the chiefs according to their ranks, put the British medals into the hands of his Excellency Governor Johnston, who hung then about their necks, at which instant was a general discharge of the guns from the fort, accompanied with all the drums and fifes of the two regiments: the Superintendant then delivered them their commissions with proper instructions and charges. The Indians, though the French Parade, (which made the present method necessary) were greatly effected with the solemnity of the ceremony, and the steady, severe and manly behaviour of the Superintendant, so different from the French. They acknowledged they had never seen any thing so grand and so Solemn. A few days afterwards they bestowed, with great power, on the Superintendant a beloved name, which signified "Great Head of the Choctaw Nation." in short the whole was begun, carried on, and finished in such a manner, as to afford very great satisfaction to all his Majesty's subjects in these parts, and does much honour to the abilities of the conductor."

NEW-YORK July 8. Postscript of a letter from Albany, dated June 24. says, "The news we had formerly from Detroit, of a second war with the Indians, is entirely groundless; some of our traders have lately met with some Indians on Lake Erie, who treated them with love and friendship."

Charlestown S. Carolina July 10. Letters from the Cherokee Country informs us, that the two messengers with the letters from Colonel Lewis and Chiswell, concerning the assassination of the Cherokee Indians formerly mentioned, were brought in the upper towns about the 2d ult.

Three Virginians likewise brought in a wounded Indian and delivered him to his relations. The dread and terror the traders were in may be easily imagined: They came all round the house of the Superintendant's deputy, who prevailed on some of the principal Indians to protect them, and appoint a meeting of all the headmen on the 5th, when Oucconnostota said, that the Virginians were the cause of the last war, &c. and said he would send no talk to Virginia, as they knew they had spilt the blood of the Cherokees, and how to wipe it away, when that was done, according to treaty, a good talk should be sent. In short, he desired that as many white men should die as they had been Indians killed. Our true and faithful friend Attakullakulla said he suspected the Indians had been in the same measure to blame themselves, he had always told them that they ought never to be in settlements without white people in company; and the same day set out for Virginia himself to accommodate matters if possible.

When Governor Fauquier's letters were read and explained to the Indians, they said they were very good, and it was very surprising the English should talk so well and yet kill their people.

CHARLESTOWN S. Carolina July 17. Letters from Pensacola in West-Florida of the 7th of June inform us, that the Creek Indians had then almost entirely left that place. The Hon. John Stuart, Esq; Superintendant, had succeeded in every thing to his wish; having among other things, obtained large grants of lands for that province from the Indians, who were the most numerous at any congress they ever held with the white people. ——— A Gentleman who was present tells us there were fourteen hundred, and from every town in the nation. The famous Mortar declared himself the Superintendant's brother and joyfully from him received a British Commission and medal, a length the French never could bring him.

Several traders having arrived with rum in the Cherokee nation, the Indians who lost their relations lately began troublesome, but as it is hoped an effectual stop will soon be put to this dangerous traffick affairs will return to their former channel. It was very lucky that there was not a single gallon of rum in the nation when the first news arrived, as otherwise many lives would have been lost. What sort of men are they who carry it?

WILLIAMSBURG July 19. On Tuesday last his honnour the Lieut. Governor gave an audience to the Little Carpenter [Attakullakulla] and Great Doctor, two headmen deputed by the Cherokee nation to enquire into the cause of the late murder of some of their countrymen in Augusta. Upon their being acquainted that the same was perpetrated by some mischievous people in that county, for the apprehending whom considerate rewards had been offered, they departed in good temper, relying on the assurances given them that all possible means would be used that justice might hereafter be done their nation.

NEW-YORK July 22. A North Carolina Newspaper of the 19th of June, has the following paragraph in it. viz.

"By late accounts from Pittsburg, we hear of Col. Crogham's arrival at Scito; he informs us that Lieut. Fraser, with his party, had left that place some time before he got there; and as there appears a very good disposition in the Indians, it was not doubted he would get safe to Fort Chartres, the place of his destination. These accounts contradict the reports which were received some time since, of his being destroyed by the Savages, which was hatched by traders to serve their own purposes."

PORTHSMOUTH New Hampshire July 22. Last Saturday Evening was committed to his Majesty's goal in this town one James Neal, an suspicion of Killing an Indian at Cohoss. 'Tis said the quarrel between them arose in the following manner. viz. Neal and the Indian agreed to hunt together for a certain time, and just as they were setting off in order to cross a small River, some business, obliged Neal to make a stop: The Indian proceeded over the river, and agreed to stop the other side till Neal got over. After a few hours he crossed the river, and found the Indian, when walking together about 14 rods, made a stop, and the Indian ('tis said being in liquor) began complaining, that he made too long a tarry before he came over, &c. and immidiately struck at Neal's head with his Tomahawk but luckily miss'd his aim, upon which he struck at his head again, but Neal fending off the blow with his hands jump'd towards the Indian, took the Tomahawk out of his hand, and started back, but the Indian still persisting to follow him with a large knife, he tho't it prudent to stand in his own defence, and immediately struck the Indian on the head with the Tomahawk, which kill'd him instantly. He afterwards surrendered up to justice.

SAVANNAH July 25. We hear from Fort Barrington that they have received accounts there, both by white people and Indians, that two white men have been lately killed near Pensacola, it is thought by Indians, and some of them are missing, and the rest of them thereabout seem to be very uneasy about the affair; one of the men killed is supposed to be Simpson an Indian trader, and linguister at Pensacola.

NEW-HAVEN July 30. A party of Indians who were lately hunting near Dewbury sent a messenger into that town to know on what terms could be allow'd to trade with the inhabitants. Before he left the town he agreed with one O'Neal to assist him to carry his Packages. Shortly after they departed, several circumstances occurred which occasioned a Suspicion that he had murder'd that Indian whom he agrees to assist, whereupon he was secured, examined and charged of the murder by Col. Bailey, who carried him to different places marked with a sign of such a transaction. After several Equivocations, when he was brought to the place where the blood was spilt, he confessed his guilt. He then pretended the Indian killed his brother in the last war also lately as they walked together he attempted to kill him also, which he prevented by destroying his adversary. O'Neal dragged the body into the river and had the goods near the bank thereof, where they were both found according to his directions. They then sent for the

Indian party, to whom it was proposed to send O'Neal to Albany or New-York that justice might be done, in order to prevent further mischief.

CHARLESTOWN S. Carolina July 31. Letters from Fort Prince-George inform us, that Salloue or the Young Warrior of Estatoe was returned from the Upper Towns, and had met with all the success he could expect in persuading the relations of those Indians who were assassinated in Virginia to forebear taking revenge, at least to wait to issue of Attakullakulla's journey to Williamsburg. These letters express great fear of mischief from the quantity of rum lately carried into Cherokee country from this province.

AUGUST 1765

NEW-YORK Aug. 5. We are informed, that Lieut. Fraser, who was sent to the Illinois, remains there until the arrival of Col. Croghan with presents for the Indians: That he is well treated and much oblig'd to the French Commandant, who, at the Hazard of his own Life, protected him from the resentment of the Savages occasioned by a report made to them, that some of his party had scalped in their march from Pittsburg twelve Indians. This Lie propagated for the Destruction of Lieut. Fraser, being resolutely confronted and refuted, and appeased them, and he remains in safety.

All was well at Detroit about 30 days since, and we hear the garrison of that place was not under any apprehensions of a visit from Pondiac.

PHILADELPHIA Aug. 14. M. Aubry the French commandant at New-Orleans, has received orders from his court not to repair or augment the fortifications under his command, and to give no more presents to any Indians whatsoever.

From Virginia we learn, that Attakullakulla with two other Cherokee headmen were arrived at Williamsburg, and that the assassins who were in custody for the murder of the Cherokees formerly mentioned had actually been rescued by a body of their accomplices, said to be near two hundred in number.

One of the Cherokees, that escaped in Virginia is got back to his own country.

Advice from different quarters informs us, that Pondiack has again commerced hostilities on the Lakes, and has stirred up several powerful nations against us. The Shawanese, it is added, appears on no good temper.

Advice from New-Orleans of June 9th says, that, a few weeks before, Pondiack was at Fort

Chartres in the Illinois, impatiently looking for the English troops who were to take possession of that country, that he might conclude a firm peace with them.

Major Farmer, with the troops under his command, left New-Orleans on the 10th day of June last, in order to proceed up the Missisippi to the country of the Illinois.

NEW-YORK Aug. 19. Extract of a Letter from Pennsborough Aug. 7, 1765.

"I have received a letter from Mr. Croghan, dated at Wiochtonan, the 13th of July; at which place he was attacked by a large body of Indians who killed two of his men, and three of the Shawanese deputies that accompanied him, wounded Maj. Smallman, and himself, and made them all prisoners. But when he informed them who he was, and on what business he was going; that he was conducted thither by the Shawanese nation, and that it was their chiefs who, were killed, they, in the most abject manner, begged forgiveness of him, as they then began to apprehend what they had done might be a means of bringing the Shawanese, Delawares, and Six Nations on them, whom they very much dread, However, he has accommodated matters with them entirely to his satisfaction, and intended to proceed to Illinois, where he expects success."

NEW-YORK Aug. 19. Extract of a letter from New-Orleans, June 19.

"Upon my arrival here, I was very much surprized to see Lieut. Ross; he was obliged to leave the Illinois, and come down the Missisippi to this place, not being able to stay there any longer in safety. A few days after arrived Lieut Fraser, from the Illinois; he was sent there by Gen. Gage, by way of Fort Pitt, he got to the Illinois without much difficulty, 5 days before Lieut. Ross left it: but upon arrival three of his men were taken prisoners by the Indians, and badly treated, both whip'd and stript; the Indians also threatened to kill them if they would not find their officer, who lay conceal'd, upon which Lieut. Fraser gave himself up to them, determined to share the same fate with his men or get them off; however, the manner of his giving himself up struck the Indians very much, and with the interest of Pondiac, he got himself & men back again; but upon arrival of an Indian Chief, (with a white woman to his wife) who told the Indian many lies, they again seized upon the men, but Pondiac obliged them to give the men back: Some days after this Lieut. Fraser got leave to let his men go down the river for Mobille, and they are arrived here safe, but he determined to stay, and Pontiac promised to protect him 'till he heard news of Mr. Groghan, who was to follow him in 12 days from Fort Pitt; but after waiting some time and hearing nothing of him, and being in continuous danger, several attempting being made to assassinate him, he was advised to go away, which he did in a batteau: He says Pondiac is a clever fellow, and had it not been for him he would never had got away alive. Mr. Ross and Fraser both agree, that it is the Indians, and not the French, that commands at the Illinois for the Indians do as they please; that many of the French, and particularly the traders, are a pack of very great villains, & do every thing in their power to set the Indians upon us. Major Farmer sets off in a day or two for the Illinois. There has been great desertions from the 34th regiment; but what remains do not seem dispirited or afraid of the expedition. ——— You may be assured the Spaniards will be in possession of this place by September next."

CHARLESTOWN S. Carolina Aug. 28. Extract of a letter from New-Orleans, dated June 9, 1765.

"About a fortnight ago arrived here, 14 men who accompanied Lieut. Fraser late Col. Fraser's highlanders from Detroit to Illinois. Lieut. Fraser was to have been accompanied by Mr. Groghan, Sir William Johnson's deputy; but the latter finding it necessary to confer with the tribes through whose country they were to pass, Mr. Fraser proceeded on his journey and arrived at Illinois the 13th of May: he was civilly received by M. de St. Ange the commandant (who has only seven men to keep possession of the fort) but whilst at supper with him he understood that some Indians had seized and going to put his men to death, upon which he went out and said he was determined to share the same fate with his people; whence upon Pondiack, pleased with his bravery, said he was a man and a warrior, and took him with his people under his protection. Mr. Fraser remains at Illinois, but all the people were sent down. Mr. Croghan was nor arrived at Illinois, when the last advices came away."

"M. De Gauterais with Mr. Sinnet deputed by Mr. Stuart Superintendant of the Southern district were met in their batteaus with presents for the Indian nations about thirty leagues bellow Illinois 15th of May: and it is to be hoped they arrived there safe in almost six days after.

SEPTEMBER-DECEMBER
1765

PHILADELPHIA Sept. 26. Extract of a letter from Fort Pitt. August 22, 1765.
"Tomorrow Capt. Thomas Sterling with 100 men of the 43d regiment leave this in battoes to take possession of the Illinois. Mr. Croghan the Indian Agent, having settled some priliminaries with the French Indians, is gone to Detroit to hold a great council."

SAVANNAH Oct. 3. Mr. Sinnet who accompanied M. de Gauterais to the Illinois with presents for the Indians, was at Pensacola about a month ago waiting an opportunity to go to charlestown. When they arrived at Illinois 13 nations of Indians were met there, who took their presents from them, and sent them back, telling them they would not allow any English troops to take possession of the fort. The Illinois were for putting them to death, but they were prevented by Pondiack.

NEW-YORK Oct. 21. On Tuesday last arrived, in 36 days from Pensacola; by whom we learn, that ten sails of Transports, with Troops, (to relieve those on that station, who are gone home) were arrived there, and that there has been a great Mortality among them, ten or twelve dying of a day, amongst which was the gallant and worthy Officer Brigadier General Bouquet, whose eminent Service and amiable character demand the tears of his country and acquaintance: ——— He arrived the 23d of August and died the 2d day of September. Out of six Officer's Ladies, who accompanied them, five were dead and the other very ill and not likely to recover.

BOSTON Dec. 16. In Capt. Scott came passenger, Nathaniel Potter, Esq; secretary to his Majesty's Garrison at Michilimackinac and to the

Western Indians: Mr. Potter left London the 23d if October last, and is going directly to New York. ——— Major Rogers, we hear, is appointed Governor Commandant of Michilimakimac, and its Dependencies, and Agent for the Western Indians and is expected in America in a few Weeks, but will not proceed to his Command till the Spring ——— He had the Honor to kiss his Majesty's Hand the 17th of October when he took Leave of the Court.

1766

PHILADELPHIA Jan. 2. On Thursday last an Express passed through this City from Fort Pitt to the General, with the agreeable and important News that Capt. Sterling, and his Party, had arrived safe at Fort Chartres, in the Illinois Country, and were received with open arms by the Natives. ——— A full confirmation this, of Colonel Croghan's influence, and judicious Negotiation with Pondiac, and other Chiefs of many numerous Western Nations.

By Letters from Detroit of a late Date, we hear, that every Thing was in the most perfect State of Peace with the Natives.

HARTFORD Connecticut Aug. 25. Accounts of the famous Pondiac or Ponteack, the present Emperor of the Indians on the Lakes.

From Major Rogers's Account of North-America.

The Indians on the Lakes are generally at peace with one another, having a wide, extended and fruitful country in their possession. They are formed into a sort of Empire, and their Emperor is elected from the eldest tribe, which is the Ottawas, some of them Inhibit our fort at Detroit but are mostly further westward towards the Missisippi. Ponteack is their present King or Emperor, who has certainly the largest empire and greatest authority of any Indian chief that has appeared on the continent since our acquaintance with it: He puts on air of Majesty and princely grandeur, and is greatly honoured and revered by his subjects. He not long since formed a design of uniting all the Indian nations together under his authority but miscarried the attempt.

In the year 1760, when I commanded and marched the first detachment into this country that was sent by the English. I was met in my way by an emissary from him, of some of his warriors and some of his chiefs, of the tribes that are under him; the purport of which was, to let me know, that Ponteack was at a small distance, coming peaceably, and that he desired me to halt my detachment till such time as he could see me with his own eyes. His Ambassadors has also orders to inform me, that he was Ponteack, the King and Lord of the country I was in.

At first salutation when he met me he demanded my business into his country, and how I dared to enter it without his leave? when I informed him that it was not with any design against the Indians that I came, but to remove the French out of the country, who had been obstacles in our way to mutual peace and commerce, and acquainted him with my Instructions for that purpose; I at the same time delivered him several friendly messages, or belts of wampum which he received, but gave me no other answer than that he stood in the path I travelled to till next morning, giving me a small string of wampum, as to say I should not march forward without his leave.

When he departed for the night he enquired whether I wanted any thing his country afforded, and he would send his warriors to fetch it? I assured him that any provisions they brought would be paid for; and the next day we were supplied by them with several bags of parched corn, and some other necessaries. At our second meeting he gave me the pipe of peace, and both of us by turn smoked with it; and he assured me he had made peace with me and my detachment; that I might pass through his country unmolested, and relieve the French garrison: and that he would protect me, and my party from any insults that might be offered or intended by the Indians; and as an earnest of his friendship, he sent two hundred of his warriors to assist and protect us in driving one hundred fat cattle, which we had brought from Pittsburg for the use of the detachment by the way of Presque Isle. He likewise sent to the several Indian towns on the west side of Lake Erie, to inform them that I had his consent to come into the country. He attended me constantly after this interview, till I arrived at Detroit; and while I remained in the country and was the means of preserving the detachment from the fury of the Indians, who had assembled at the mouth of the Strait with intent to cut us off.

I had several conference with him, in which he descovered strength of judgement, and a thirst after knowledge. He endeavoured to inform himself of our military order and discipline. He often intimated to me that he could be content to reign in his own country in subordination to the King of Great-Britain and was willing to pay him such annual acknowledgement as he was able, in furs, and to call him uncle. He was curious to know our methods of manufacturing, cloth, Iron, &c. and expressed a great desire to see England, and offered me a part of his country if I would conduct him there. He assured me he was inclined to live peacefully with English while they used him as he deserved, and to encourage their settling in his country; but intimated if they treated him with neglect, he should shut off the way, and exclude them from it; in short, his whole conversation sufficiantly indicated that he was far from thinking himself a conquered prince, and that he expected to be treated with the respect and honour due to a prince or emperor, by all that came into his country, or treated with him.

In 1763, this Indian had the art and address to draw a number of tribes into a confederacy, with a design first to reduce the English from upon the lakes, and then to establish himself in his imperial authority; and so wisely were his measures taken, that, in fifteen days time, he reduced or took ten of our garrisons, which were all we had in this country, except Detroit: and had he carried this also, nothing was in the way to complete his sceme. Some of the Indians left him, and by his consent made a seperate peace; but he would not be active or personally concerned in to, saying that when he made a peace, it should be such an one as would, be serviceable and honourable to himself, and to the King of Great-Britain: But he has not yet proposed his terms.

In 1763, I went to throw Provisions into the garrison at Detroit, I sent this Indian a bottle of brandy by a Frenchman, his counsellors advused him not to taste it, insignuating, it was poison, and sent with a design to kill him; but Ponteack with a nobleness of mind, laughed at their suspicions, saying it was not in my power to kill him, who had lately saved my life.

In that late war of his, he appointed a commissary, and began to make money, or bills of credit, which he hath since puntually redeemed. His money was the figure of what he wanted in exchamge for it, drawn upon bark, and the shape of an Otter (his arms) drawn under it.

Were the proper methods taken, this Indian might be renderee, very serviceable to the British trade and settlements in this country, more exactly so than any one hath ever been in alliance with us on the continent

NEW-YORK Nov. 6. Extract of a Letter from Detroit September 8, 1766.
"A few days ago Pondiac and his chiefs of the several nations here, arrived from Oswego, where they have been in council with Sir William Johnson, & all seem very well contented with the treatment they met with there."

PENNSYLVANIA Chronicle August 14, 1769.
Philadelphia. Extract of a letter from Fort Pitt, dated the 15th of July 1769.
Pondiack is certainly killed by two kaskaskias, as he was going from the Fort to his Cabbin.

INDEX

----, Charles 238
ADAMS, Henry 68
ALISON, 6 282 Robert 280-281
ALLEN, James 100
ALLISON, 2
ALLMONG, Jacob 85
AMHERST, 106 Gen 44 94 109 177 Jeffry 4 10 58 76 90 102
ANDERSON, 31 62 Daniel 16 Ens 62-63 William 16
ANSTRUN, George 153
ARMSTRONG, 255 Col 87 90 206 241 John 35 William 254
ASHBY, Capt 220
ASHEN, Levie 268
ASHLIN, Lee 13
ASKY, Ens 188
AUBRY, M 305 Mr 292
BABEE, Mons 62
BAILEY, Col 303
BAIN, Capt 136 Lt 62
BAKER, Jacob 210 218
BALDWIN, Abraham 243 249 Daniel 249 Jane 249
BALL, Capt 53
BALLEY, Frantz 100

BANARD, Lt 135
BARNET, Hose 243 Lena 243 Sarah 243
BASSET, Capt 58
BAWYER, Capt 86
BENNEFIELD, 257
BERNARD, Fra 29 124 234 Francis 28 121 233
BEZZO, Mr 73
BLANE, Lt 4
BOLTON, Robert 216
BOONE, Gov 93 Thoman 89 Thomas 3 98 130-131 133
BOSTWICK, 72
BOUQUET, Brig Gen 309 Col 34 50 52 54-55 58-59 68-69 76 126 141 177 232 241 244-245 250-254 259 264-265 267 273 275-277
BOWERS, Capt 115 Lemuel 100 116
BRADSTREET, Col 205 223 227-228 237 240 244-245 247 256 262 264-265 269 293
BRADY, Capt 186 188
BREHM, Lt 118-119
BRENNOM, James 254

BRINK, Esther 92 Garret 92 Stephen 92
BROWN, Lazurus 140 Lt 62-64
BROWNE, 218
BRYAN, Hugh 215
BULKLEY, Richard 79
BULL, Capt 213 249 Col 168 Gov 241 Lt Gov 110 Samuel 260 William 215
BUQUET, Col 43
BURKE, Maj 262
BURTON, Brig Gen 217 Col 237
BUTLER, Joseph 287
BYRNS, Capt 269
CALENDER, Capt 279 Mr 280 282
CALHOON, Mr 19 Thomas 7 17
CALHOUN, Capt 222 247 Mr 132 140
CALLENDER, Capt 7
CALVIN, Hezekiak 285
CAMPBALL, Lt 54
CAMPBEL, John 76
CAMPBELL, Capt 10 25 42 47 49 292 Catherine 260 Col 270 Donald 53 George 81 James 136 289 John 53 146 Lt 82 273 Maj 87 112 Robert 30
CARTER, Elizabeth 243 Nathaniel 115 Sarah 243
CATCHEL, Lt 62
CHAMBERLAIN, Thropbilus 285
CHAPMAN, Abigail 243 Col 1 4 6-7 9
CHARLOTTE, Queen Of

CHARLOTTE (cont) England 278
CHAROBER, Lt 188
CHEVILLET, Col 131
CHISWELL, 300 Col 254
CHRISTIAN, William 113
CHRISTIE, Ens 41 51 Mr 25-26
CLARK, James 18
CLAWS, Capt 217
CLAYTON, Capt 92
CLOUPER, 221
CLOYD, David 205 Mrs 205
COCHRAN, Garvin 214
COCHRANE, Capt 254 Garvin 293
COCKRAN, Capt 82
CODY, Arthur 131
COILLAWAY, Job 103
COLBERT, Capt 67 88
COLDEN, Cadwallader 249 268 Lt Gen 106
COLLINS, Capt 70-71
COLVIL, John 112
CONPLA, 249
CORNALL, Mr 218
CORTWRIGHT, William 115
CRAWFORD, Hugh 17 Mr 7 19
CRESAP, Col 28 35 Michael 189 Mr 36
CROCHER, 100
CROGHAM, Col 302
CROGHAN, Col 305 311 Mr 24 306 308-309
CROW, William 219
CULLINS, Luke 69
CUNNINGHAM, Capt 86
CUYLER, 62 Lt 8 16
D'ABADIE, Gov 137 Mr 274
D'ABBADIE, M 292
D'ABBAEDIE, M 212

D'BRAHM, William 215
DALYELL, Capt 46 48 61-65 84
DALZEL, Capt 59
DARTAQUET, Mons 300
DAVERS, Robert 25 49-50
DAVIDSON, Agnes 188
    Edward 151 Lt 128
DAVIES, Elias 281-282
DAVIS, Robert 10
DAWSON, Capt 269
DAYTON, Lt 82-83
DEATON, 81
DECKER, Andrew 115
DEGAUTERAIS, M 308-309
DEHAVEN, 254
DELAGAUTERAIS, Mons 289
DELES, 70
DENIKE, Capt 115
DEPOE, Capt 99
DESAINTANGE, M 307
DESJOUNE, Baron 5
DEVAUX, James 216
DEVEAUX, James 151
DILLESTER, Mary 251
DINWIDDIE, Hugh 240
DOBBS, Arthur 3 89 98
    George 30 Gov 51 133
DOBSON, 112 Capt 294
    George 189
DONEGALL, 171
DOW, Lt 53-54 59 76
DUNCAN, John 225 243
    Sarah 243 William 115
DUNN, Patrick 7
DUNNING, Mr 36
EGREMONT, Lord 5
ELSICK, Capt 26
ENOS, Philip 101
ERWIN, Mr 104
ETHRINGTON, Capt 47
EWEN, Capt 93

FAIRFAX, Lord 32
FALSTAFFE, John 258
FARMAR, Robert 151
FARMER, Maj 274 293-294 299 306-307
FAUGUIER, Lt Gov 87
FAUQUIER, Francis 3 89 98 295 Gov 291 298 301 Lt Gv 295
FIELD, Capt 87
FIFE, Hans 146
FINCHER, John 67
FINLER, Christopher 111
FISHER, 62 Mr 10
FORBES, 5 Gen 147 184 Maj 50 157 271 Rev Mr 260 William 147
FORMAN, John 69
FOSTER, Col 76
FOWLER, David 285
FRANCE, King Of 261
FRANKLIN, William 99
FRASER, Col 307 Lt 302 305-307 Mr 308
FRASIER, Lt 82
FRAZIER, 81
FUNSTON, Lt 260
GAGE, 80 Brig Gen 102 Gen 121 200 202 205 243-244 264-265 274 306
GAMBLE, Lt 191
GARDINER, Capt 110-111
GASCOIGN, Capt 215
GEORGE, 3d King Of England 29 King Of England 15 57 234 278
GERMENY, Mr 218
GIBBONS, Mrs 252
GILLIVEAY, Capt 88
GIN, Joshua 260
GLADWIN, Col 117 210 Maj

317

GLADWIN (cont)
　10 25 41-42 47-48 118
　127-128 185
GLASS, David 103
GORDON, Mr 25 50
GORHAM, 110
GRAHAM, Capt 54 Capt Lt
　59 John 31 53 Mungo 88
GRANT, 5 Capt 61-63 65
　269 James 273 Lt 50
　Robert 53 76
GRAS, Alexander 153
GRAY, Capt 62-65 Mr 2
GREAT BRITAIN, King Of
　313-314
GROGHAM, George 17 145
GROGHAN, Mr 24 307
GUIN, Samuel 92
GUN, Elisha 284
GYLER, Lt 41
HACER, Benjamin 92
HAGENBUSH, 100
HALIFAX, Earl Of 274
HANCOCK, Mr 66
HARNESS, Michael 70
HART, Mr 54
HAY, Capt 68 252
HENRY, Mr 73 William 114
HEWLICK, 194
HEZLET, Andrew 96 100
HICKENBOTTOM, Capt 113
HICKS, Gershorn 207
HOBLER, Frantz 68
HOLMES, Ens 41 47 John
　282
HOPE, Capt 48
HORSEY, Mr 83
HOWE, 280
HOWELL, Daniel 249 John
　249
HUGHES, Capt 287 Solomon
　257 260

INDIAN, Allakullakulla 3
　Arajungas 197
　Atakullakulla 54 254
　Atanas 94
　Attakullakulla 110 247
　301-302 304-305
　Aughnawawis 198 Bear
　161 Betty 163 Capt
　Bull 185 190 Capt
　Johnny 142 Captain
　Bull 174 Chonedagaw
　198 Cow Keeper 226
　Dawet Shagorakaongo
　283 Eclambuit 57 Evil
　Doer 260 George 163
　Great Doctor 302 Great
　Warrior 289 293 Great
　Wolf 142 Gwedelnes
　Agwerondonewas 283
　Harry 163 John 163
　Judd's Friend 276-277
　Kaanijes 198 Keehowee
　155 King Beaver 16
　King Heigler 75
　Kittagusta 247 Little
　Carpenter 3 54 254 302
　Long Warrior 226
　Meserwanderoment 57
　Mistificah 88 Mohikas
　John 134 Mortar 283
　289 299 301 Moytoy 131
　Mulmaleis 142
　Oghseguaraghta 11
　Ottassite 271 276-279
　Ottessite 278
　Oucconnostota 289 301
　Oucconostota 254
　Oucconstota 247
　Ouconnostata 293
　Papunechang 103-104
　Peggy 163 Peter 163
　Pondiac 64 117 185

INDIAN (cont)
  296-298 307 311 314
  Pondiack 265 305 308
  314 Ponteack 311-312
  314 Pontiac 64-65 307
  Red Horse 28 88
  Salloue 187 219 287-
  288 304 Sally 163
  Saquayanguaraghta 11
  Saure Woraromegasa 57
  Sayenqueraghta 198
  Seed 254 Seriboana 197
  Settiquo 254 Shehaes
  163-164 166 Shingas 16
  142 Singas 142
  Sogheres 11 Struther's
  Friend 88 Taanjaqua
  198 Tagaanadie 198
  Tagannondie 198
  Teedyuscung 174
  Teskekeman 142
  Teskekemen 142
  Tidyessang 185
  Toguascanta 11
  Toquerole 11 Turtle
  Heart 142 Volgomet 282
  Wannughsila 197
  Wanughsisaue 198 White
  Eyes 208 Wholanawidzie
  260 Wild Sue 163 Will
  Soc 169 Wingeenum 16
  Wingeman 142 Wolf 6 89
  Wolf King 88 107 137
  147 157 161 283
  Wyanjoy 163
  Wyendougjeta 16 Young
  Twin 156 Young Warrior
  90 150 155 187 209
  214-215 219 231 287-
  288 298 304
INGLES, Capt 86 113
INGLIS, Capt 97

IRVING, William 153
ISTASSI, M 274
JAMES, 207
JAMETT, Lt 72-73
JEFFRIES, Stephen 30
JENKINS, Lt 41 47
JENNETT, Lt 47
JOHNSON, 36 Capt 81 148
  194 202 208 Francis
  226 Guy 225 John 191
  193 Lt 110 Snow 236
  William 4 40 45-46 71
  90 102 109 126 146 148
  161 173-175 185-186
  190-191 193-197 199
  203 205 209 213 218
  223 225 227-230 233
  236-237 240 243-245
  249 251 265-266 268-
  269 275-277 287 291
  297 307 314 Wm 198
JOHNSTON, 269 Capt 80 83
  George 40 131 Gov 272
  287 300 James 215
  Thomas 82
JOINER, Capt 87
JONES, 221
KEED, William 103
KELLY, Eleanor 260 Sarah
  260
KENNEDY, Edward 191
KEPPEL, Gen 50
KERN, Capt 56 67 114
KIESSER, Capt 93
KINBERLIN, Jacob 113
KING, Thomas 263
L'ABADIE, M 156
LAHUNT, 81
LAKE, 62
LAWSEN, ---- 132
LECHORN, Col 239
LEE, Henry 72

LEGARD, Henry 153
LENS, Capt 246
LESLY, Lt 47
LEVY, 2 134 Mr 74
LEWIS, Andrew 86 295
　Capt 222 Col 291 294-
　295 300
LLOYD, 221 Henry 260
LOCKYER, Col 293
LOFTUS, Maj 136 146-147
　158 211-214 222 226
　231 271 274 299
LOGAN, Alexander 36
LORING, Commodore 55
LUCAS, Capt 226
LUKE, Lt 64
M'CLELLAN, William 253
M'CLURE, 296 Alexander 7
M'CORMICK, 7
M'DOUGAL, Lt 62
M'DOUGALL, Capt 25
M'GEE, Mr 6 23-24
M'INTOSH, Lt 59
M'KEE, Alexander 6
MACDONALD, Capt 252
MAGEE, Capt 154
MALOONY, Nicholas 242
MARKS, Nicholas 84
MARTIN, Clement 93 John
　55
MARTINE, 62
MAXWELL, 280 Mr 282
MCCLOUD, Capt 82
MCDOUGAL, 49
MCDOUGALE, Lt 10
MCDOWALL, John 280
MCGILLVRAY, Capt 93
MCQUEEN, Mr 218
MEKLY, Jacob 85
MENTIEUR, Capt 194
MENZIER, Lt 53
MILLEDGE, John 287

MILLEGES, Capt 242
MILLER, John 250
　Nicholas 68
MILLS, Mr 140
MITCHEL, Joseph 188
MOFFAT, Capt 86
MONCKTON, Gen 190
MONCRIEF, Maj 118
MONTEUR, Capt 263
MONTOUR, Capt 198 206
　208 268
MONTREFOR, Capt 82 129
MONTRESOR, Capt 117
MORGAN, Hillarous 242
MORRIS, Capt 263
MURRAY, Gen 83
MYERS, Hyam 154
NARTHLOW, 62 Lt 63
NEAL, 303 James 302
NEGRO, Tony 209
NEWNEZ, Lt 93
NIVERNOIS, Duke Of 5
NOBLE, Mr 125
NOX, William 111
NUNEZ, Moses 88
O'NEAL, 303-304
OAKES, Mr 72 74
OLIVER, A 29 234
ONEAL, Arthur 260
ORMSBY, John 271
OTTER, Joannah 243 Sarah
　243
OURRY, Capt 8 252
PAINTER, Lt 128
PARK, Silas 114
PARKE, Mr 262
PARMER, Maj 125
PATTEN, James 111
PATTON, William 259
PAULEY, 49 Lt 19
PAULI, Ens 41
PAULY, Mr 49

PAURY, Ens 62
PAWLEY, ---- 132
PAWLY, Ens 2
PAYNTER, Lt 118
PECTANG, 171
PENN, Gov 129 268 John 166 Mr 163 William 162
PERCIPCOL, Henry 153
PERKINS, John 287
PETER, Capt 263-264
PHILIPS, Capt 86
PILLITON, Gabriel 146
PIPER, 186 Capt 188
PITMAN, Lt 211
POLLAN, 280 Mr 279
POMPEY, 134
PONTUCK, Monsieur 263
POST, Frederick 147
POTTER, Mr 310 Nathaniel 309
POUNT, Francis 153
PRECTOR, 282
PRENTICE, Capt 7 Mr 134
PRESTON, Lt 269
PREVOST, Capt 188 Col 107 James 214
PRICE, Ens 23 25 Mr 25 209 278 293 295
PRINGLE, Robert 260
PROCTOR, William 298
PROVOST, Col 125 135 147
PUMMEROY, 36
PUTNAM, Col 262 265 Gol 238 Israel 239 264 Lt Col 262
QUERY, Thomas 111
RAHN, Capt 93
RAND, Joshua 114
RANDOLPH, John 295 Peter 87
REA, Capt 269
REAVE, Richard 256
REID, Col 246 Lt Col 251
RICHARDS, Lt 87
RICHARDSON, Col 75 Richard 75 William 75
RIPPY, Samuel 188
ROBERSON, Capt 10
ROBERTSON, 50 Capt 49 Col 157
ROBESON, Capt 25
ROBINSON, Capt 173 Lt 158 Lt Col 158 Thomas 67 William 31
ROGERS, Capt 99 Maj 10 44 46 50 62 65 108 117 126 140-141 148 310-311 Mr 142
ROLLE, Denys 260
ROSCO, 81 Lt 82-83
ROSS, Lt 306
RPOBERTSON, Col 137
RUSSEL, James 150
RUSSELL, John 175
RUTHERFORD, Robert 28
RYAN, Elinor 112
SAUNDERS, Capt 57
SCHIFLER, George 101
SCHLOSSER, Ens 47
SCHNEBELL, Casper 215
SCOTT, Capt 309
SHAW, Lt 148
SHEFFER, Ens 67
SHELBY, Capt 218
SHEPARD, Benjamin 243
SHEPERD, Benja 249
SHIMMER, Charles 260
SHOEMAKER, Jacob 92
SIMBLETT, John 118
SIMPSON, Mr 287
SIMS, Adam 186 Andrew 188
SINNET, Mr 308-309
SINNOT, Peter Acton 289

SLITERMAN, Jeremiah 151
SMALL, Maj 265
SMALLMAN, Maj 7 240 306
   Mr 134
SMITH, 7 Daniel 101 Ens
   232 John 163 Mr 282
   Thomas 250 Titus 285
   William 280-281
SNEIDER, 85
SOLOMON, Mr 73
SPENCER, 3
STAPLETON, 101
STAUNTON, Capt 56
STEDMAN, Mr 82
STENTON, John 96 100
STEPHEN, Col 70 72 112
STEPHENS, Col 56 Magaret
   188
STERLING, Capt 311
   Thomas 309
STEVENS, Col 35
STEWART, Charles 111
   John 87
STIMBLE, Isaac 246
STINSON, Lt 251
STOUGHTON, Lt 110-111
STOUTON, Lt 111
STRUTCHESS, Mr 218
STUART, Capt 89-90 105
   Charles 289 James 218
   John 3 106 209 225
   272-273 278 283 287
   289 293 299 301 Mr 308
SUMERVILLE, Capt 151
SUMPTER, Mr 5
TALLEY, John 21-22 121
TASHLER, Adam 84-85
TAYLOR, Capt 90
TELFAIR, William 153
TERMOR, Maj 136
THOMAS, 221 William 95
TRACEY, Mr 72-73

TREE, Jacob 101
TRIM, Ezra 243
UPDEGRAVE, Catherine 243
   Peter 243
VANCAMP, Col 115
VANGADA, Peter 92
VAUGH, Col 297
VILLEMONT, M 274
WALTON, Ens 115 John 69
WARD, Joshuah 153
WEISER, Conrad 179
WELCH, Mr 134
WELDER, Mr 35
WELSH, Mr 7
WELTON, Jacob 70 John 70
   Jonathan 70
WENDELL, John 16
WESTBROOK, Benjamin 115
   Capt 108
WHEELOCK, Elizr 286 Mr
   284 Rev Mr 285
WHITE, Capt 269
WIKIN, Maj 127
WILDING, James 115
WILKINS, Maj 81 110 118
   128 185 Sally 214
WILLIAMS, Dr 118 Mr 128
WILLIAMSON, Andrew 140
   James 102
WILSON, Maj 71 116
WILTON, Rev Mr 260
WINSTON, Mr 134
WOLFE, Nicholas 215
WOOLY, Joseph 285
WRIGHT, Gov 241 248
   James 3 20-22 106 119
   121 260
WYLLY, Samuel 66-67

Other Heritage Books by Armand Francis Lucier:

1767 Chronicle

Boston, the Red Coats, and the Homespun Patriots, 1766–1775

*Central Colonies Chronicle: The Freeman, the
Servants, and the Government, 1722–1732*

*French and Indian War Notices Abstracted from Colonial Newspapers
Volume 2: 1756–1757
Volume 3: January 1, 1758 to September 17, 1759
Volume 4: September 17, 1759 to December 30, 1760
Volume 5: January 1, 1761 to January 17, 1793*

Jolly Old England

*Journal of Occurrences: Patriot Propaganda on the
British Occupation of Boston, 1768–1769*

*Newspaper Datelines of the American Revolution
Volume 1: April 18, 1775 to November 1, 1775
Volume 2: November 1, 1775 to April 30, 1776
Volume 3: May 1, 1776 to November 1, 1776
Volume 4: November 1, 1776 to January 30, 1777*

*Pontiac's Conspiracy and Other Indian Affairs: Notices
Abstracted from Colonial Newspapers, 1763–1765*

www.ingramcontent.com/pod-product-compliance
Lightning Source LLC
Chambersburg PA
CBHW060942230426
43665CB00015B/2035